CARTOON HEADCASE:

CARTOONS TO MAKE YOU HAPPY

To Sue with very best wishes!
John King

BY JOHN KING

ISBN:
ISBN-9781717892805

ACKNOWLEDGEMENTS

SIMON KING: PHOTOGRAPHY
GRAPHIC DESIGN

PETER KING: WEB DEVELOPMENT

CHECK OUT CARTOON HEADCASE:

 INSTAGRAM.COM/CARTOON_HEADCASE

 FACEBOOK.COM/CARTOONHEADCASE

 WWW.CARTOONHEADCASE.COM

CONTACT ME ON INFO@CARTOONHEADCASE.COM
I'D LOVE TO HEAR FROM YOU! I CAN LET YOU KNOW WHEN...

MORE BOOKS ARE COMING!

ENDORSEMENTS

"BUY THIS BOOK"!

    – THE AUTHOR

"WHY ASK US FOR A REVIEW"?

    – A GARDENING MAGAZINE

DEDICATION

THIS BOOK IS DEDICATED TO GRAHAM AND MALCOLM HILLS. THANKS FOR YOUR FRIENDSHIP SPANNING DECADES, AND FOR ALL THE HUMOUR TRAFFIC THAT HAS KEPT OUR CREATIVE JUICES FLOWING. 😊

THE CARTOON HEADCASE

MISSION STATEMENT:

A SMILE ON EVERY FACE, AND A BOOK IN EVERY TOILET

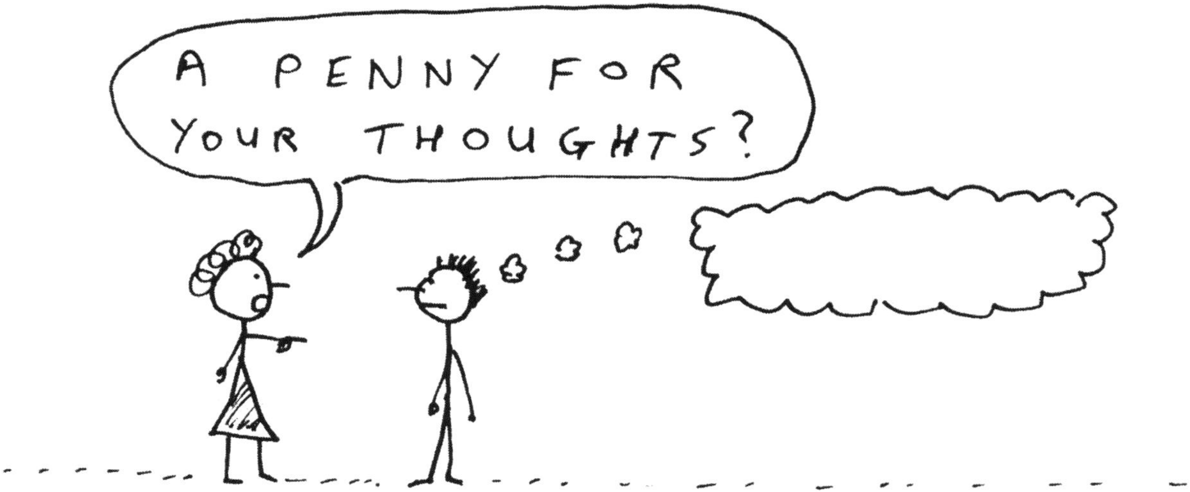
A PENNY FOR YOUR THOUGHTS?

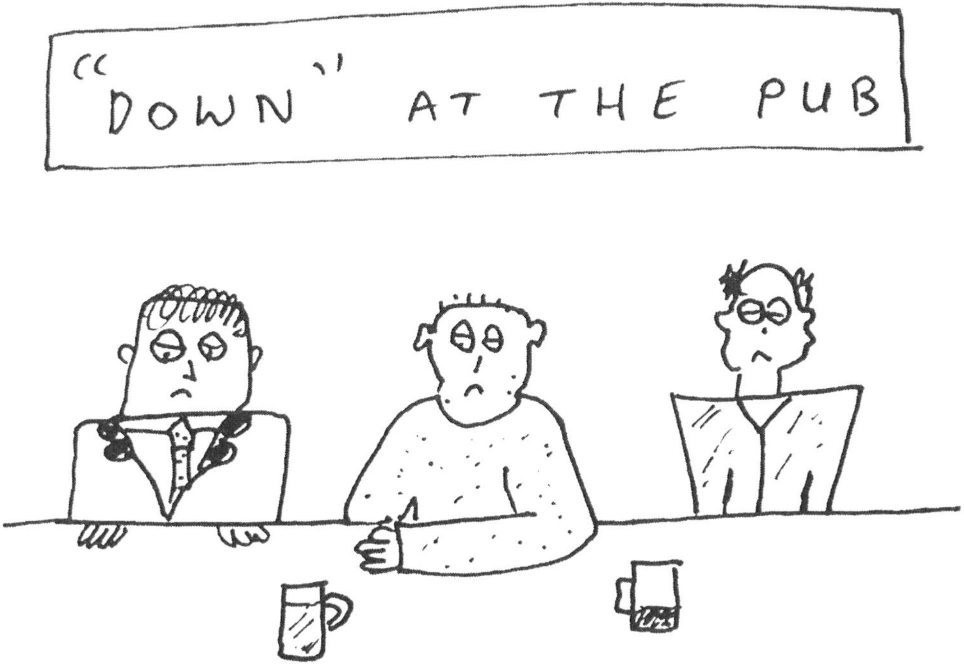
"DOWN" AT THE PUB

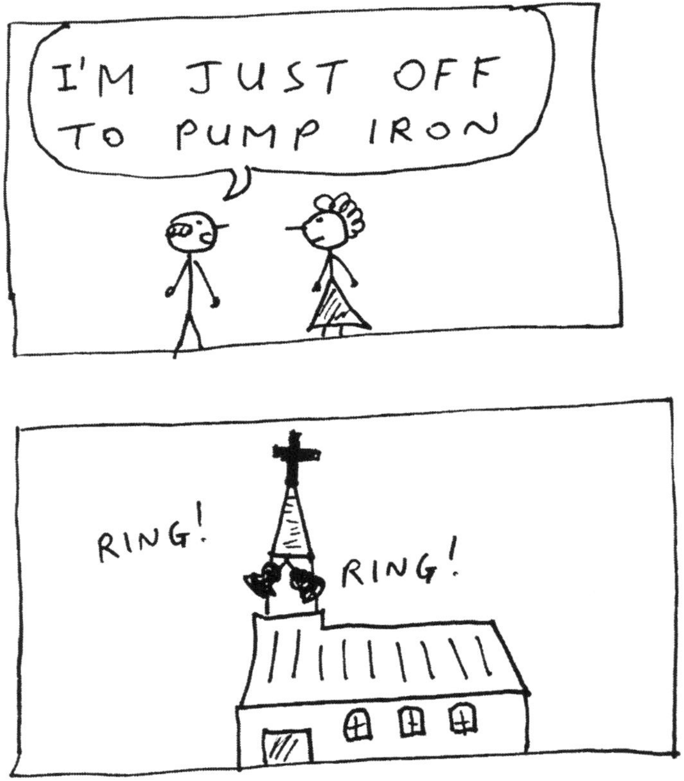
I'M JUST OFF TO PUMP IRON
RING!
RING!

THIS PAGE IS INTENTIONALLY LEFT BLANK

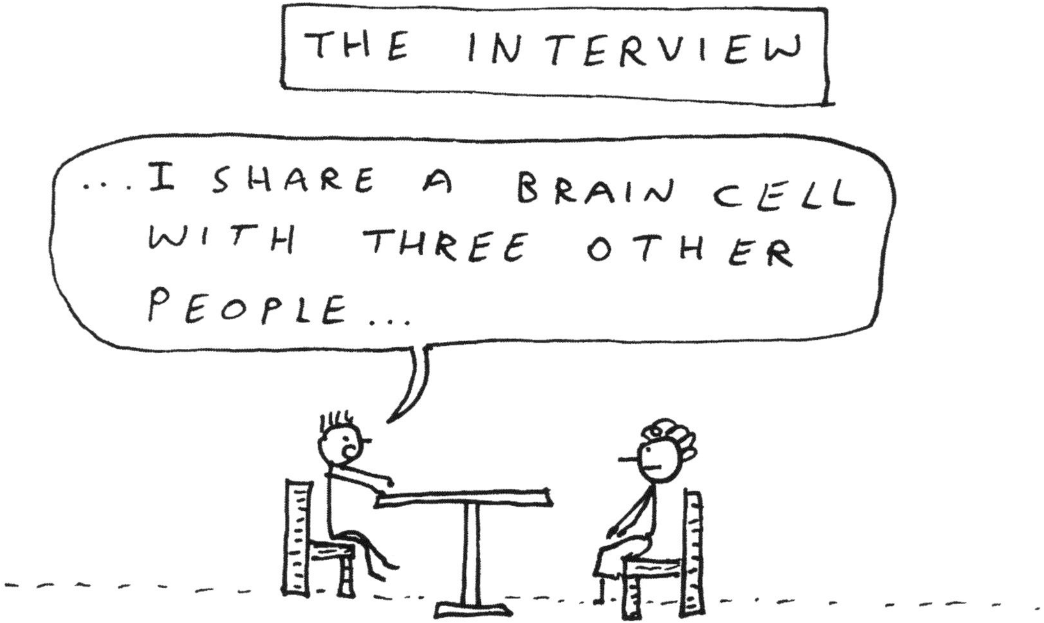
THE INTERVIEW
...I SHARE A BRAIN CELL WITH THREE OTHER PEOPLE...

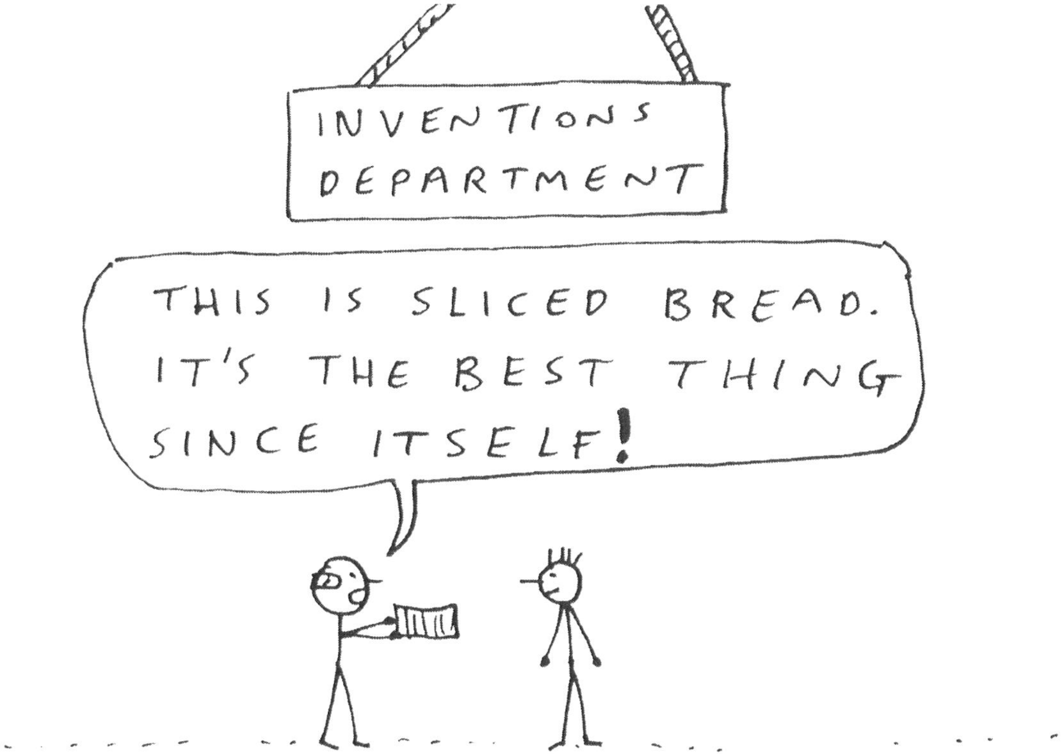
INVENTIONS DEPARTMENT
THIS IS SLICED BREAD. IT'S THE BEST THING SINCE ITSELF!

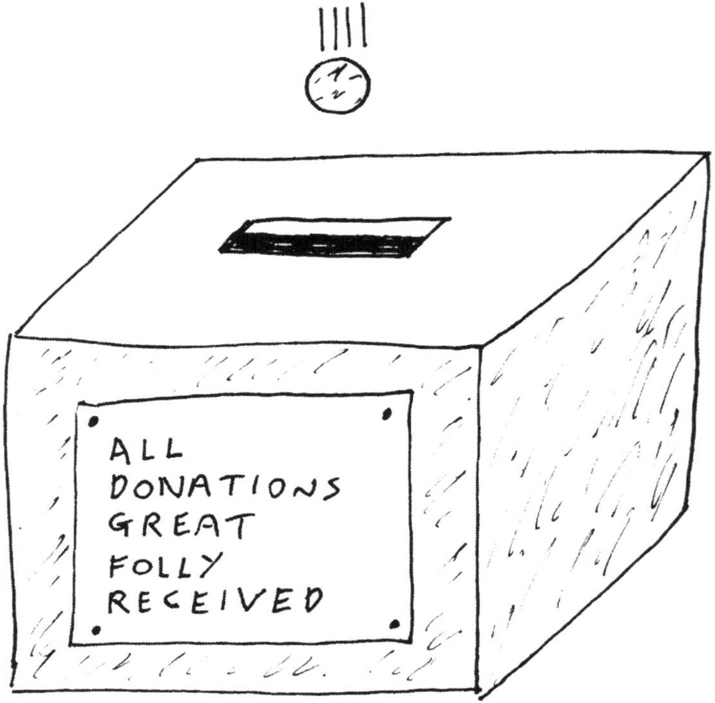
ALL
DONATIONS
GREAT
FOLLY
RECEIVED

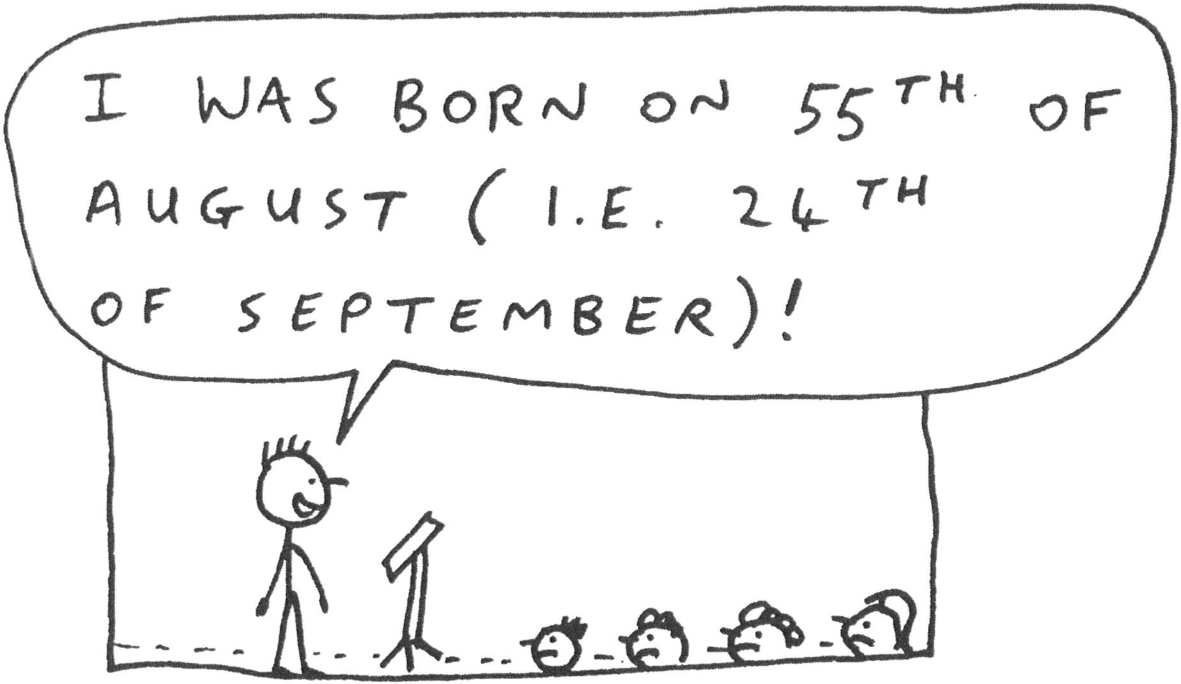
I WAS BORN ON 55TH OF AUGUST (I.E. 24TH OF SEPTEMBER)!

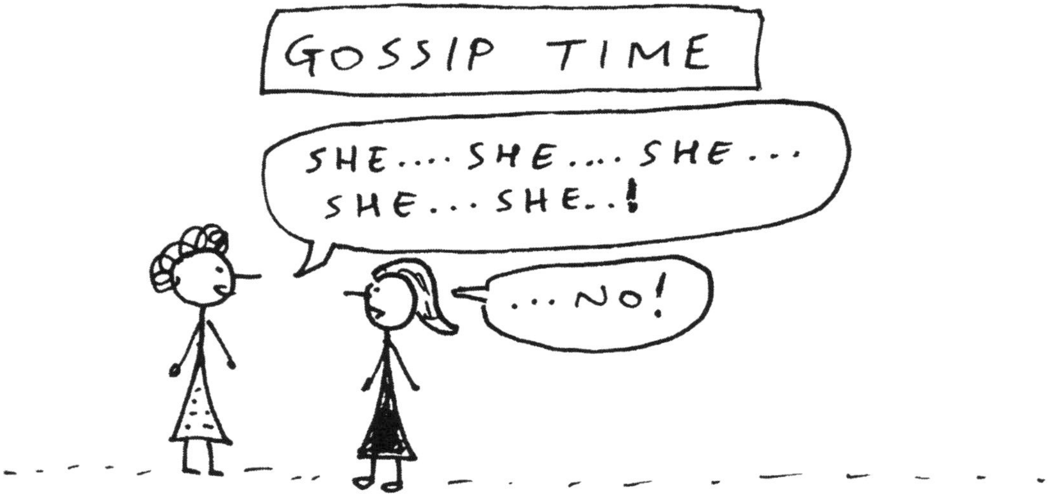
GOSSIP TIME
SHE.... SHE.... SHE...
SHE... SHE..!
...NO!

THE NEXT FUNNY STORY RELATES TO WHEN I WAS ON THE BOARD FOR THE COMMITTEE OF THE CHAMBER OF COMMERCE ON THE CONSOLIDATION AND AMALGAMATION OF ..!
INTELLIGENT PEOPLE ALWAYS GIVE YOU TOO MUCH INFORMATION

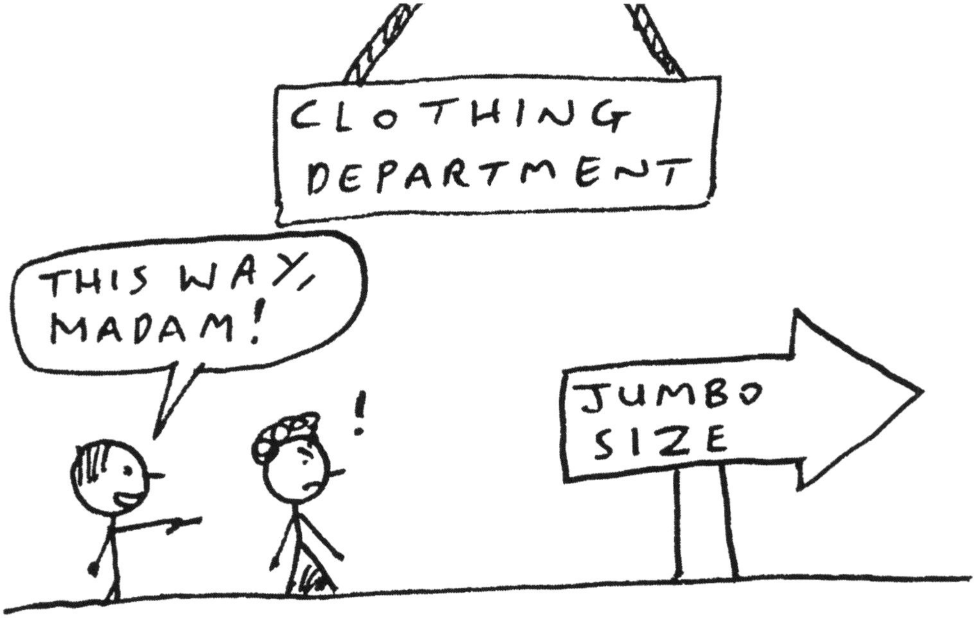
CLOTHING DEPARTMENT
THIS WAY, MADAM!
!
JUMBO SIZE

WHY DO YOU KEEP BEING PATRONISING, CRITICISING ME AND PUTTING ME DOWN?
BECAUSE I CARE!

MUM - YOU ALWAYS END YOUR SENTENCES WITH A PUT-DOWN!
NO I DON'T, SILLY!

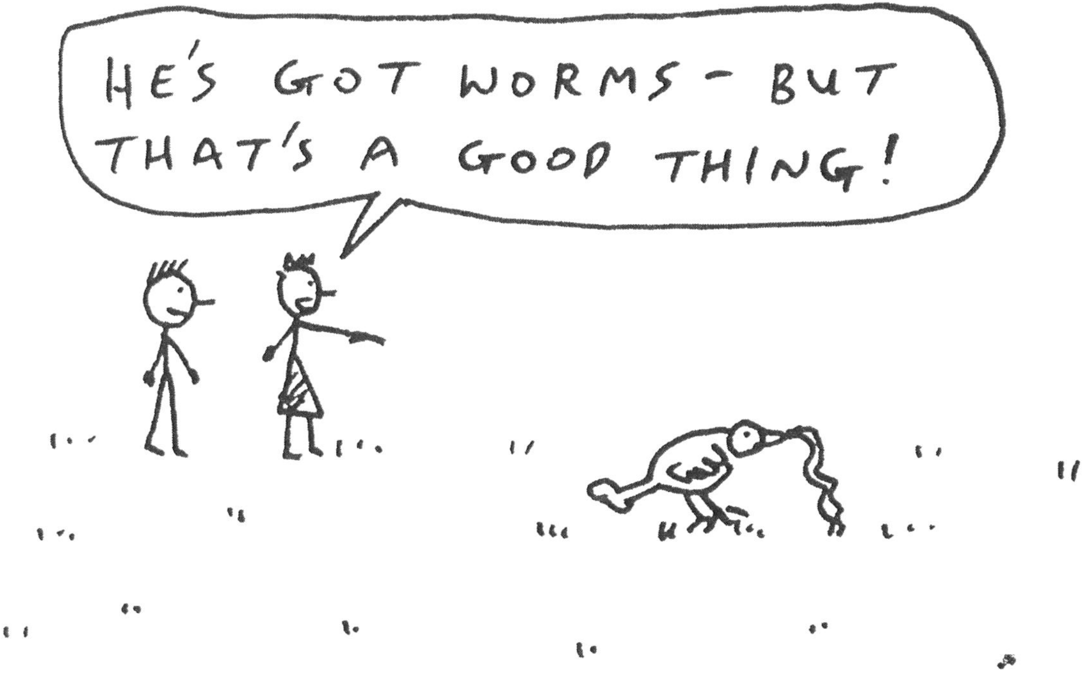
HE'S GOT WORMS - BUT THAT'S A GOOD THING!

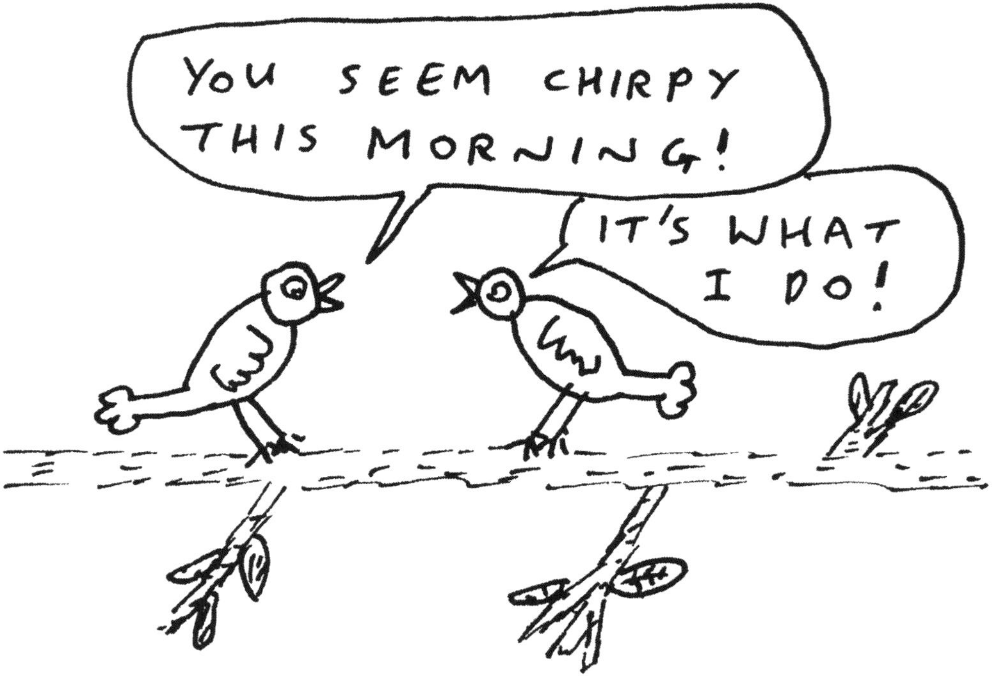
YOU SEEM CHIRPY THIS MORNING!
IT'S WHAT I DO!

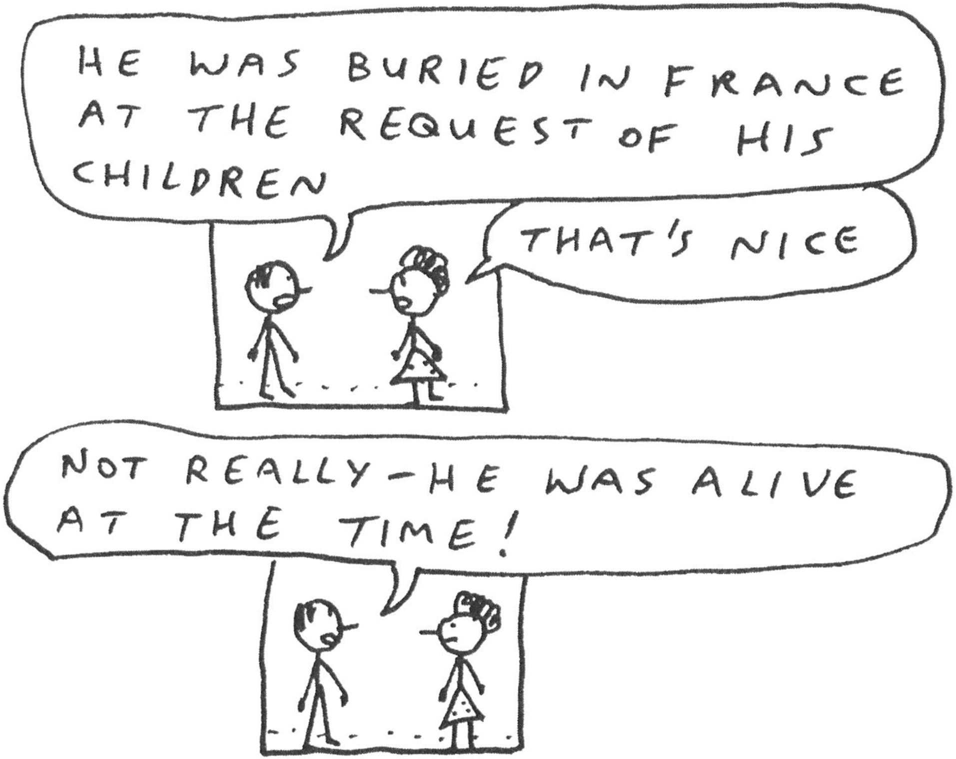
HE WAS BURIED IN FRANCE AT THE REQUEST OF HIS CHILDREN
THAT'S NICE
NOT REALLY—HE WAS ALIVE AT THE TIME!

YOUR PROBLEM IS YOU THINK THE WORLD REVOLVES AROUND YOU!
YOUR PROBLEM IS YOU'RE CONFUSING THE EARTH WITH THE ORBITING PLANETS!

HE DIED, FALLING THROUGH A CEILING INTO A PIRANHA TANK
IT'S HOW HE WOULD HAVE WANTED IT

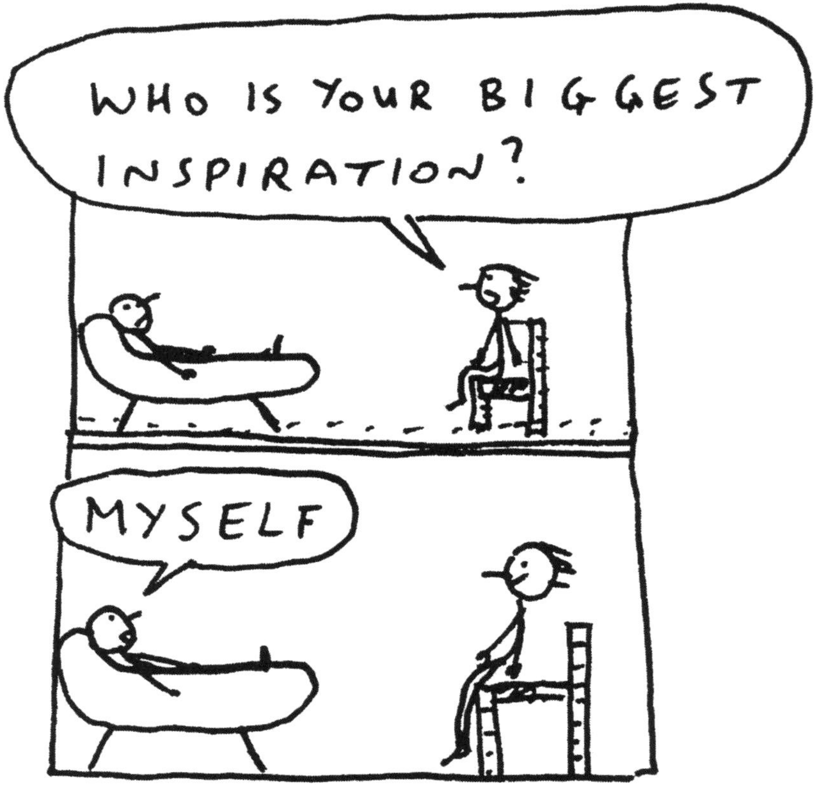
WHO IS YOUR BIGGEST INSPIRATION?
MYSELF

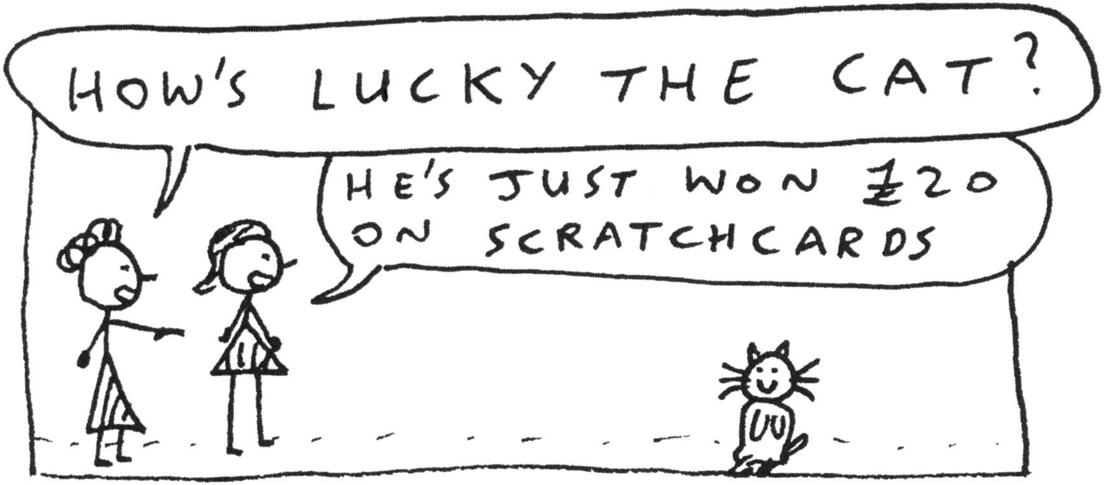
HOW'S LUCKY THE CAT?
HE'S JUST WON Ƶ20 ON SCRATCHCARDS

THE ANCIENT ROMANS HAD WIGS, FALSE TEETH AND CENTRAL HEATING. WHAT DOES THAT TELL YOU?
BALD PEOPLE COULD TALK IN COMFORT!

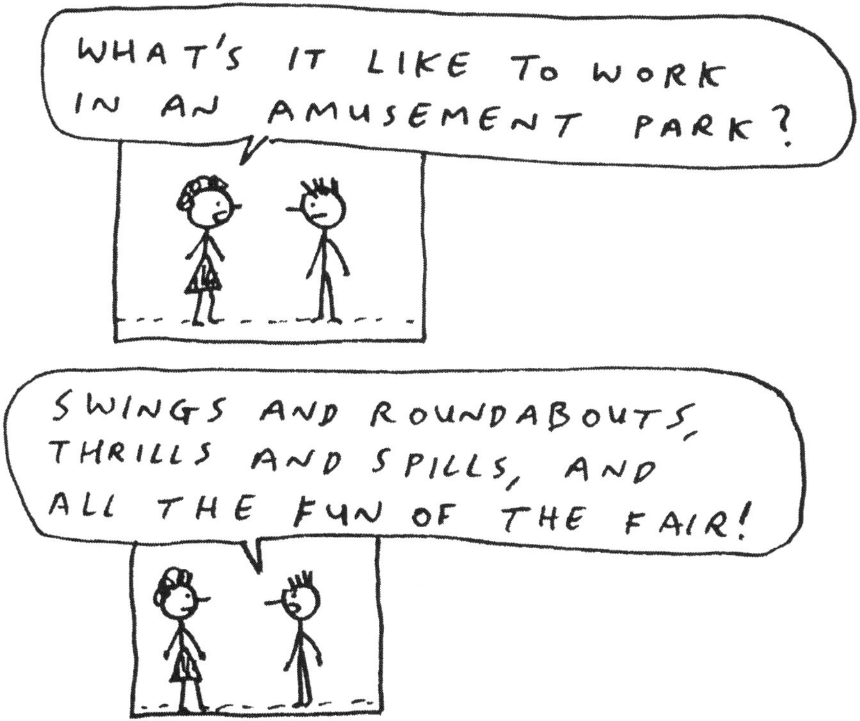
WHAT'S IT LIKE TO WORK IN AN AMUSEMENT PARK?
SWINGS AND ROUNDABOUTS, THRILLS AND SPILLS, AND ALL THE FUN OF THE FAIR!

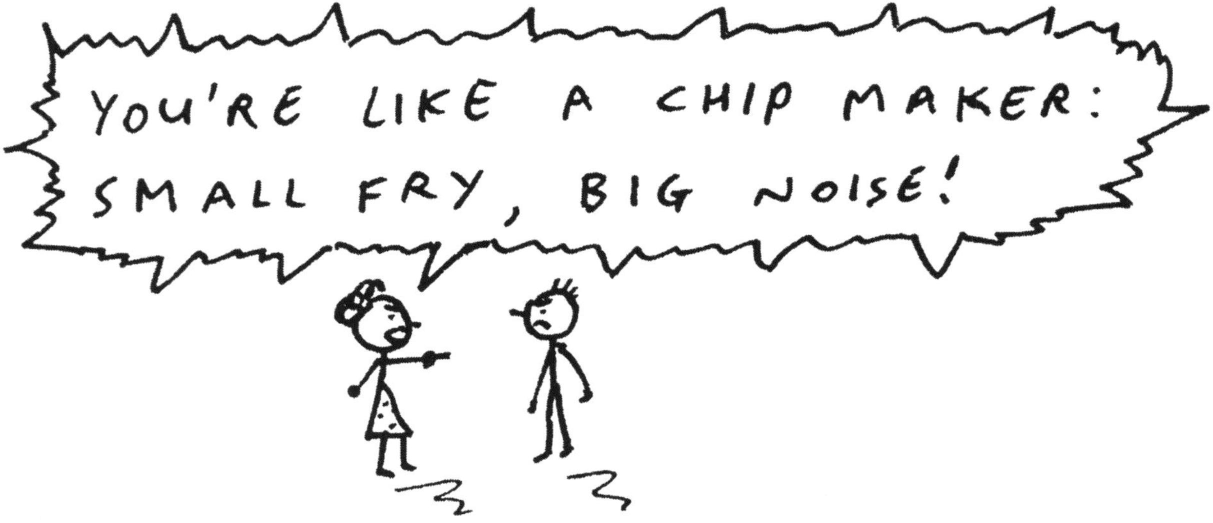
YOU'RE LIKE A CHIP MAKER: SMALL FRY, BIG NOISE!

WHAT DO YOU THINK OF THE MANAGEMENT?
THEY'RE COUCH POTATOES, CHINLESS WONDERS AND STUFFED SHIRTS!

I'M LOOKING FOR A BLACK CAT IN A COAL BUNKER
I'M LOOKING FOR A WHITE CAT IN A SNOW STORM

THIS BOOK IS SALTED WITH... IS SEASONED AND SPICED WITH... AND HAS A PEPPERING OF...

DOCTOR, I KEEP THINKING I'M A COATHANGER
IT'S TIME YOU CAME OUT OF THE CLOSET!

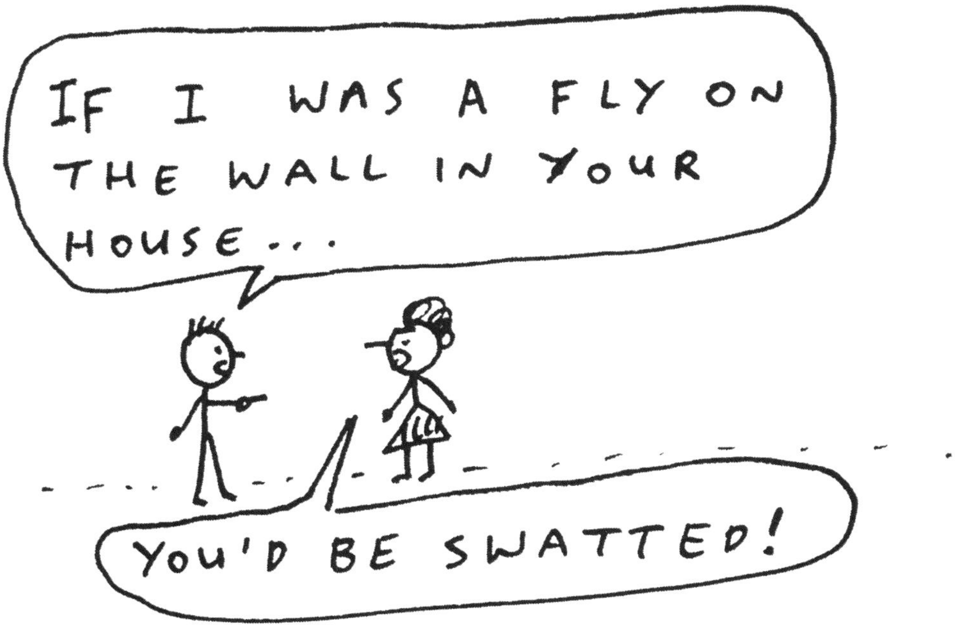
IF I WAS A FLY ON THE WALL IN YOUR HOUSE...
YOU'D BE SWATTED!

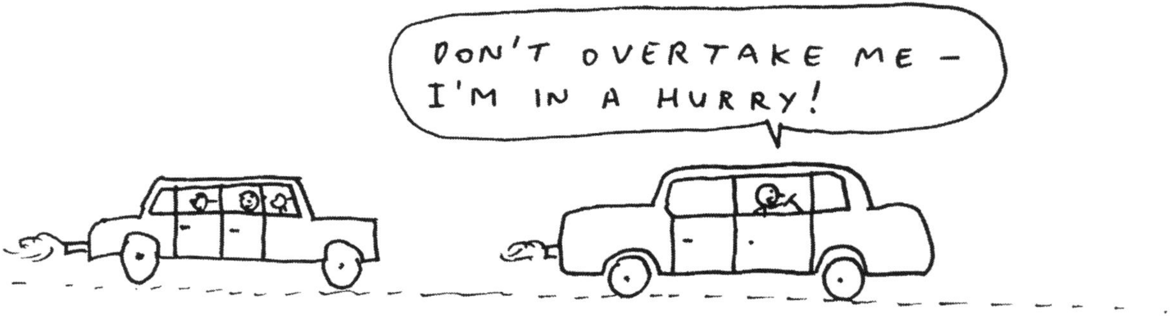
DON'T OVERTAKE ME – I'M IN A HURRY!

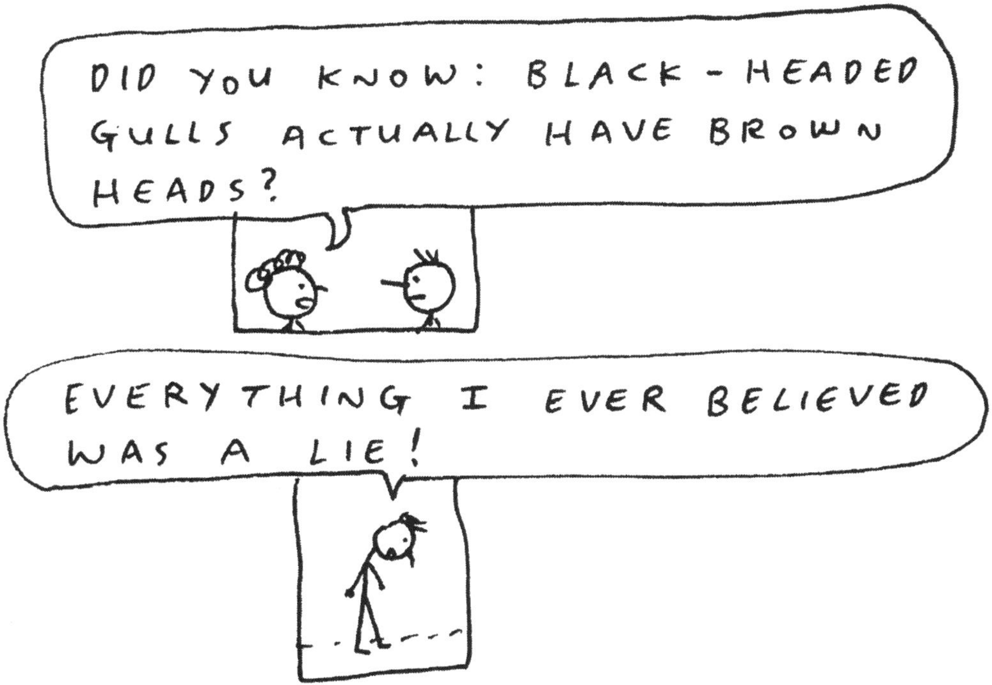
DID YOU KNOW: BLACK-HEADED GULLS ACTUALLY HAVE BROWN HEADS?
EVERYTHING I EVER BELIEVED WAS A LIE!

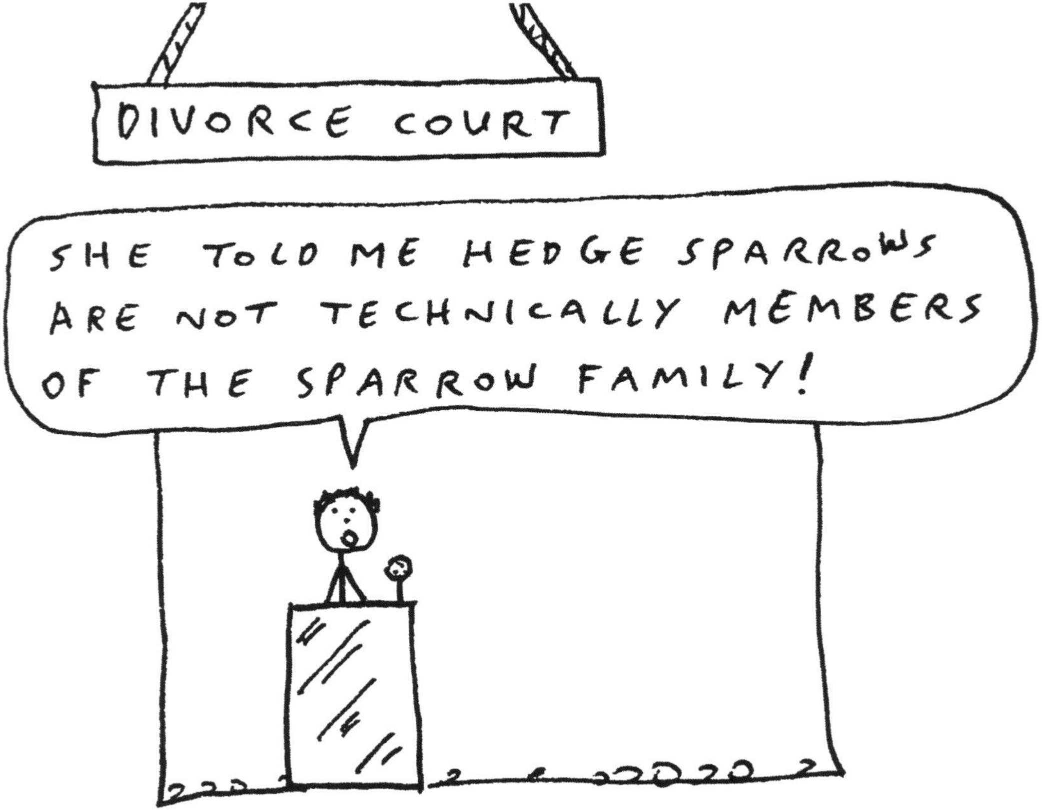
DIVORCE COURT
SHE TOLD ME HEDGE SPARROWS ARE NOT TECHNICALLY MEMBERS OF THE SPARROW FAMILY!

I WILL INVENT THE WHEEL, AND KILL DINOSAURS WITH MY CLUB!
PRO-ACTIVE MAN

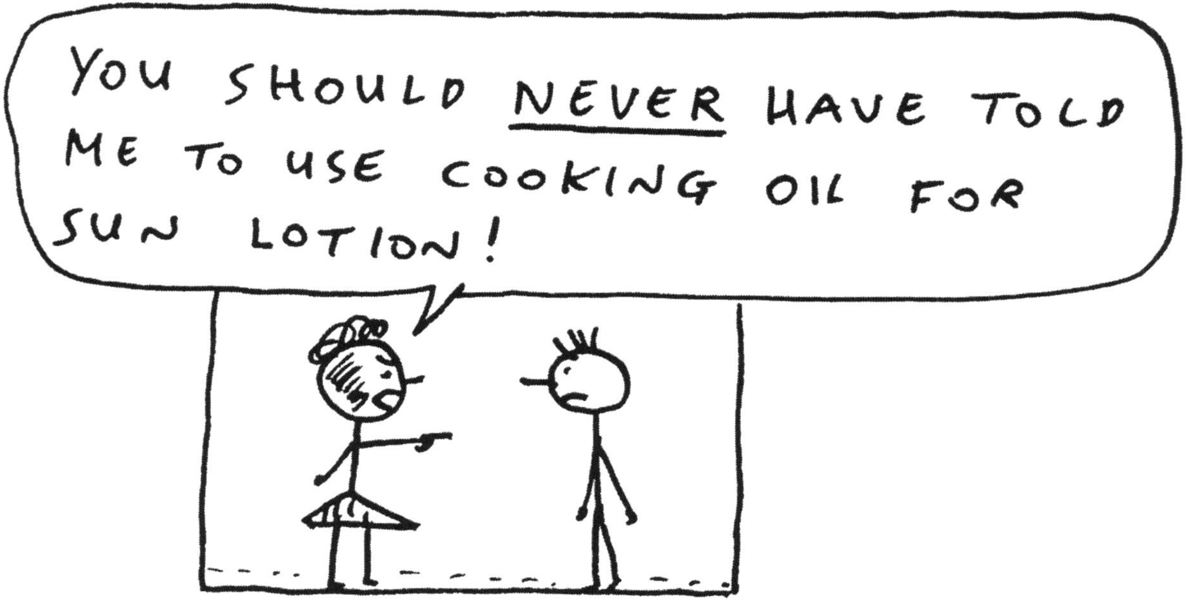
YOU SHOULD NEVER HAVE TOLD ME TO USE COOKING OIL FOR SUN LOTION!

YOU'RE ON A HIDING TO NOWHERE, BETWEEN A ROCK AND A HARD PLACE, AND IN A CATCH 22 SITUATION!

YOUR TIME-DELAYED INCONTINENCE IS AN ACCIDENT WAITING TO HAPPEN!
DOCTORS

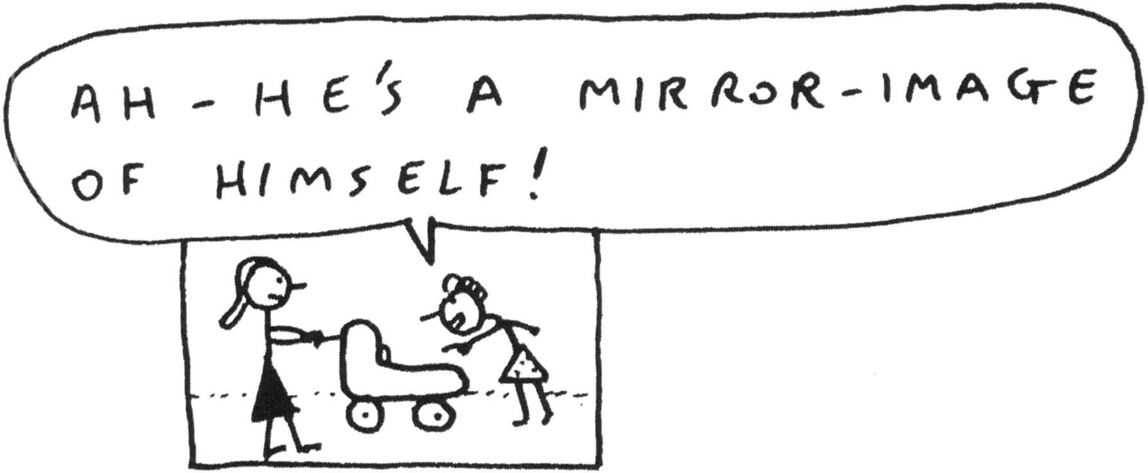
AH - HE'S A MIRROR-IMAGE OF HIMSELF!

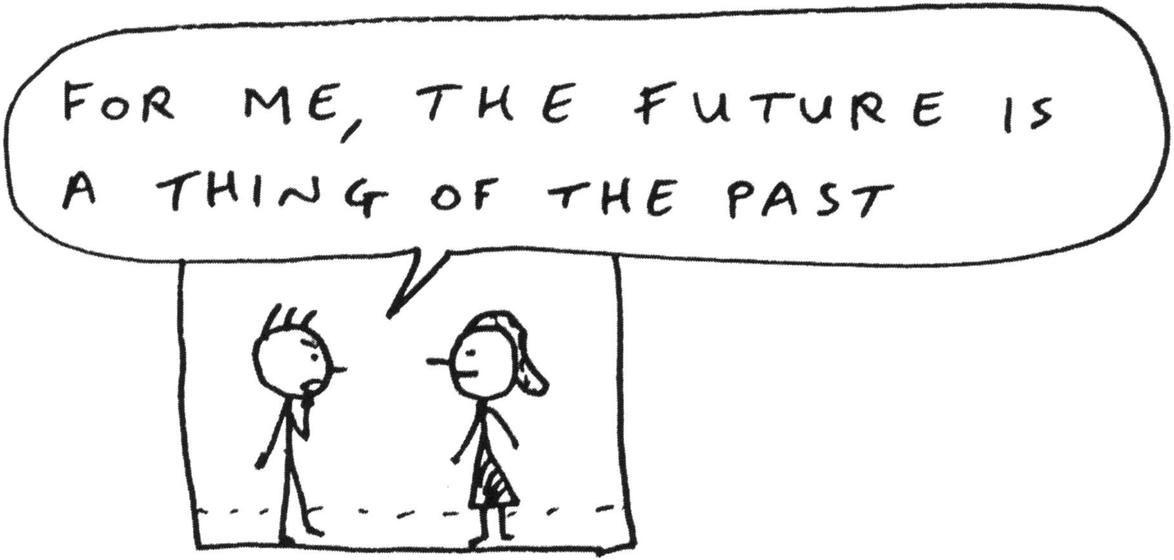
FOR ME, THE FUTURE IS A THING OF THE PAST

STOP TELLING US HOW TO SUCK EGGS!
DON'T TELL THE PRESIDENT HOW TO RUN THE COUNTRY!
HECKLERS

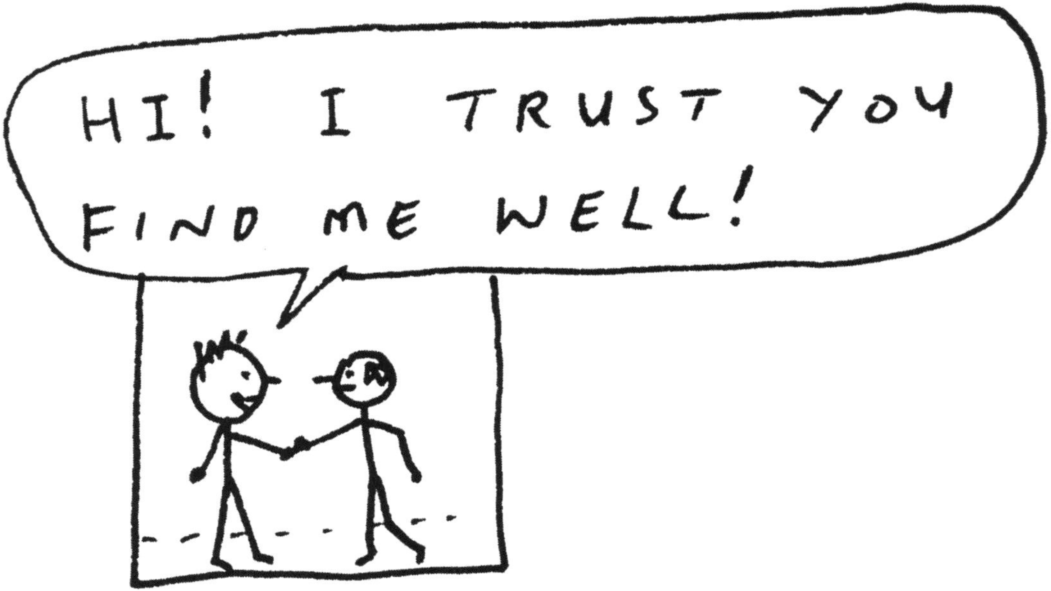
HI! I TRUST YOU FIND ME WELL!

ABOUT THE AUTHOR:

HE IS SUCCESSFULLY MARRIED
WITH SUCCESSFUL CHILDREN
AND SUCCESSFUL GRANDCHILDREN.
HE HAS A SUCCESSFUL JOB AND
MANY SUCCESSFUL HOBBIES
WHICH HE DOES IN HIS
SUCCESSFUL FREE TIME

WHERE DO YOU GO ON HOLIDAYS?
WHERE THERE'S ONLY FOOLS AND HORSES, MAD DOGS AND ENGLISHMEN, AND ANGELS FEAR TO TREAD!

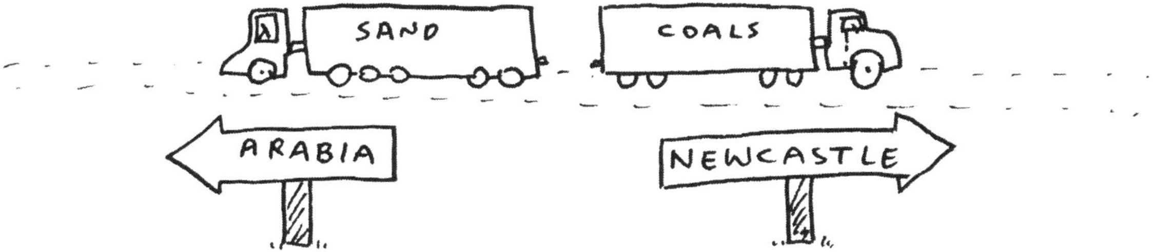
SAND
COALS
ARABIA
NEWCASTLE

LADIES AND GENTLEMEN... AND HERE HE IS... RIGHT HERE... RIGHT NOW... I GIVE TO YOU... YOUR OWN... YOUR VERY OWN... LET'S GIVE IT UP FOR...!

HIS NOSE IS ALWAYS OUT OF JOINT, BUT HIS HEART IS IN THE RIGHT PLACE!

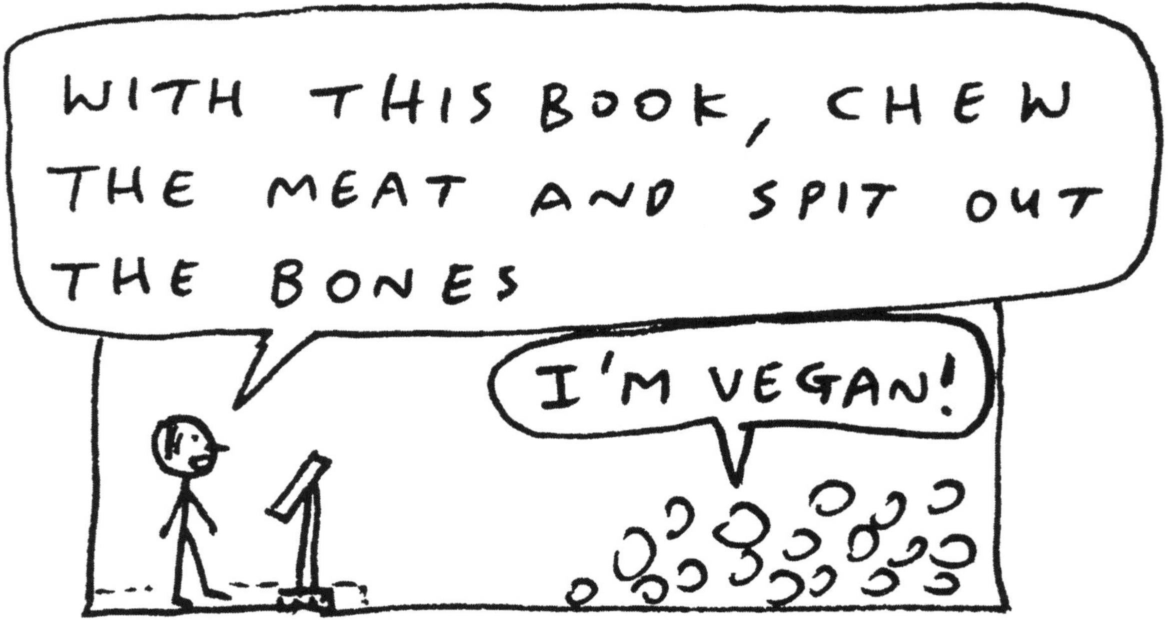
WITH THIS BOOK, CHEW THE MEAT AND SPIT OUT THE BONES
I'M VEGAN!

WHAT HAPPENED TO YOU?!
JUST HAD A FIGHT WITH A LION!
YOUR JEANS LOOK KIND OF COOL!

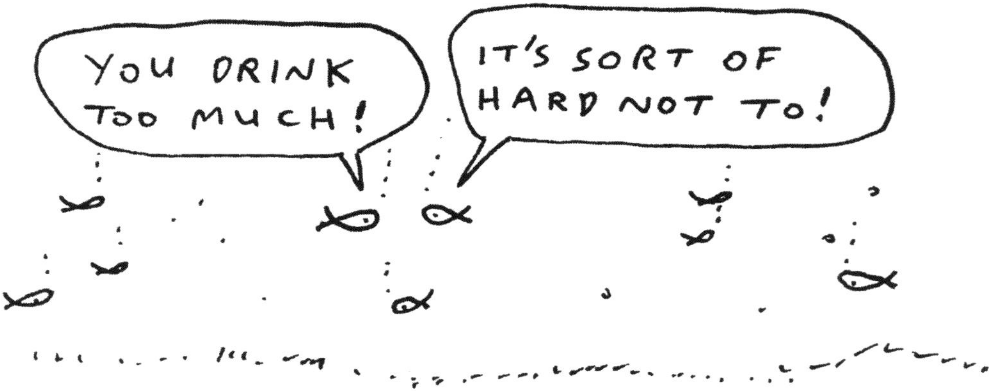
YOU DRINK TOO MUCH!
IT'S SORT OF HARD NOT TO!

THIS LESSON'S GONNA BE A CROSS BETWEEN A JOY RIDE AND A CRASH COURSE!

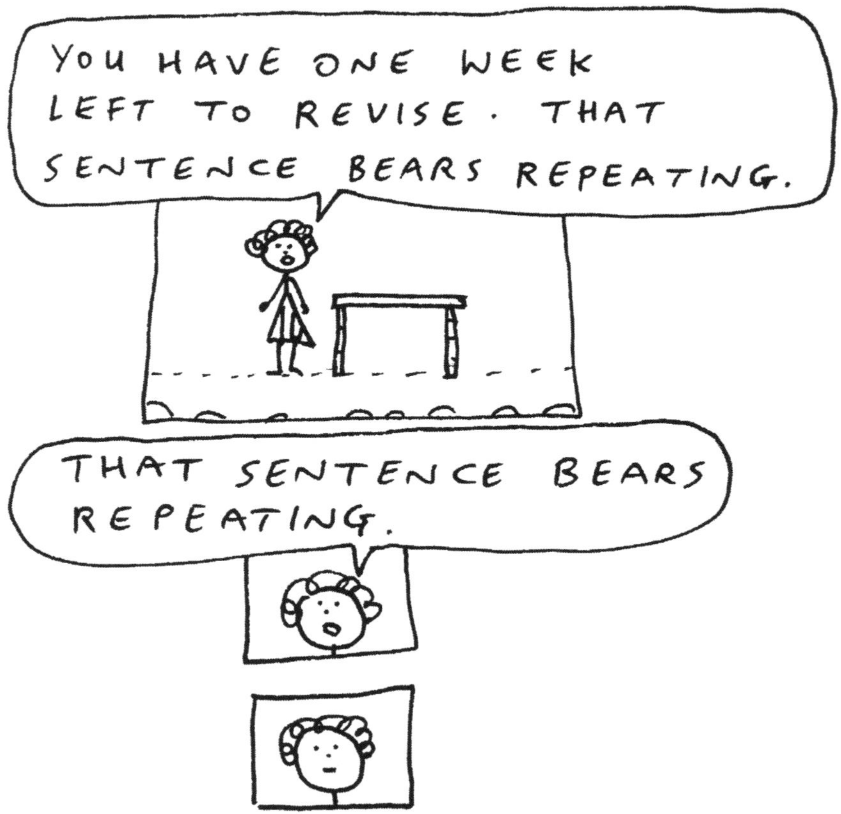
YOU HAVE ONE WEEK LEFT TO REVISE. THAT SENTENCE BEARS REPEATING.
THAT SENTENCE BEARS REPEATING.

IF YOU KNOW OTHER PEOPLE LIKE YOU, YOU SHOULD ALL BE PUT TOGETHER

WELCOME TO THE COURSE! GET INTO GROUPS OF TWO OR THREE AND INTRODUCE YOURSELVES. IF YOU DON'T KNOW WHO YOU ARE, ASK SOMEONE IN CHARGE!

FOR THIS EXAM, YOU HAVE BETWEEN HALF AN HOUR AND THIRTY MINUTES

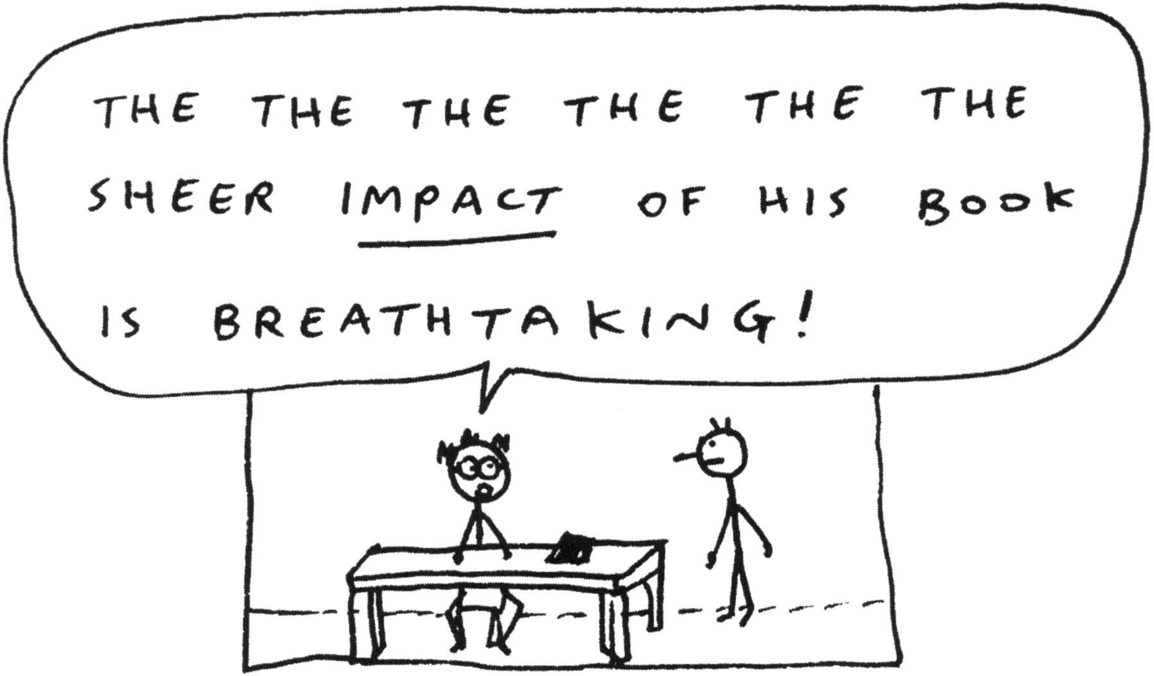
THE THE THE THE THE THE SHEER IMPACT OF HIS BOOK IS BREATHTAKING!

IF YOU'RE NOT LEADING THEM DOWN THE AISLE, YOU'RE LEADING THEM UP THE GARDEN PATH!

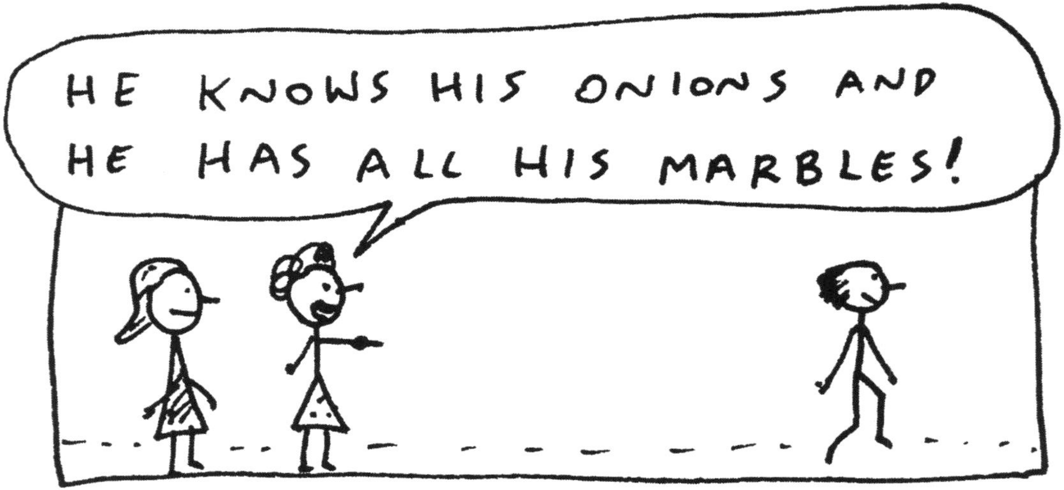
HE KNOWS HIS ONIONS AND HE HAS ALL HIS MARBLES!

HOW WAS YOUR FIRST DAY AT STACKING PLANKS?
THEY SAID I WAS A NATURAL!

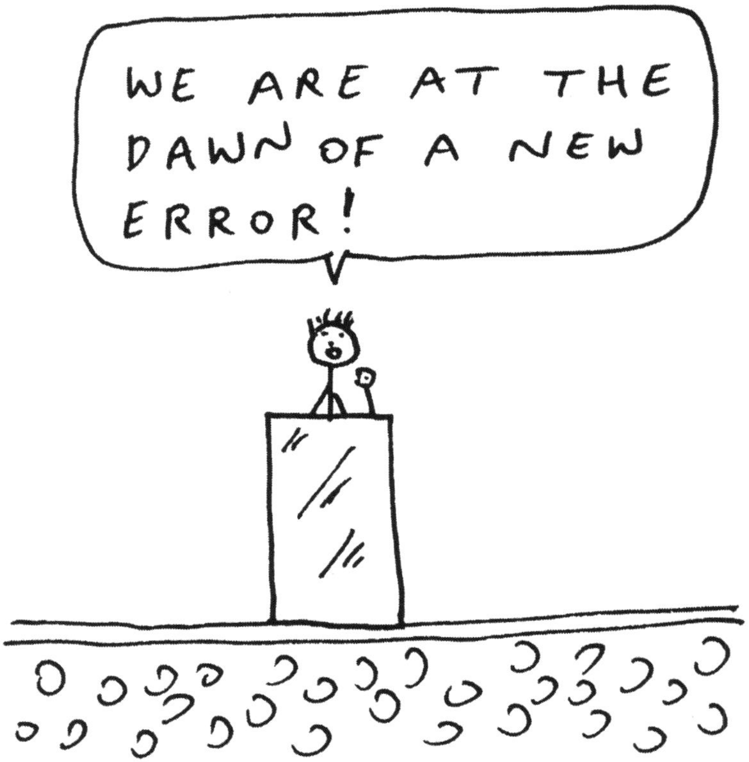
WE ARE AT THE DAWN OF A NEW ERROR!

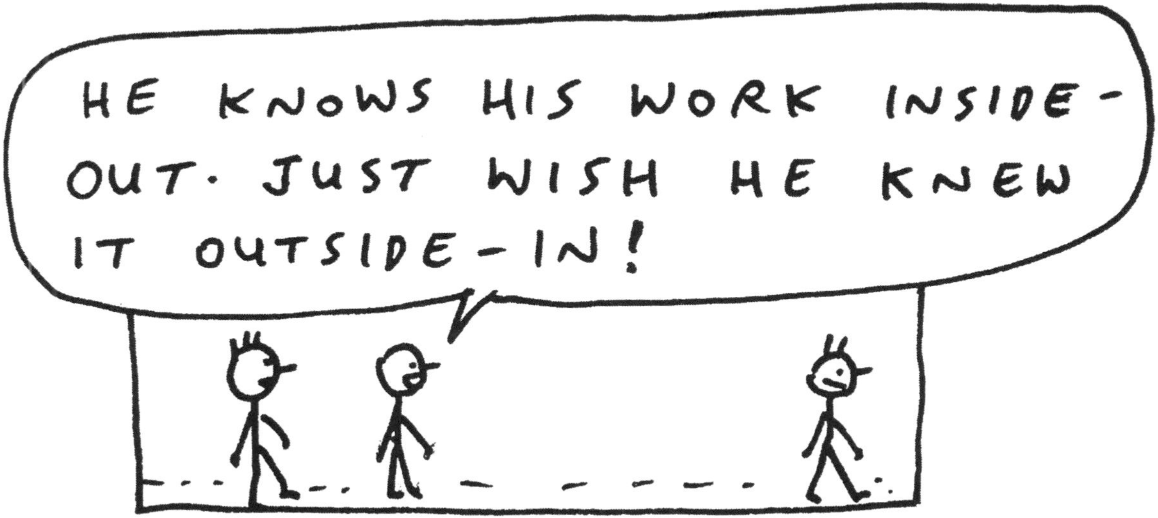
HE KNOWS HIS WORK INSIDE-OUT. JUST WISH HE KNEW IT OUTSIDE-IN!

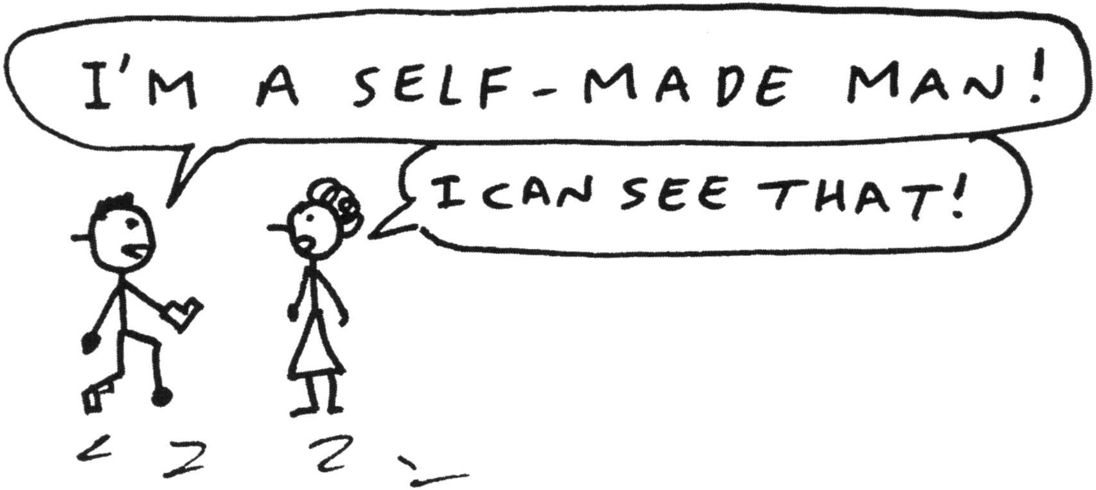
I'M A SELF-MADE MAN!
I CAN SEE THAT!

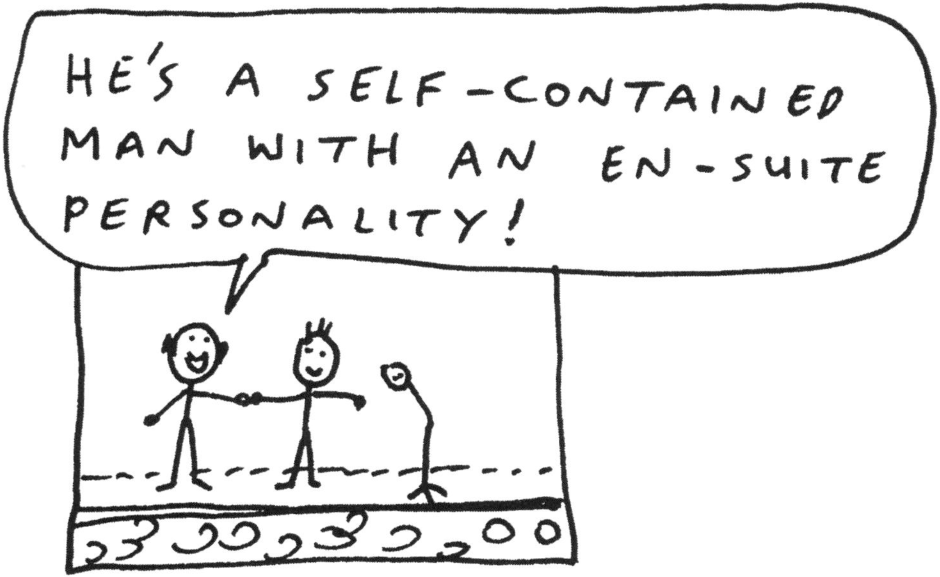
HE'S A SELF-CONTAINED MAN WITH AN EN-SUITE PERSONALITY!

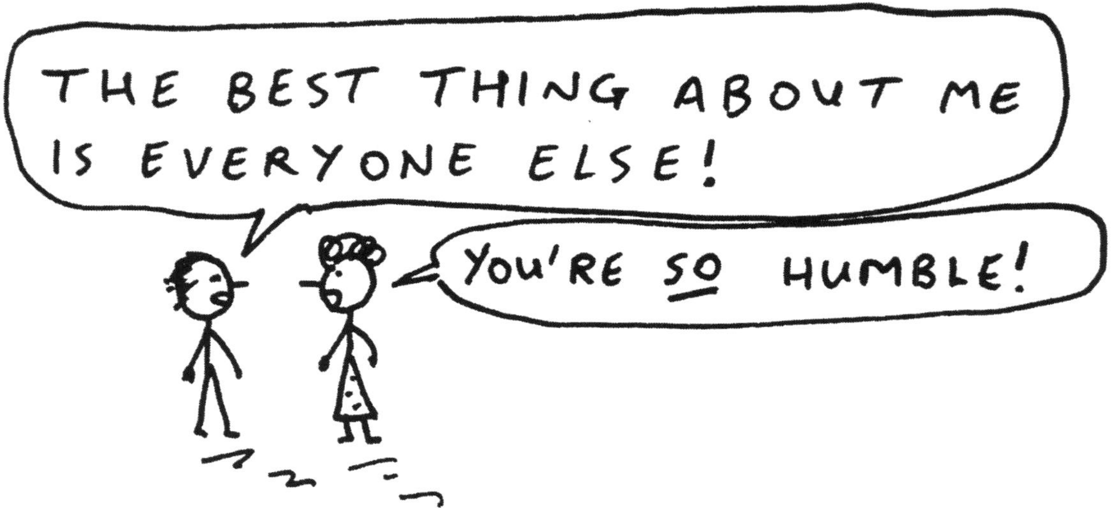
THE BEST THING ABOUT ME IS EVERYONE ELSE!
YOU'RE SO HUMBLE!

YOU HAVE A MAGNETIC PERSONALITY
THANKS!
IT REPELS

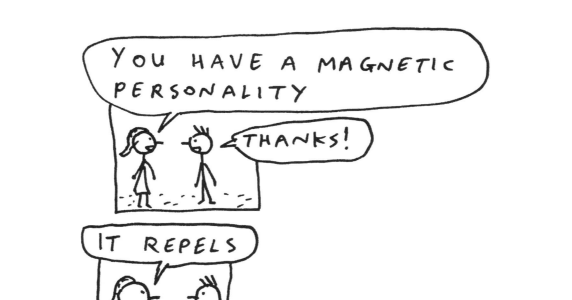

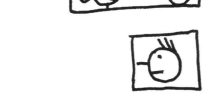

PHONE CHAT

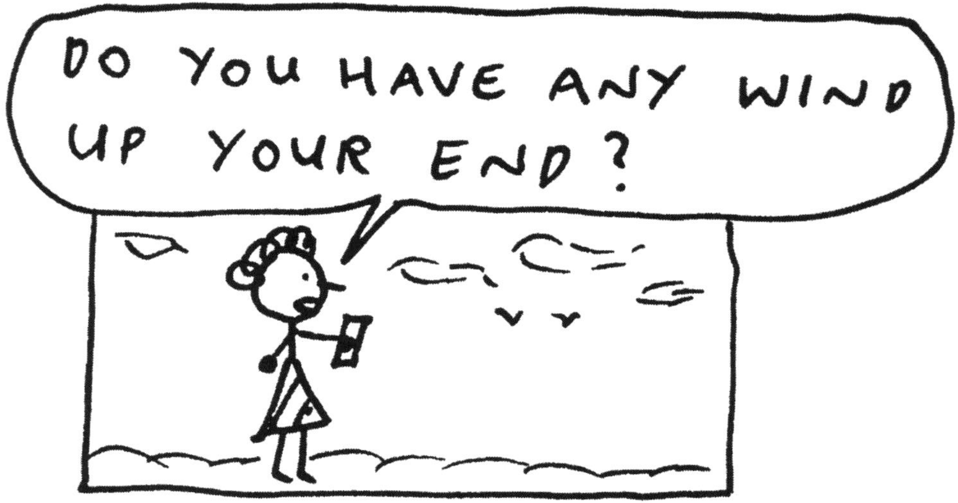
DO YOU HAVE ANY WIND UP YOUR END?

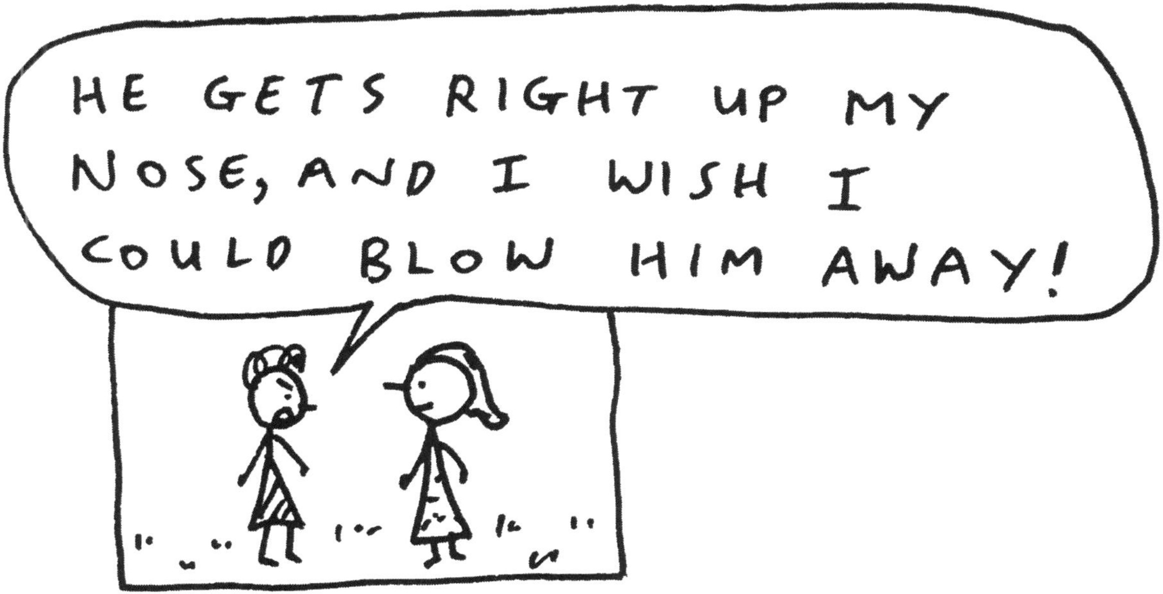
HE GETS RIGHT UP MY NOSE, AND I WISH I COULD BLOW HIM AWAY!

ARE THE DOGS HAPPY WITH THEIR NEW HOME?
THEY MADE ENCOURAGING NOISES!

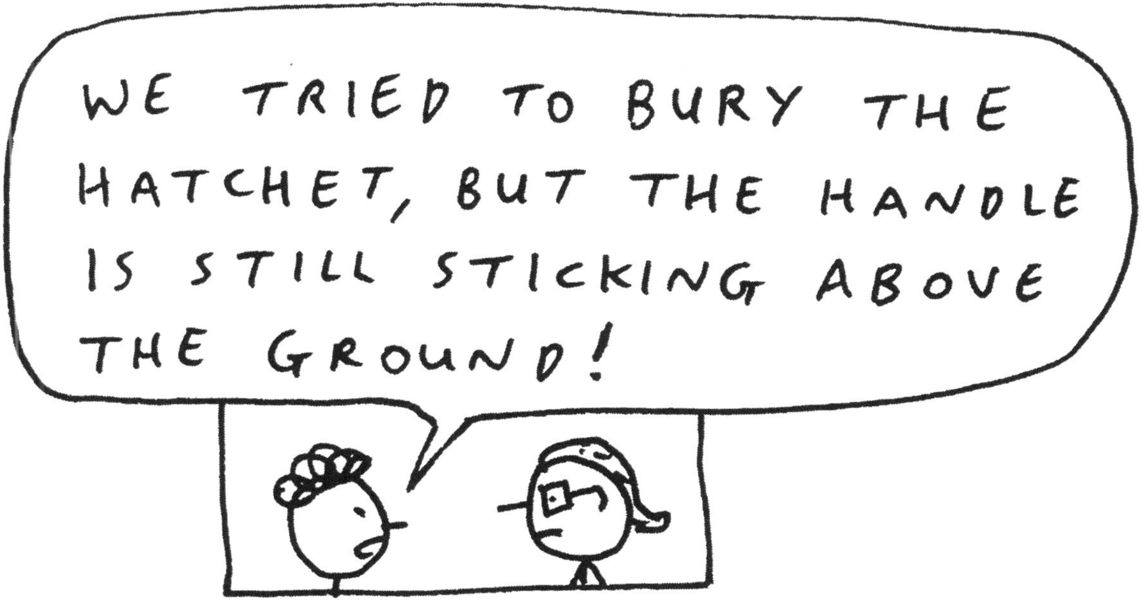
WE TRIED TO BURY THE HATCHET, BUT THE HANDLE IS STILL STICKING ABOVE THE GROUND!

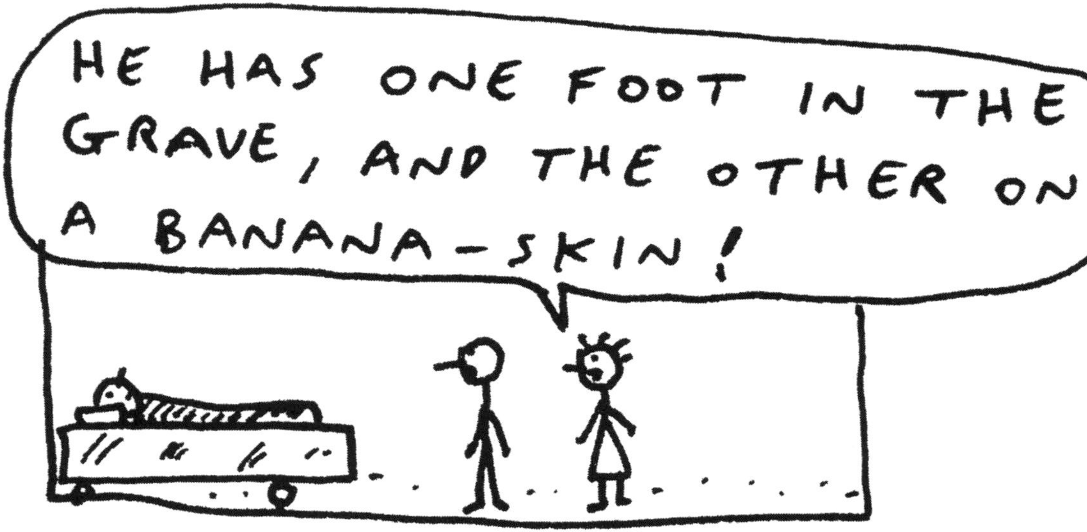
HE HAS ONE FOOT IN THE GRAVE, AND THE OTHER ON A BANANA-SKIN!

"THE FRONT PAGE WAS DOG-EARED, THE WORD "FLUX" WAS BLURRED ON PAGE SIX AND THE BOOK EDGES LOOKED BURNED LIKE A PIRATE'S MAP"

BOOK REVIEW

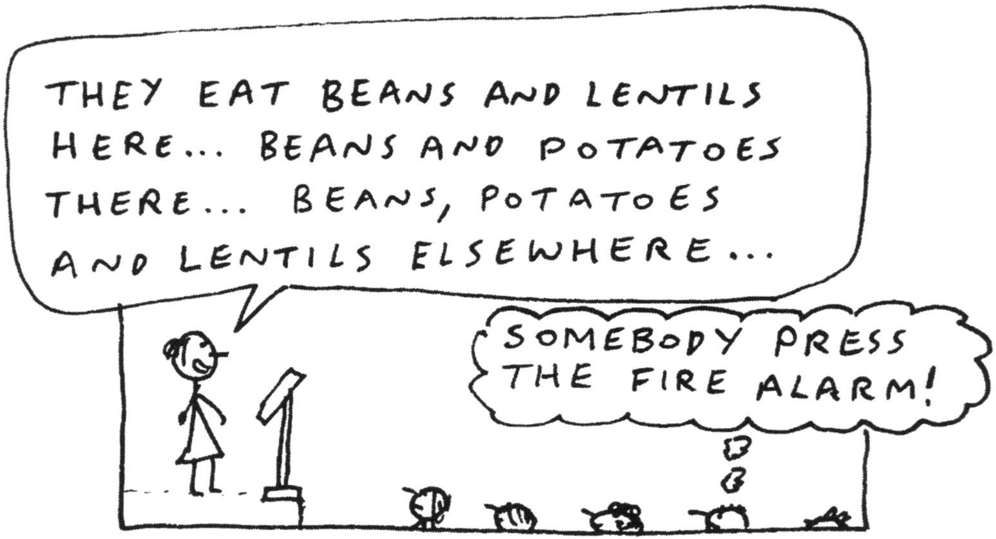

GEOGRAPHY LESSON

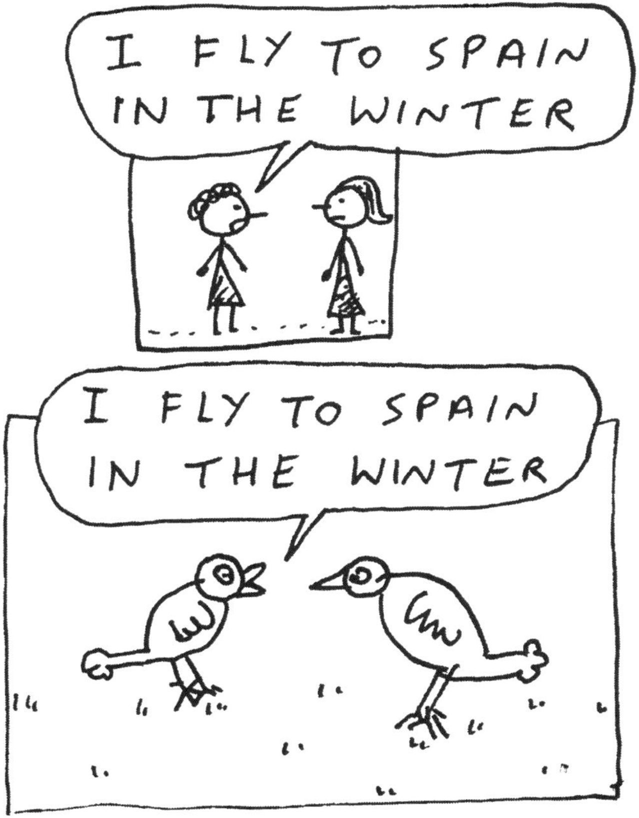
I FLY TO SPAIN IN THE WINTER
I FLY TO SPAIN IN THE WINTER

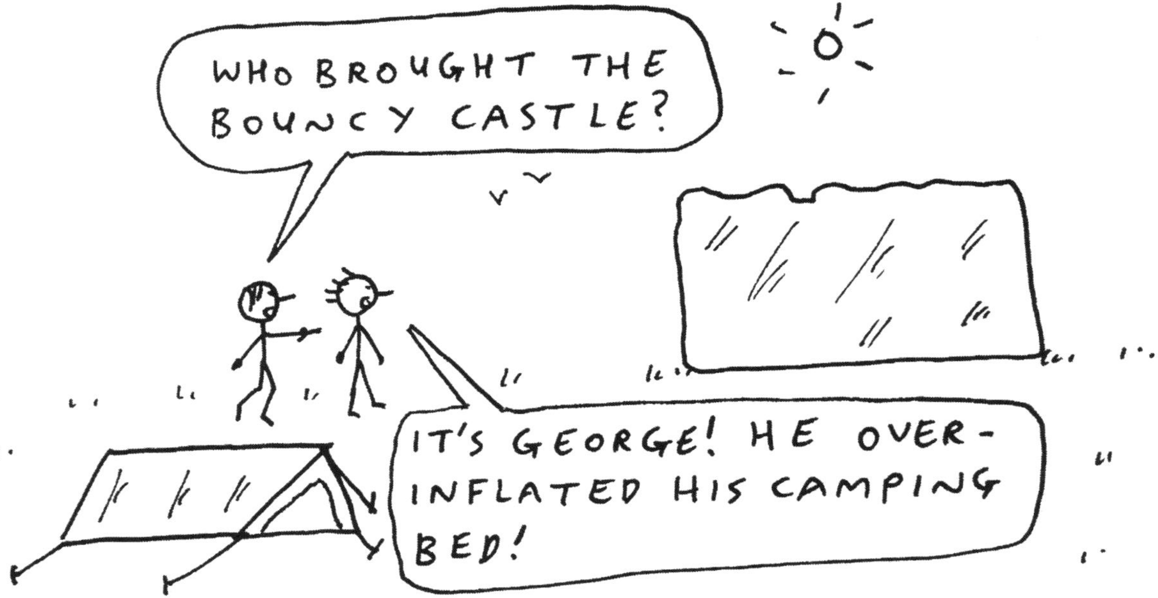
WHO BROUGHT THE BOUNCY CASTLE?
IT'S GEORGE! HE OVER-INFLATED HIS CAMPING BED!

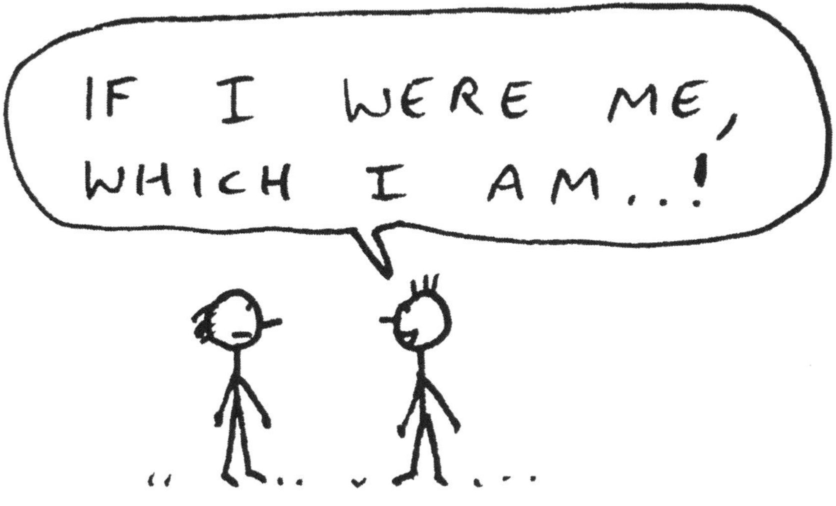
IF I WERE ME, WHICH I AM..!

WALTER WAFFLE

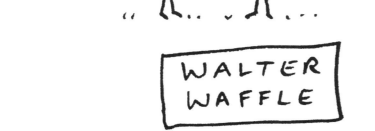

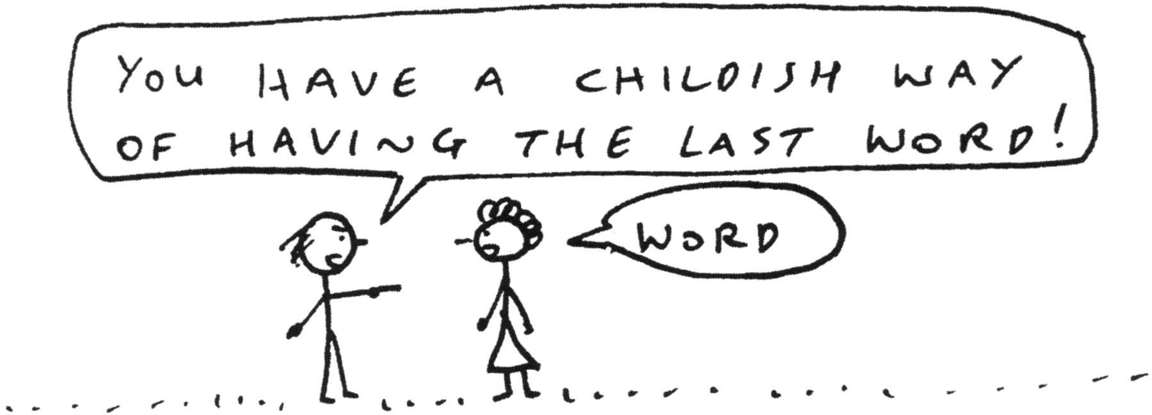
YOU HAVE A CHILDISH WAY OF HAVING THE LAST WORD!
WORD

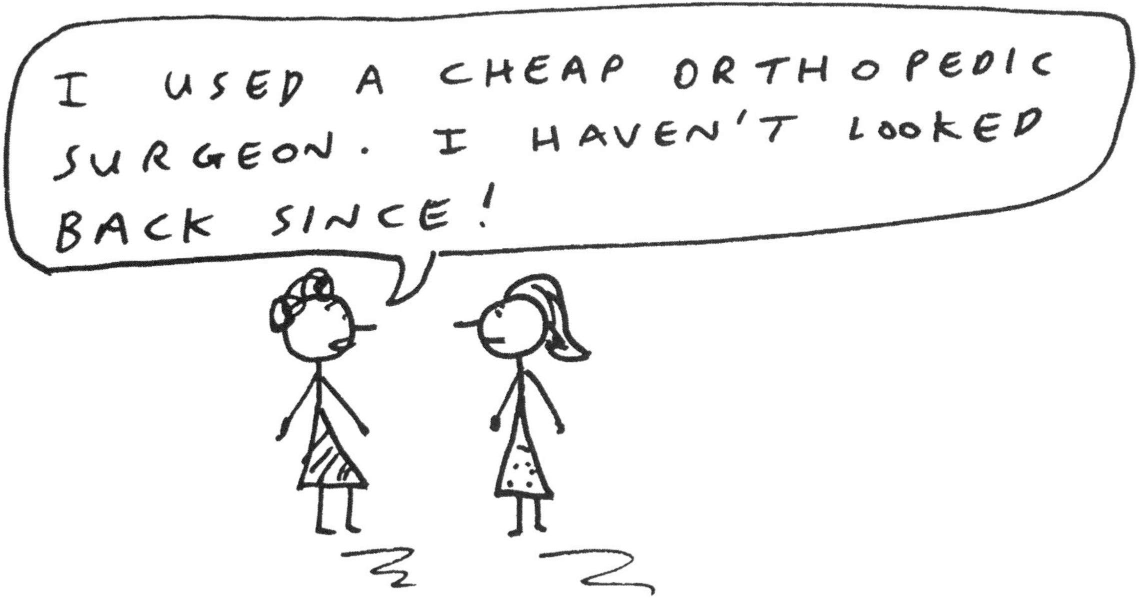
I USED A CHEAP ORTHOPEDIC SURGEON. I HAVEN'T LOOKED BACK SINCE!

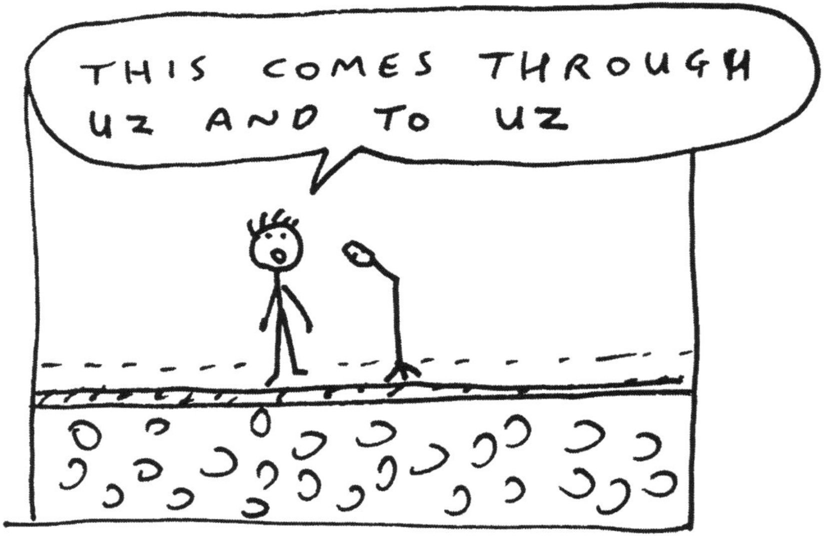
THIS COMES THROUGH UZ AND TO UZ

FUNNY ACCENT

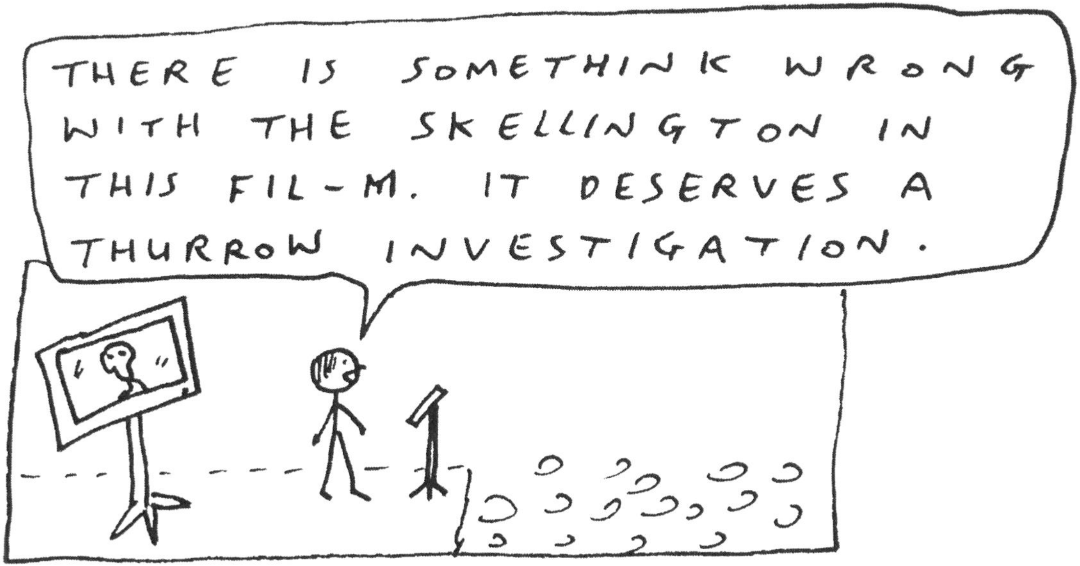

KRANKY PRONOUNCIATION

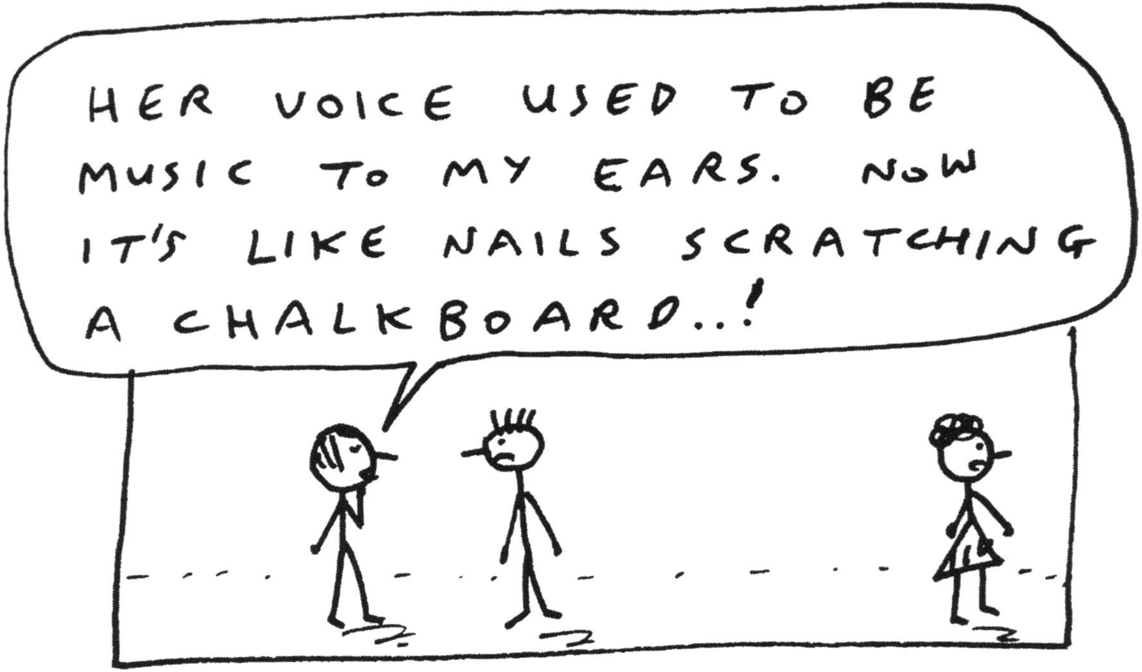
HER VOICE USED TO BE MUSIC TO MY EARS. NOW IT'S LIKE NAILS SCRATCHING A CHALKBOARD..!

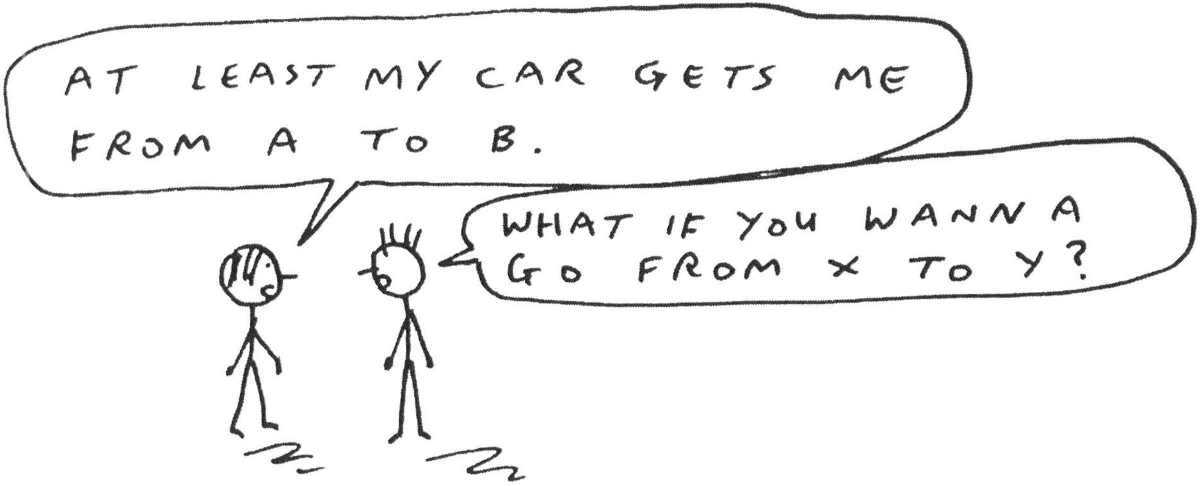
AT LEAST MY CAR GETS ME FROM A TO B.
WHAT IF YOU WANNA GO FROM X TO Y?

MY GARDEN HAS SUCH A SLOPE, I WEAR SHOES THAT ARE BUILT UP AT THE FRONT!

HE ALWAYS HAS A SWEATY UPPER LIP, AND A SMILE SO BIG YOU CAN HEAR IT!

THE ONLY THING THAT DOESN'T NEED REPLACING IS THE FLUFFY DICE!

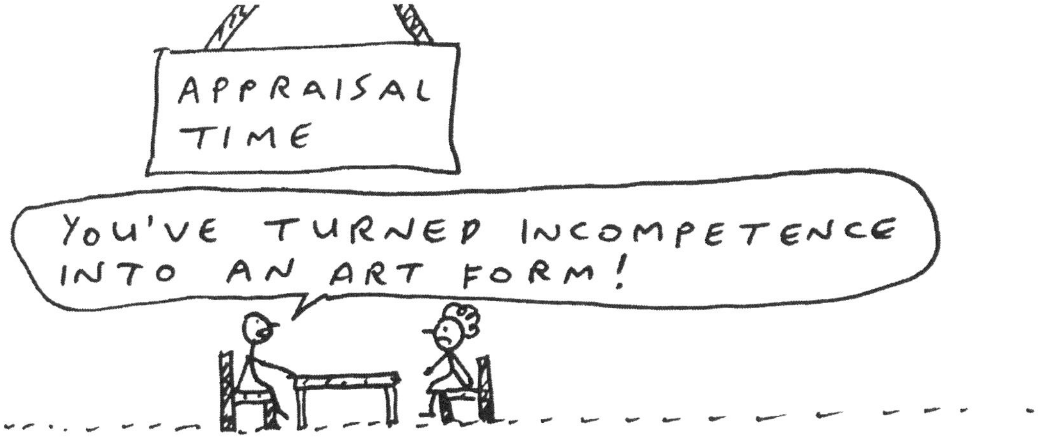
APPRAISAL TIME
YOU'VE TURNED INCOMPETENCE INTO AN ART FORM!

NOW THAT I'M INTERNATIONALLY ACCLAIMED, I WANT TO MAKE AN IMPACT ABROAD

BECAUSE MY SON IS TALL, I'M WORRIED PEOPLE WILL EXPECT TOO MUCH OF HIM
NOT NOW THEY'VE MET THE FATHER!

HE DIED AFTER BLOWING UP AN ENTIRE CONTINENT BY MISTAKE.
THE WORLD WILL BE A SMALLER PLACE

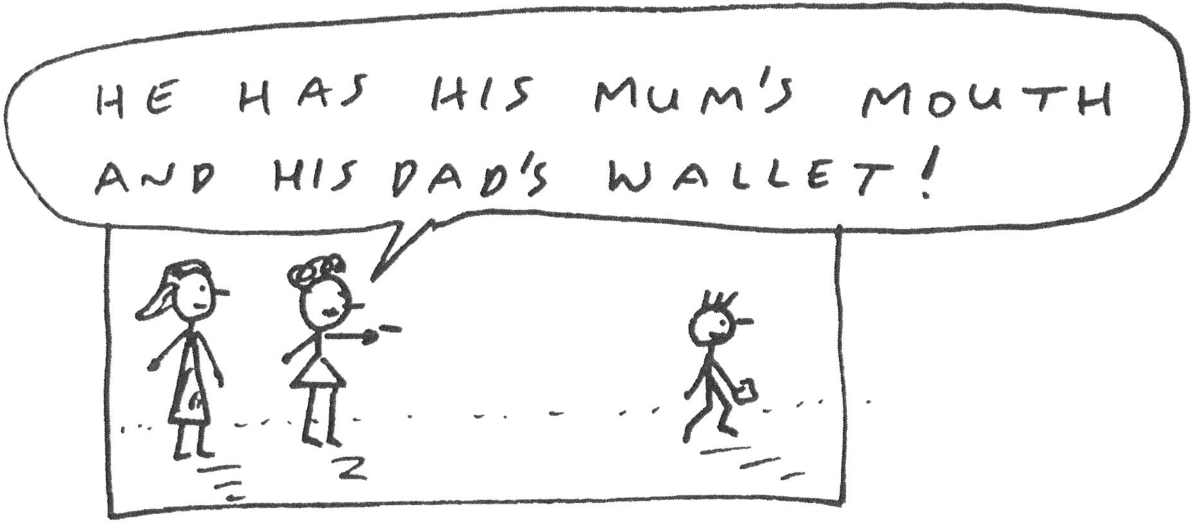
HE HAS HIS MUM'S MOUTH AND HIS DAD'S WALLET!

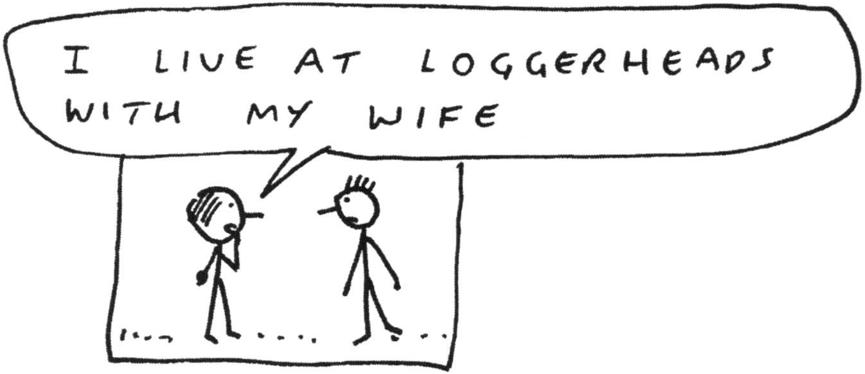
I LIVE AT LOGGERHEADS WITH MY WIFE

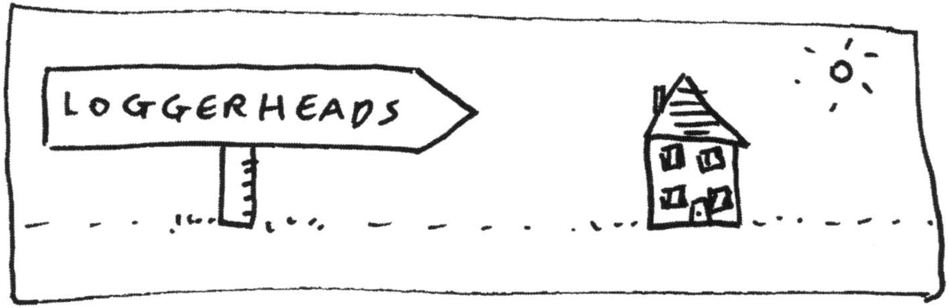
LOGGERHEADS

BUSINESS CONSULTANT
IF YOU CUT TOO MANY CORNERS, YOU'LL GO ROUND IN CIRCLES

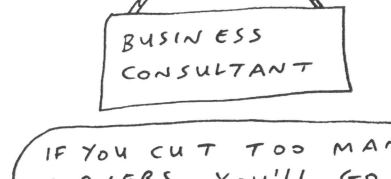

ONE DAY YOU'LL FALL OFF THAT CLIFF, AND YOU'LL THANK ME FOR TELLING YOU!

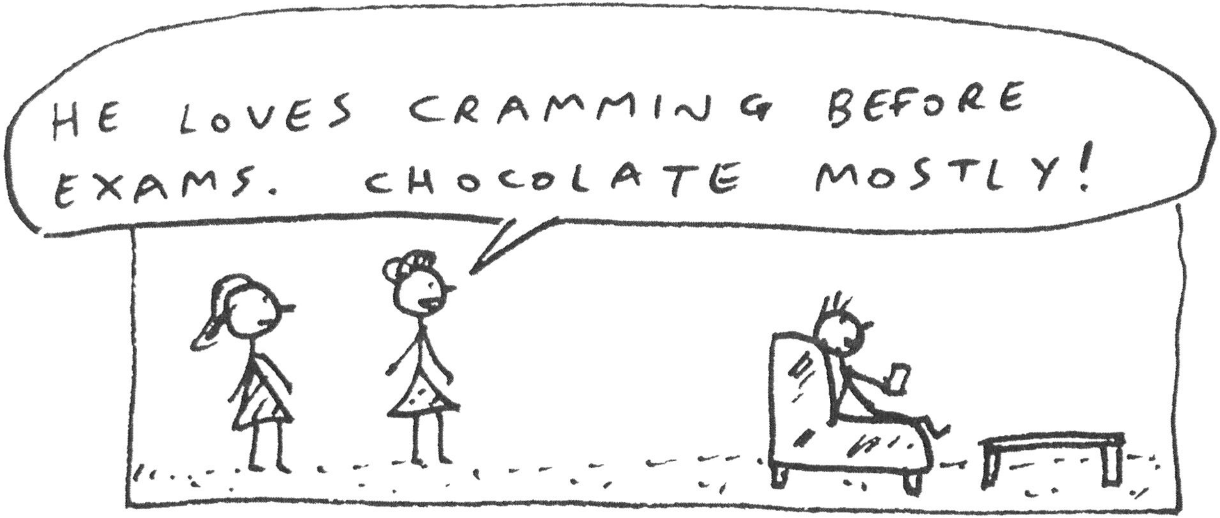
HE LOVES CRAMMING BEFORE EXAMS. CHOCOLATE MOSTLY!

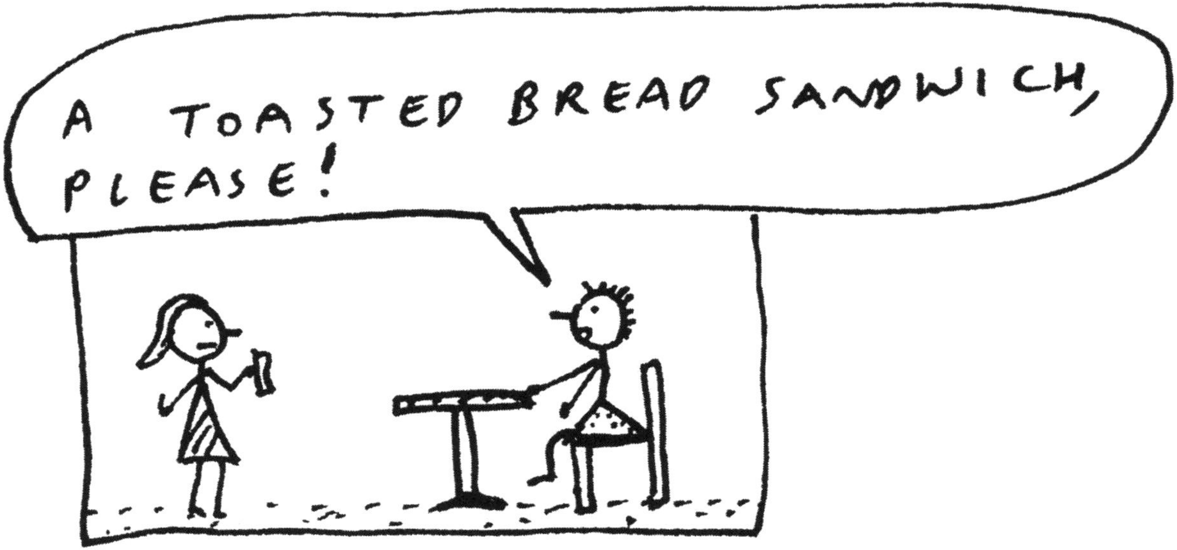
A TOASTED BREAD SANDWICH, PLEASE!

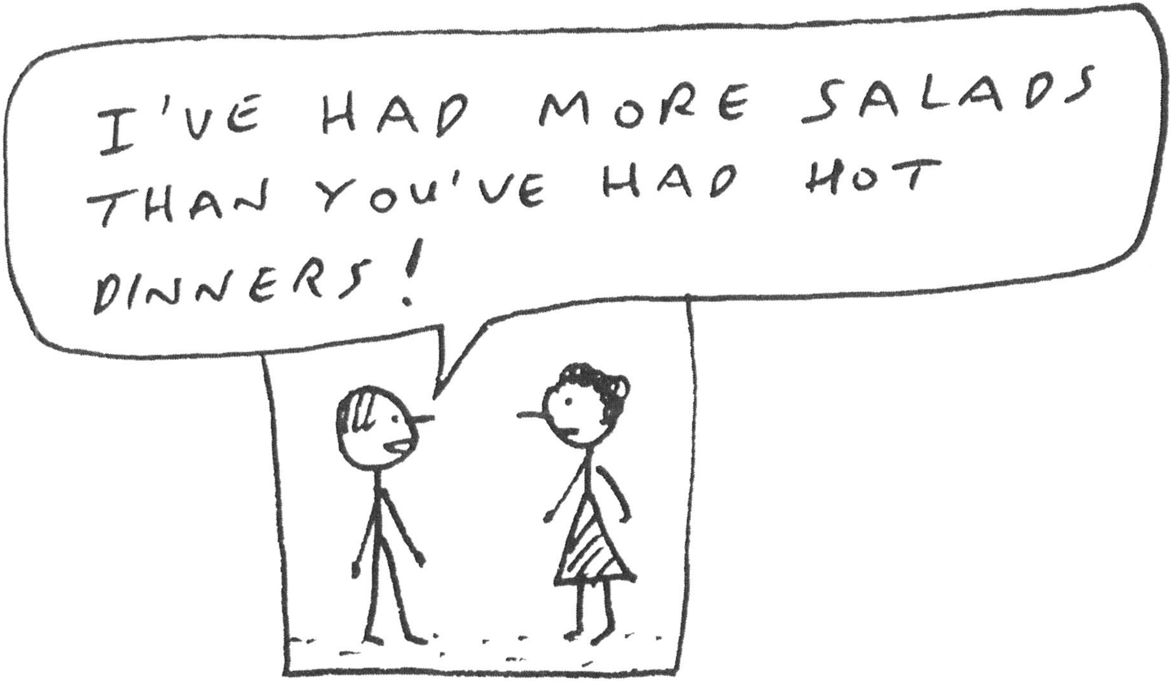
I'VE HAD MORE SALADS THAN YOU'VE HAD HOT DINNERS!

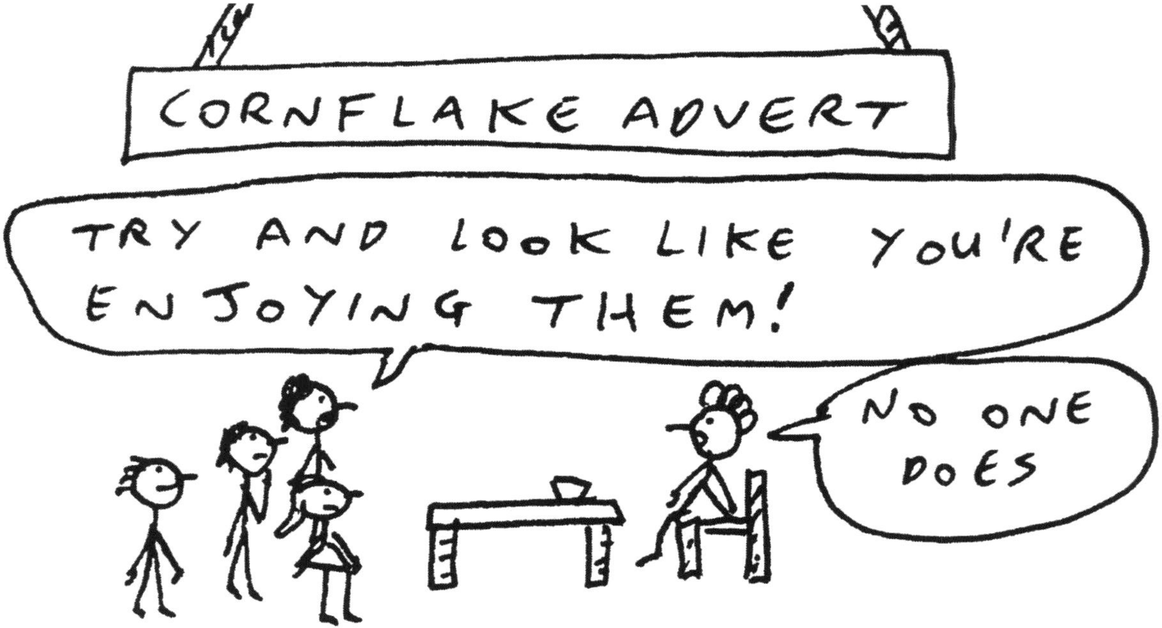
CORNFLAKE ADVERT
TRY AND LOOK LIKE YOU'RE ENJOYING THEM!
NO ONE DOES

THERE'S TOO MUCH MONEY IN THE WORLD, AND CHILDREN EXIST TO USE IT UP!

I BOUGHT OLIVIA A "FEED 'N' WEE" DOLL, AND NOW SHE'S USING IT AS A WATER PISTOL!

MY NEW SHOES HAVE BEEN HURTING THE BACKS OF MY FEET!
HAVE YOU TRIED HEEL GRIPS?
YEAH, BUT THEY KEEP COMING OFF IN THE BATH!

I RECENTLY LOST MY PERSONAL ALARM. IT TOOK ME THREE WEEKS TO REALISE WHY MY DEODERANT WAS SO NOISY!

I'VE BEEN PRESCRIBED SOME TABLETS THAT ARE SO BIG, ALL YOU NEED ARE A COUPLE OF POTATOES – AND THAT'S MY MAIN MEAL SORTED!

EVERYTHING WENT INTO
NOAH'S ARK IN TWO'S...

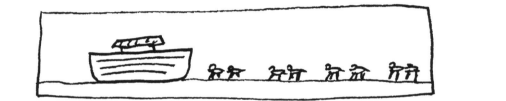

APART FROM THE BEERS

PACKS OF SIX

ALIEN INTERROGATION
WHY DO MEN WEAR TIES?
TO HOLD THEIR SHIRT TOGETHER?
NOPE
TO HOLD THEIR TROUSERS UP?
NO

MY WIFE SAID I'D SEE STARS IF I LOOKED UP THE CHIMNEY BREAST.
SHE WAS RIGHT – I MET A BRICK ON IT'S WAY DOWN!

THE POLITE WAY OF SAYING IT, IS "HE COULDN'T ORGANISE A PRIZE-GIVING IN A TROPHY SHOP"!

SURGICAL TRAINING
KEEP ONE EYE ON YOUR PATIENT, AND THE OTHER ON YOUR COLLEAGUES

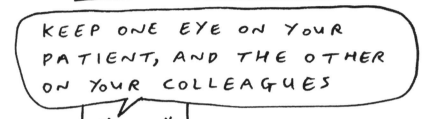

BRAINWASHED
? ! ? !
DISHWASHED

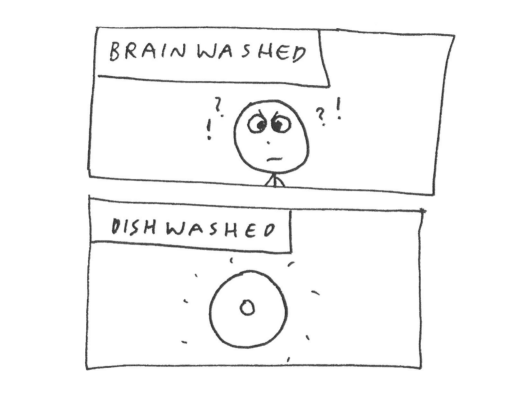

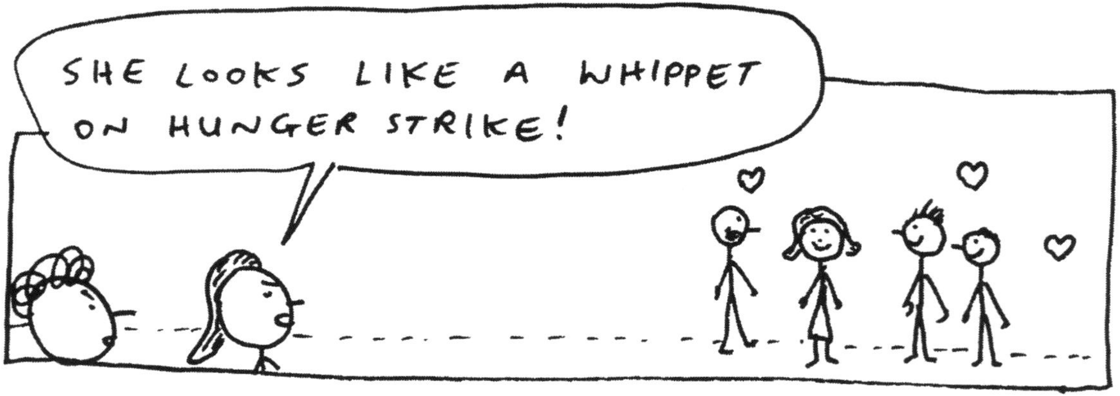
SHE LOOKS LIKE A WHIPPET ON HUNGER STRIKE!

AND TODAY, WE'RE GOING TO KNIT A QUILT OUT OF OLD STOCKINGS!
CREATIVE HOUR

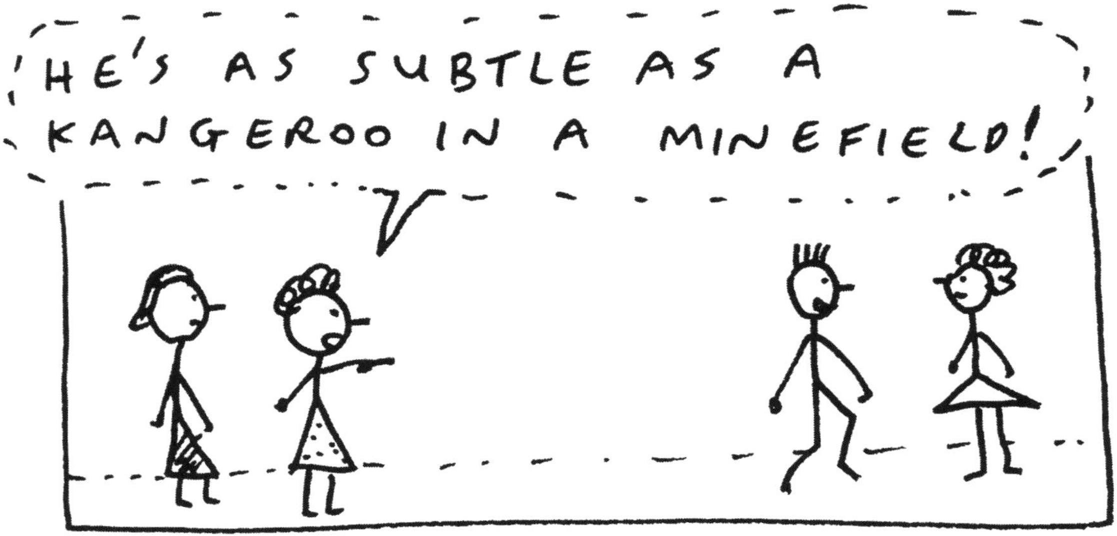
HE'S AS SUBTLE AS A KANGEROO IN A MINEFIELD!

AS WELHAUSEN SAYS IN THE PREFACE TO "THE STUDY OF SOCIAL CLASS IN RELATION TO GENERATIONAL ETHICS OF GENDER ROLES AND EMPLOYMENT," THIS IS "INTERESTING"

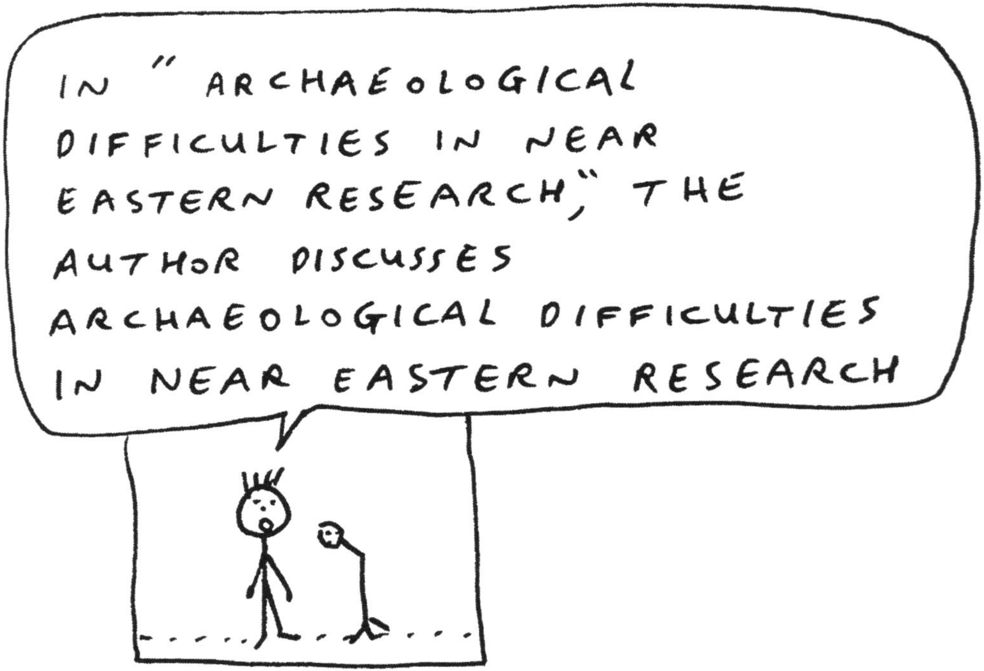
IN "ARCHAEOLOGICAL DIFFICULTIES IN NEAR EASTERN RESEARCH," THE AUTHOR DISCUSSES ARCHAEOLOGICAL DIFFICULTIES IN NEAR EASTERN RESEARCH

CAN I ASK YOU A QUESTION?
YOU JUST DID!
CAN I ASK YOU ANOTHER?
THAT WAS ANOTHER!
YOU ARE ANNOYING
THAT IS A STATEMENT

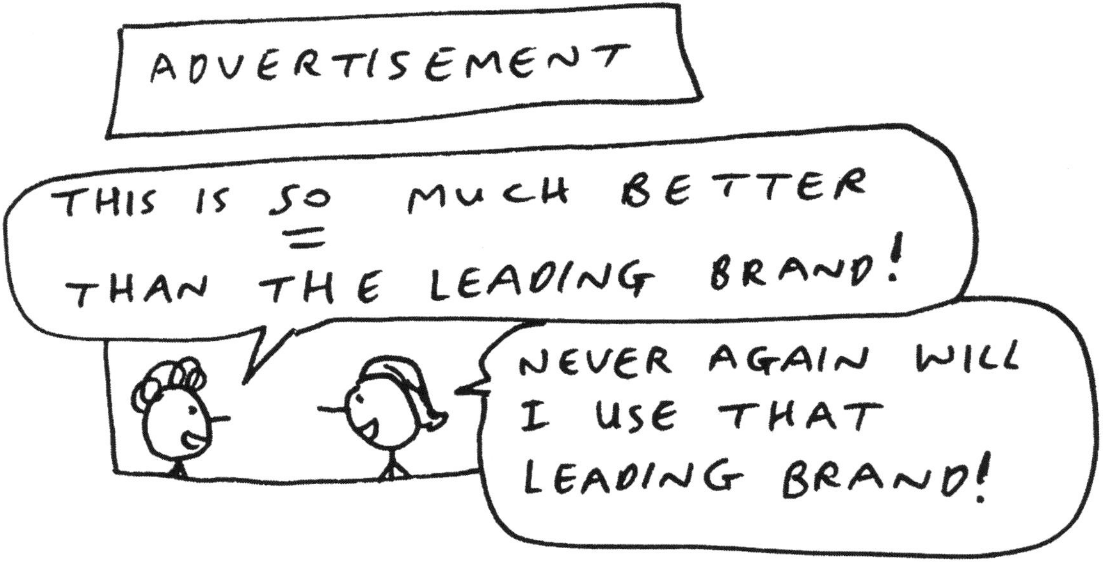
ADVERTISEMENT
THIS IS SO MUCH BETTER THAN THE LEADING BRAND!
NEVER AGAIN WILL I USE THAT LEADING BRAND!

ADVERTISEMENT
BUY MY PRODUCT OR I WILL HAUNT YOU WHEN I DIE!!
ROFALDULOX $2-99

AND SO, CHILDREN, HENRY THE EIGHTH BLAH, WHO CARES, YAWN, BAD ATTITUDES, WAFFLE WAFFLE, CREAKY CLASSROOM...
TEACHER'S LAST DAY

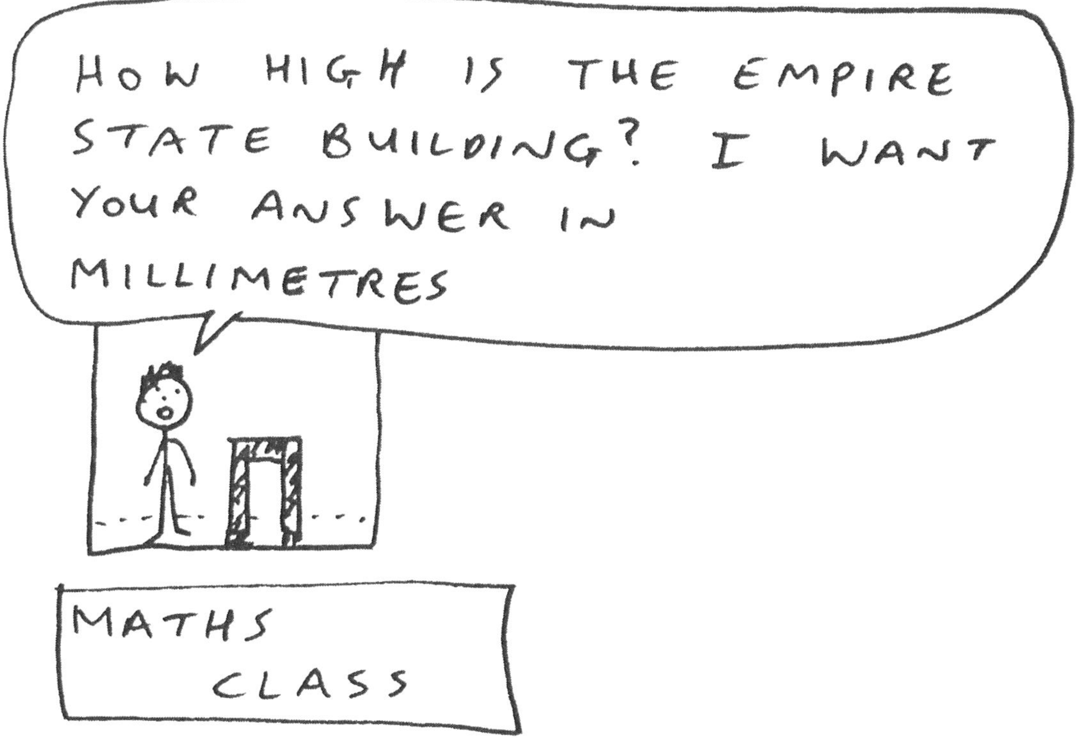
HOW HIGH IS THE EMPIRE STATE BUILDING? I WANT YOUR ANSWER IN MILLIMETRES
MATHS CLASS

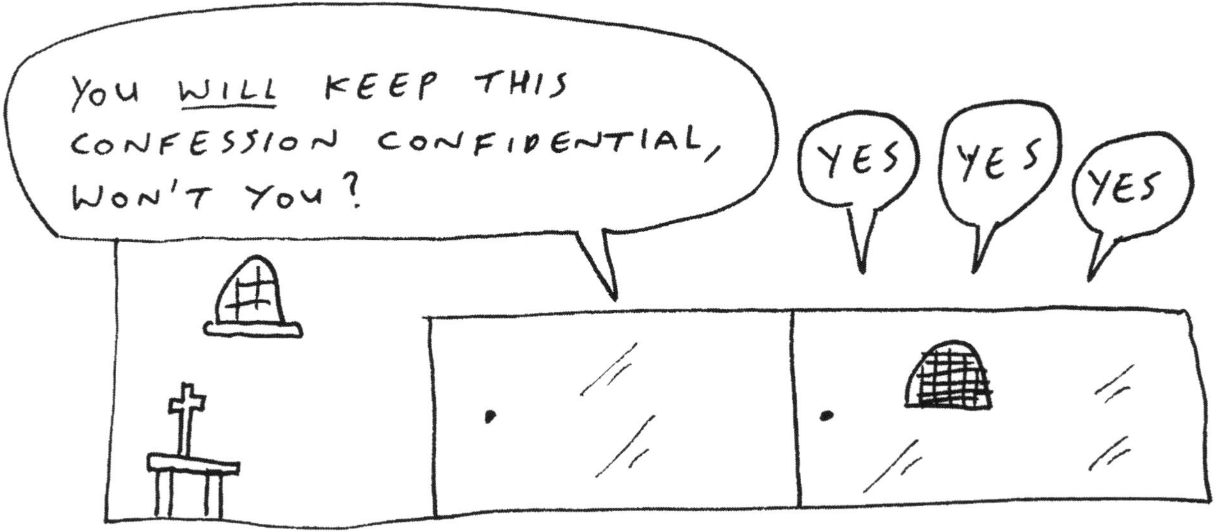
YOU WILL KEEP THIS CONFESSION CONFIDENTIAL, WON'T YOU?
YES
YES
YES

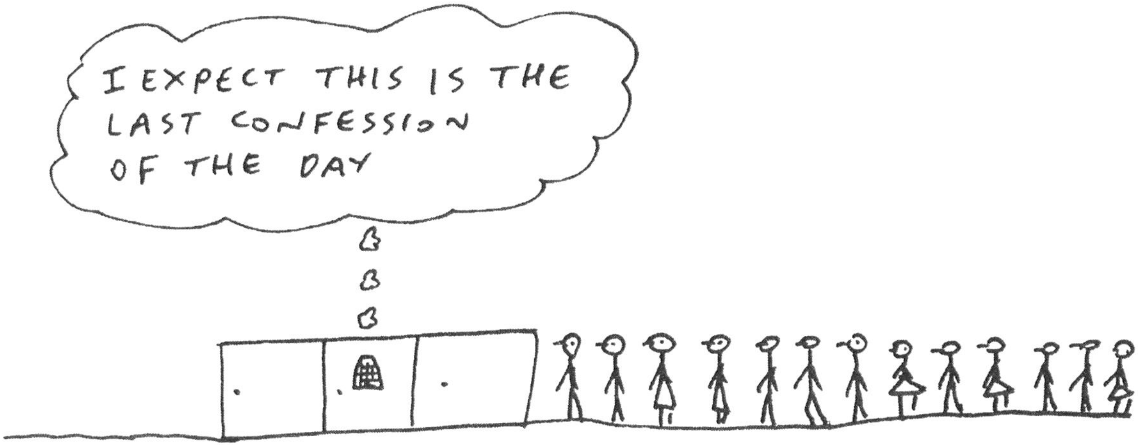
I EXPECT THIS IS THE LAST CONFESSION OF THE DAY

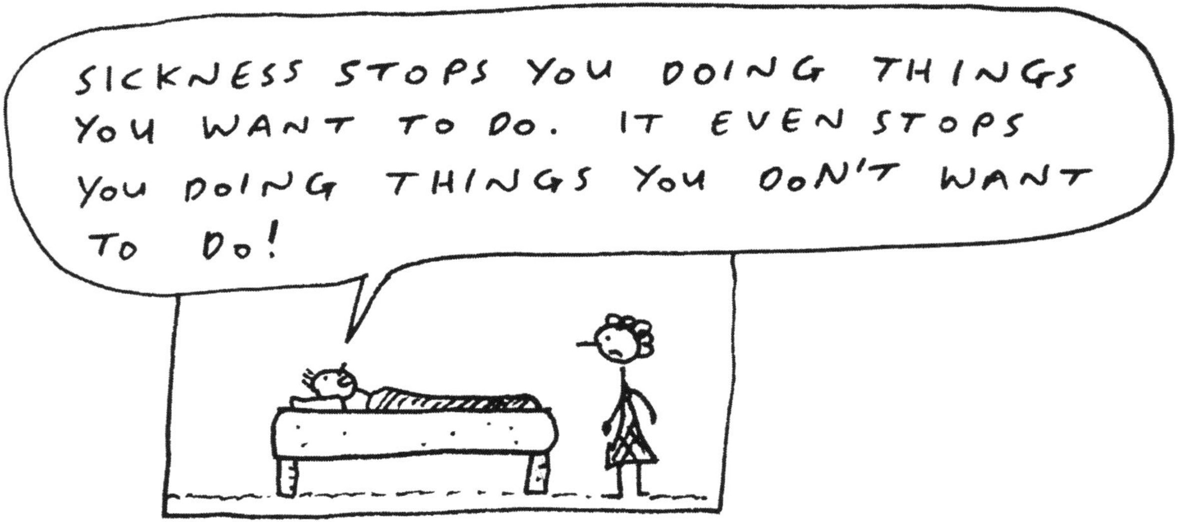
SICKNESS STOPS YOU DOING THINGS YOU WANT TO DO. IT EVEN STOPS YOU DOING THINGS YOU DON'T WANT TO DO!

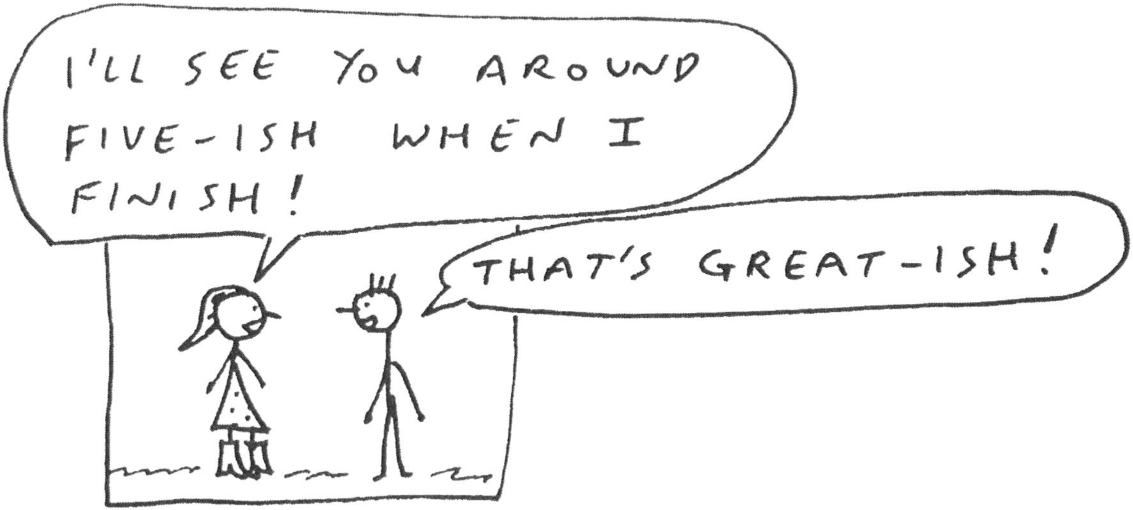
I'LL SEE YOU AROUND FIVE-ISH WHEN I FINISH!
THAT'S GREAT-ISH!

AND HOW ARE YOU THESE DAYS?
MUCH THE SAME...
FIVE FOOT SIX, BLONDE HAIR AND GLASSES

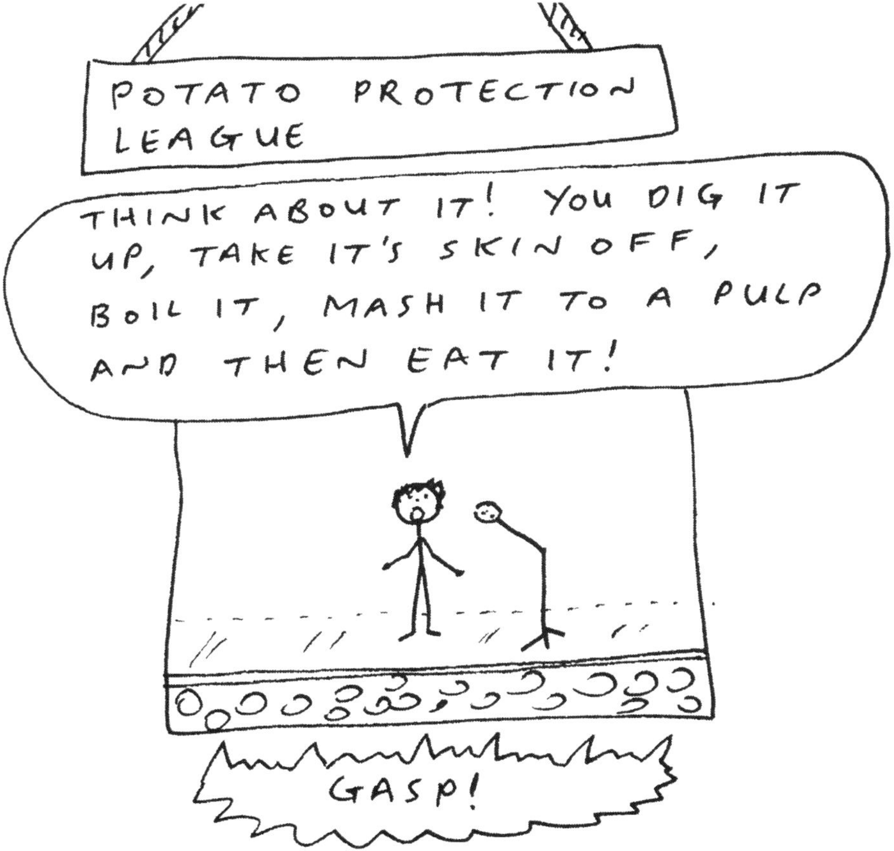
POTATO PROTECTION LEAGUE
THINK ABOUT IT! YOU DIG IT UP, TAKE IT'S SKIN OFF, BOIL IT, MASH IT TO A PULP AND THEN EAT IT!
GASP!

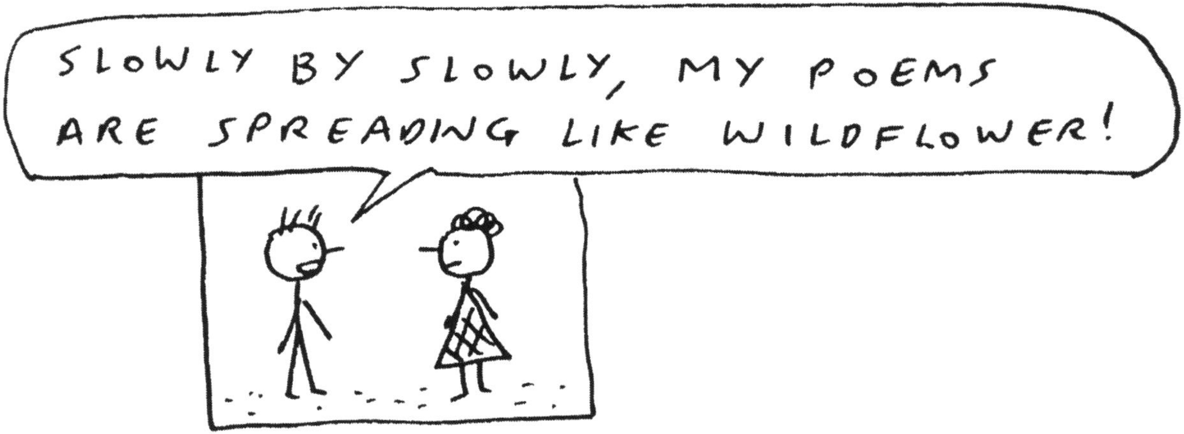
SLOWLY BY SLOWLY, MY POEMS ARE SPREADING LIKE WILDFLOWER!

UNDERWEAR CONVENTION
WE'VE MADE THESE FROM PARACHUTES, TO PROVIDE MAXIMUM WIND RESISTANCE!

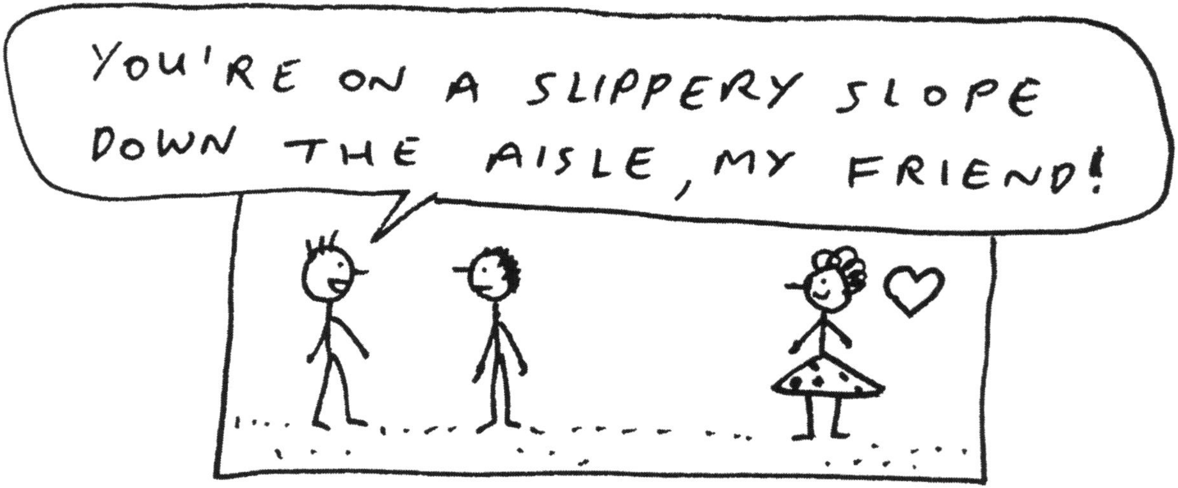
YOU'RE ON A SLIPPERY SLOPE DOWN THE AISLE, MY FRIEND!

SOMETIMES I LIE THERE, LOOKING UP AT THE STARS, AND I ASK MYSELF...
WHY AM I STILL OUTSIDE?

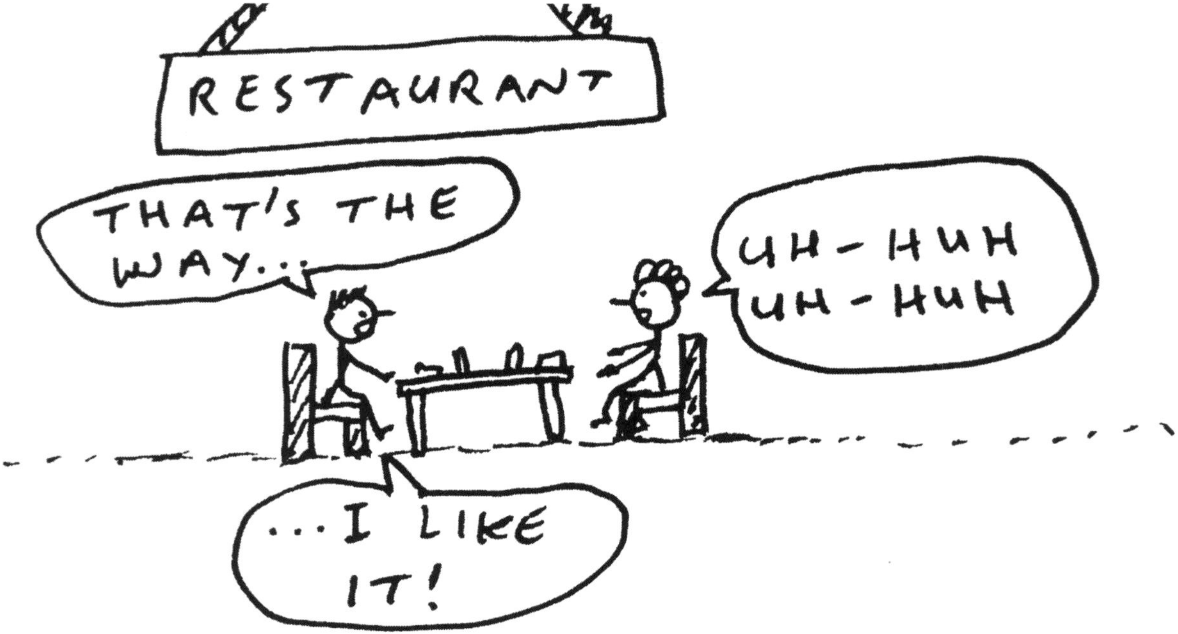
RESTAURANT
THAT'S THE WAY...
UH-HUH UH-HUH
...I LIKE IT!

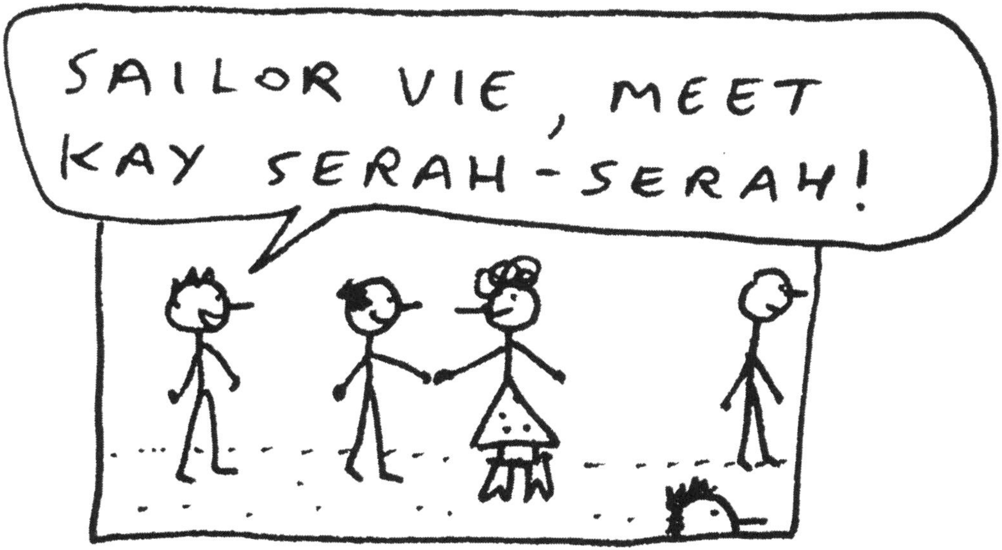
SAILOR VIE, MEET KAY SERAH-SERAH!

FLAMINGOES FIND
IT EASY TO BITE
THEIR TOENAILS

BLACK
HEADED
GULL

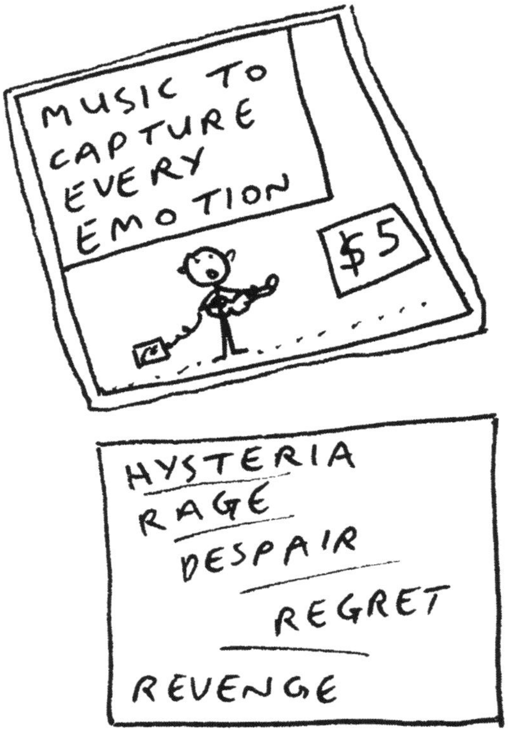
MUSIC TO CAPTURE EVERY EMOTION
$5
HYSTERIA
RAGE
DESPAIR
REGRET
REVENGE

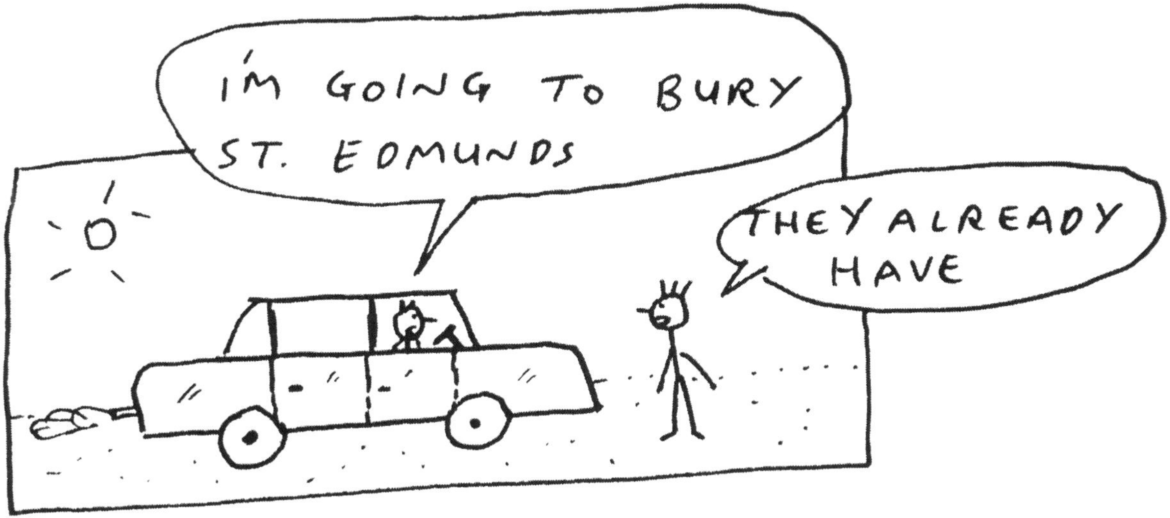
I'M GOING TO BURY ST. EDMUNDS
THEY ALREADY HAVE

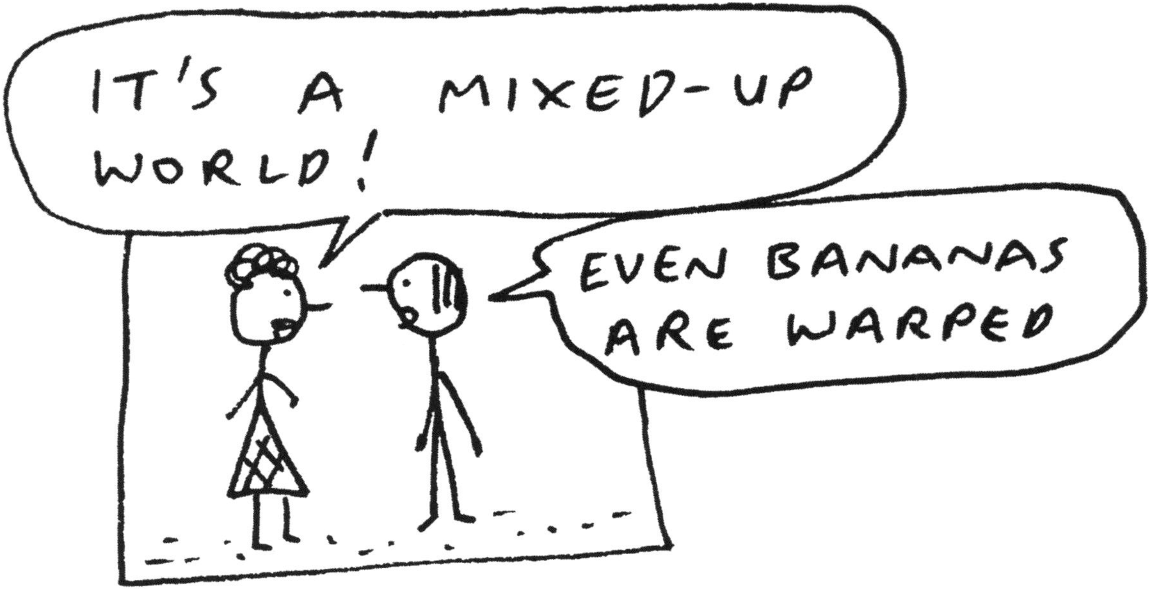
IT'S A MIXED-UP WORLD!
EVEN BANANAS ARE WARPED

I'M STONED AS THE CHURCH FONT!
INCENSE IS AS BAD AS CANNABIS!
THE CHURCH HAS GONE TO 'POT'!

HIGH CHURCH

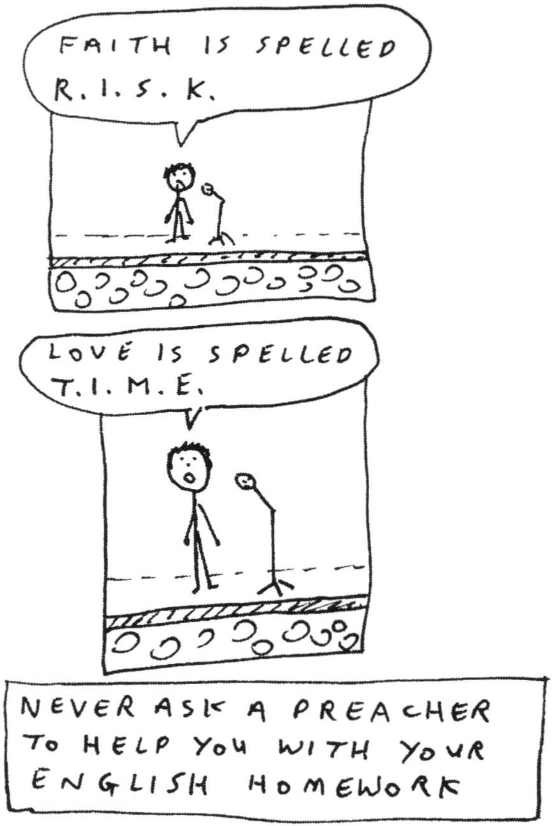
FAITH IS SPELLED R.I.S.K.
LOVE IS SPELLED T.I.M.E.
NEVER ASK A PREACHER TO HELP YOU WITH YOUR ENGLISH HOMEWORK

I DON'T THINK YOU REALISE MARTIN LUTHER AND MARTIN LUTHER KING WERE TWO DIFFERENT PEOPLE!
?!
HISTORY HOMEWORK

WHY DON'T YOU PUT YOUR EGO ON YOUR DONOR CARD- IT'S BIG ENOUGH FOR SEVERAL PEOPLE!

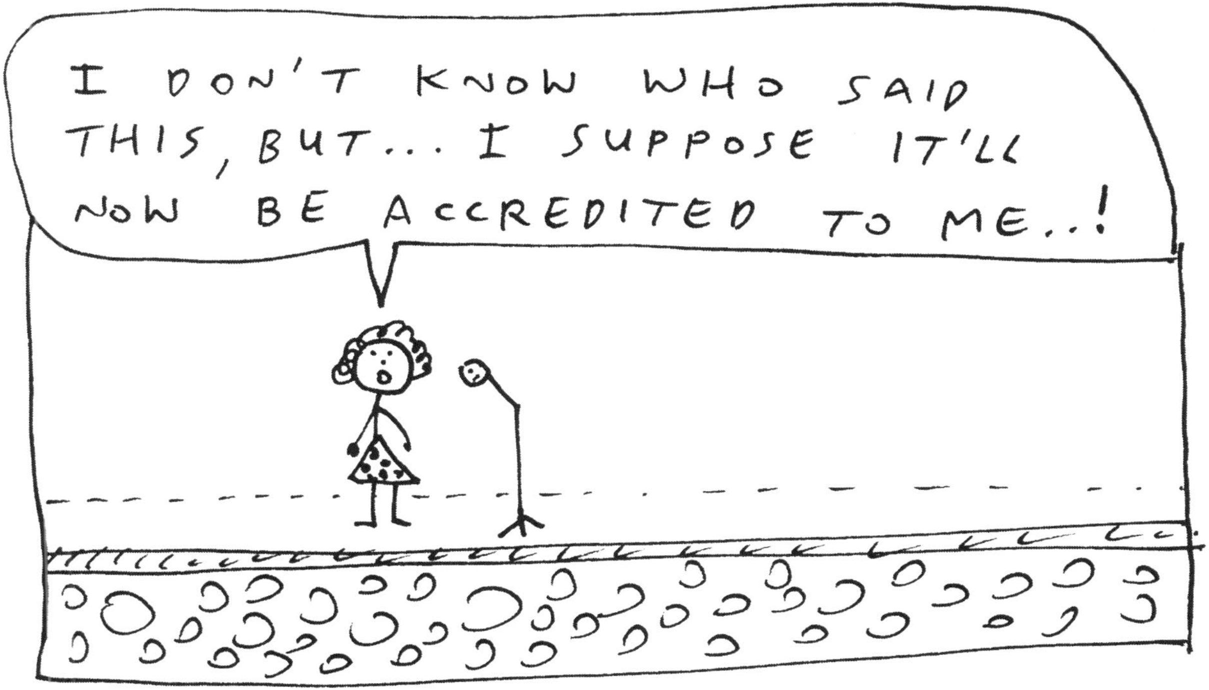
I DON'T KNOW WHO SAID THIS, BUT... I SUPPOSE IT'LL NOW BE ACCREDITED TO ME..!

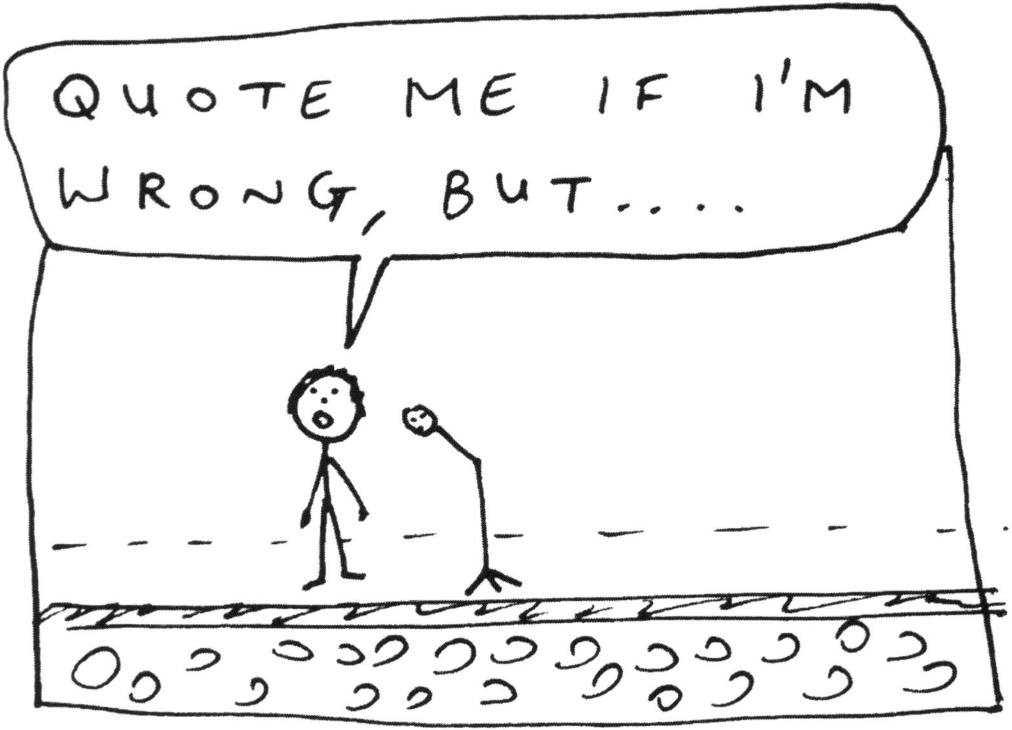
QUOTE ME IF I'M WRONG, BUT....

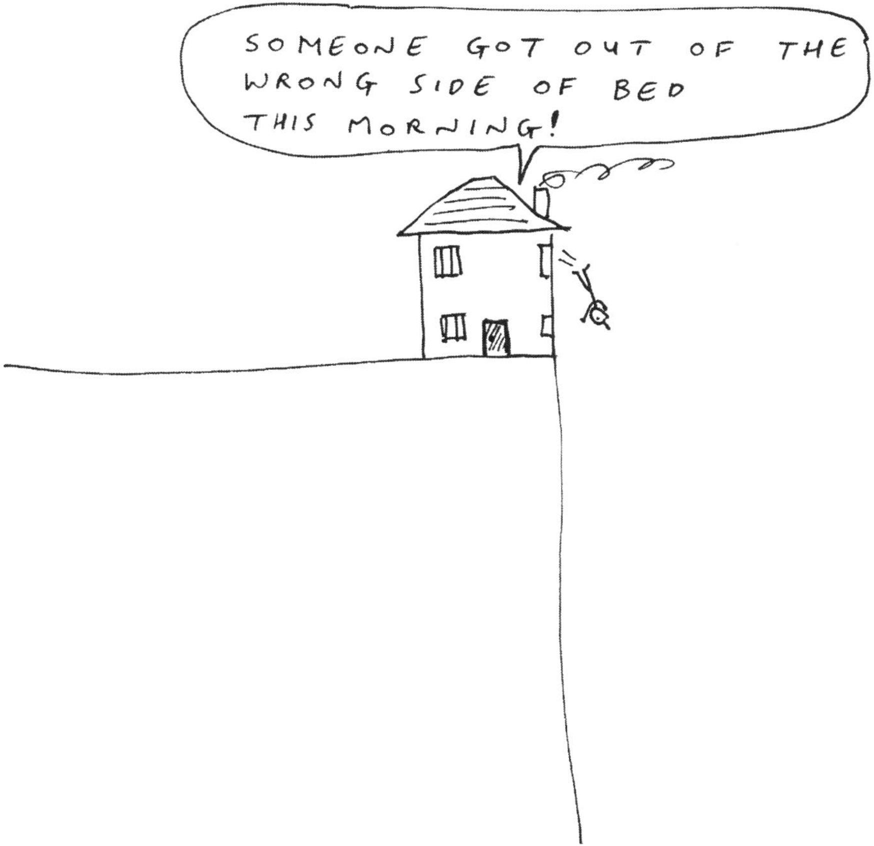
SOMEONE GOT OUT OF THE WRONG SIDE OF BED THIS MORNING!

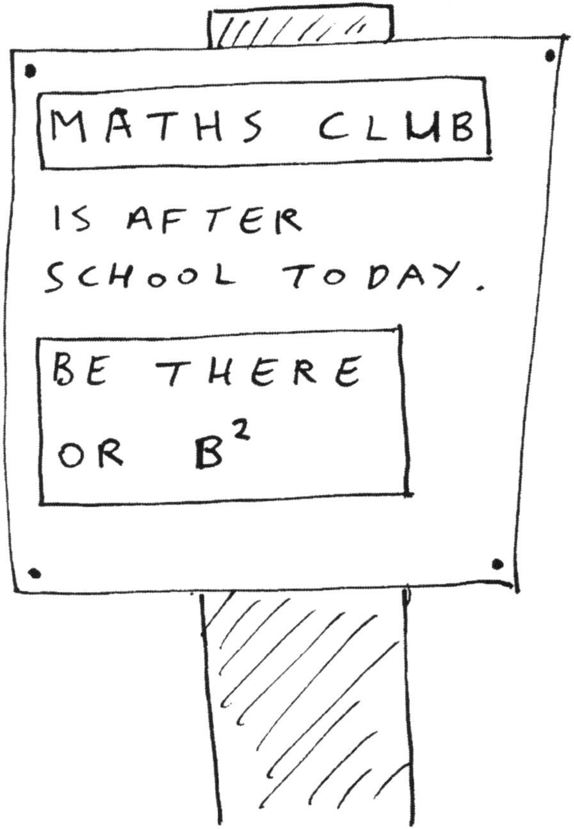
MATHS CLUB
IS AFTER SCHOOL TODAY.
BE THERE OR B^2

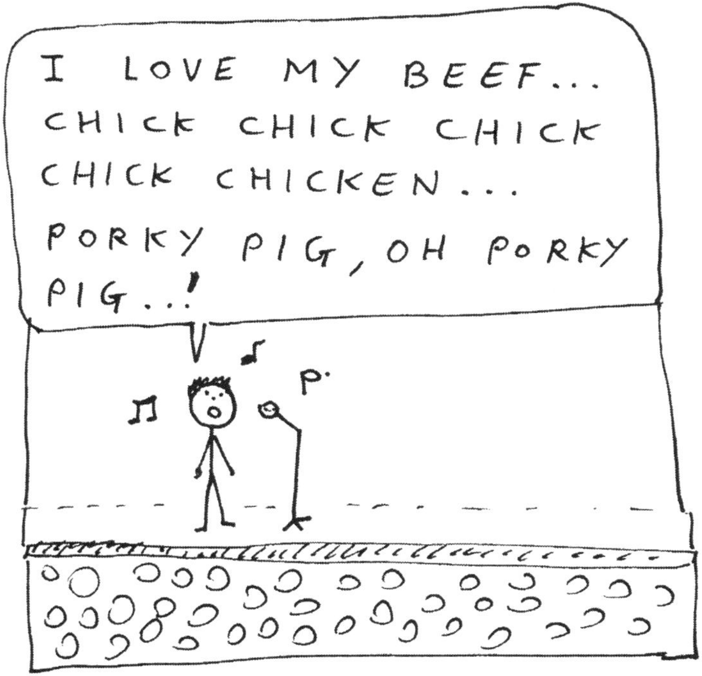
I LOVE MY BEEF... CHICK CHICK CHICK CHICK CHICKEN... PORKY PIG, OH PORKY PIG...!

A MEDLEY OF MEAT

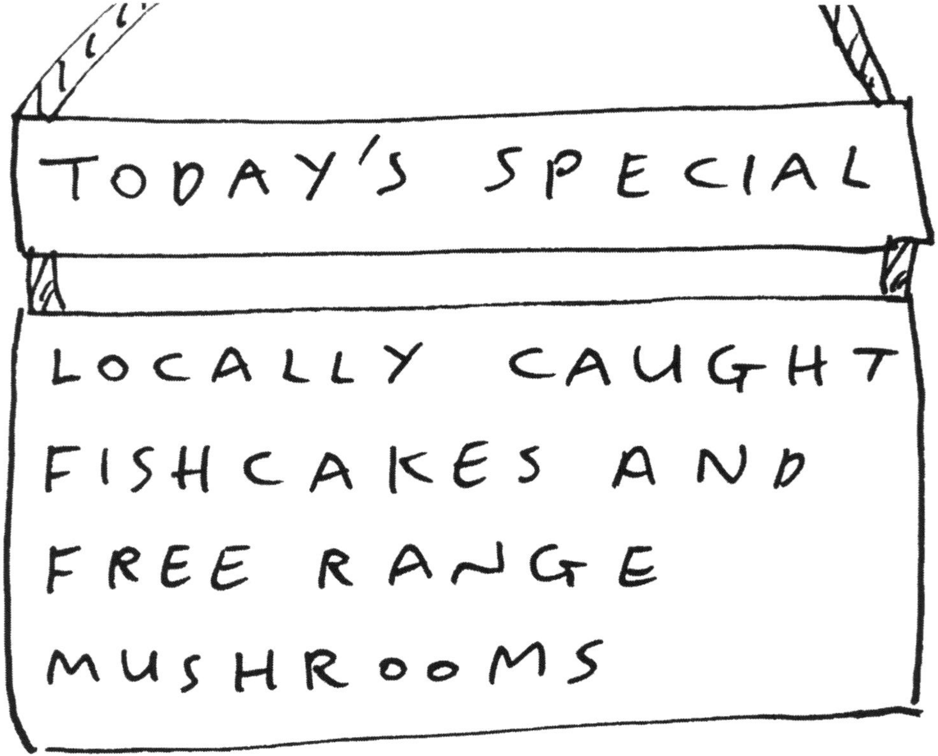
TODAY'S SPECIAL
LOCALLY CAUGHT FISHCAKES AND FREE RANGE MUSHROOMS

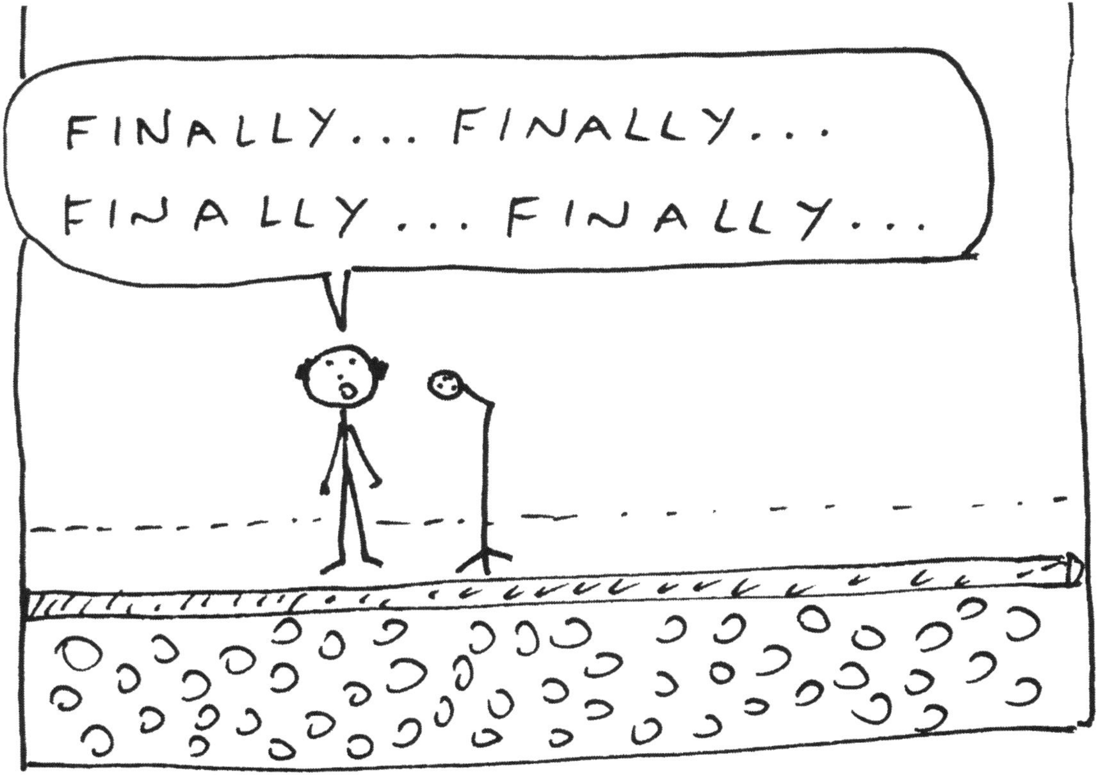
FINALLY... FINALLY...
FINALLY... FINALLY...

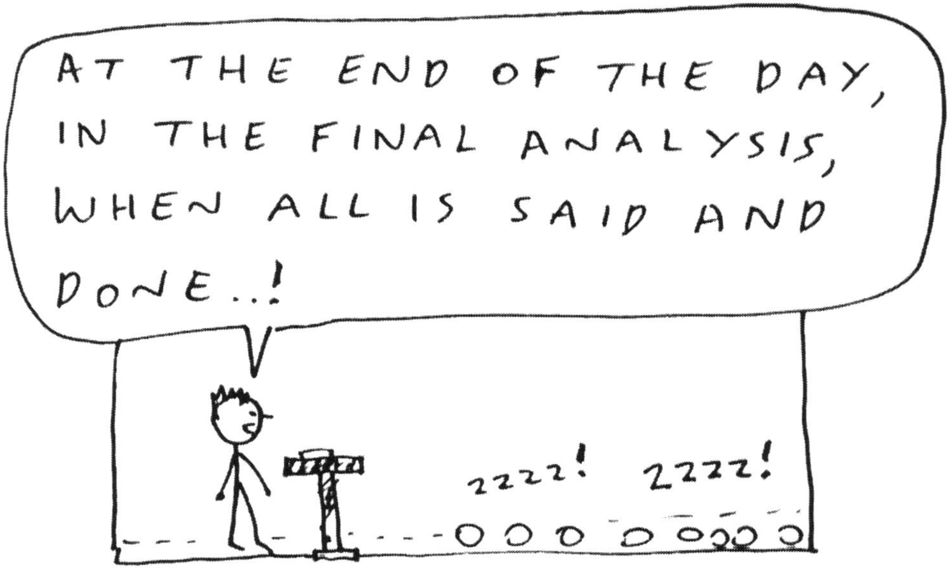
AT THE END OF THE DAY, IN THE FINAL ANALYSIS, WHEN ALL IS SAID AND DONE..!
ZZZZ! ZZZZ!

FRIDAY AFTERNOON AT SCHOOL

BUSINESS CONFERENCE
WE'RE GOING TO MERGE OUR TWO OFFICES INTO A SINGLE BUSINESS UNIT. THEY WILL THEN OPERATE INDEPENDENTLY FROM THE TWO LOCATIONS

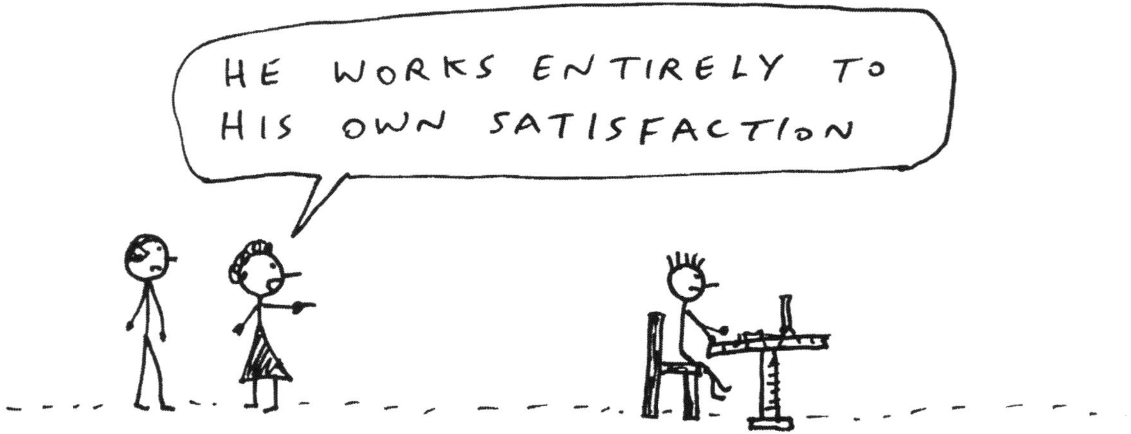
HE WORKS ENTIRELY TO HIS OWN SATISFACTION

HUMAN RESOURCES
IN OUR EXPERIENCE, AGREEMENT IS THE BEST WAY OF BRINGING DISAGREEMENTS TO AN END.

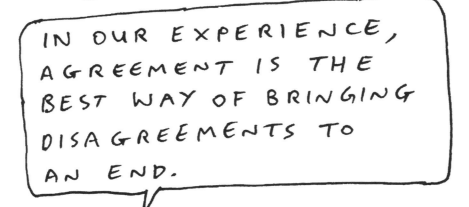

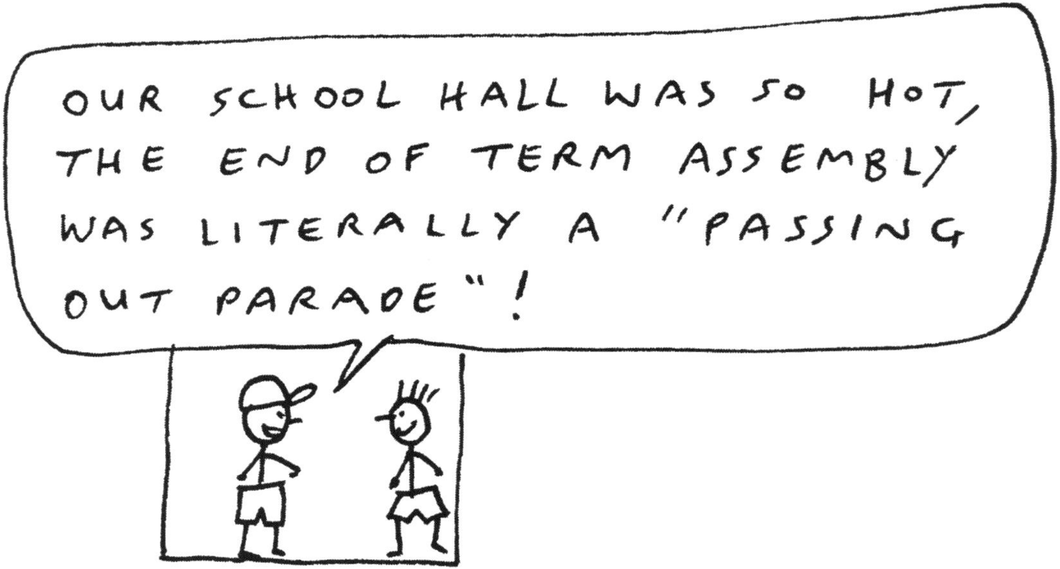
OUR SCHOOL HALL WAS SO HOT, THE END OF TERM ASSEMBLY WAS LITERALLY A "PASSING OUT PARADE"!

I'VE TAKEN OUT A GRIEVANCE AGAINST MY BOSS
BUT YOU'RE SELF-EMPLOYED!

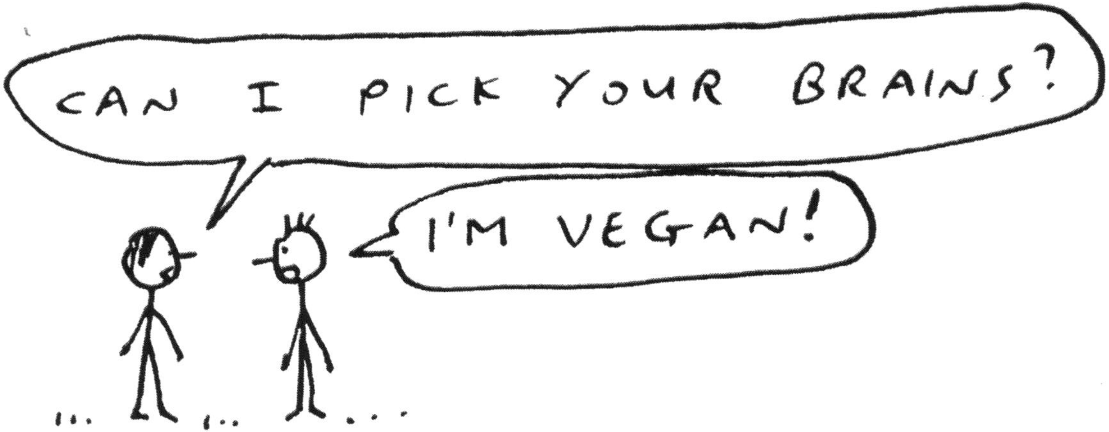
CAN I PICK YOUR BRAINS?
I'M VEGAN!

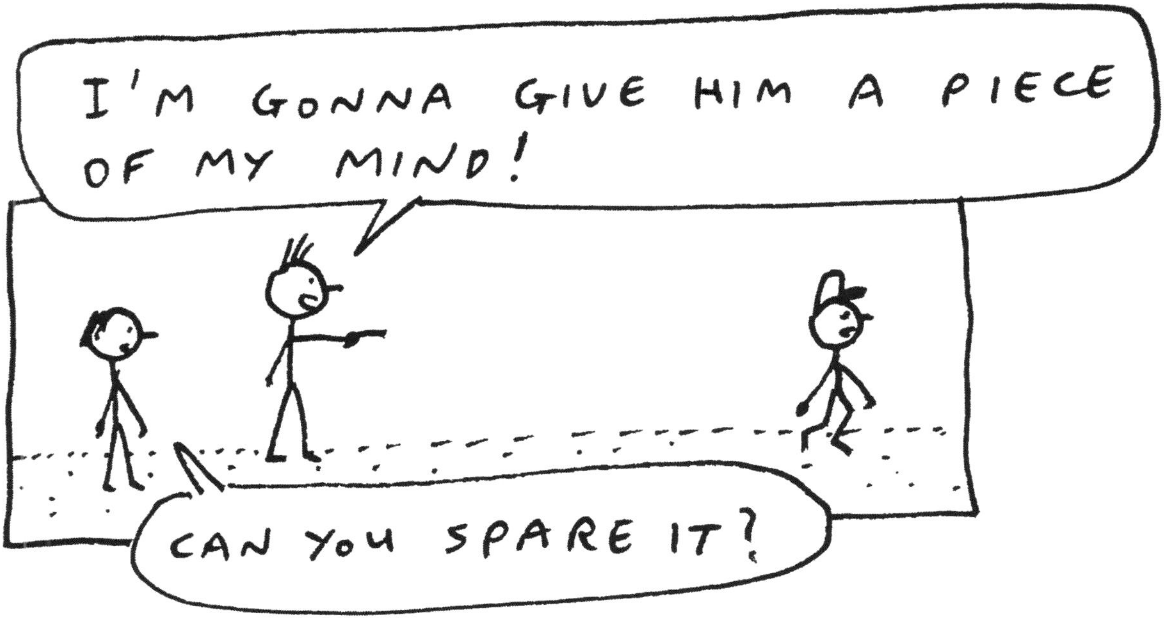
I'M GONNA GIVE HIM A PIECE OF MY MIND!
CAN YOU SPARE IT?

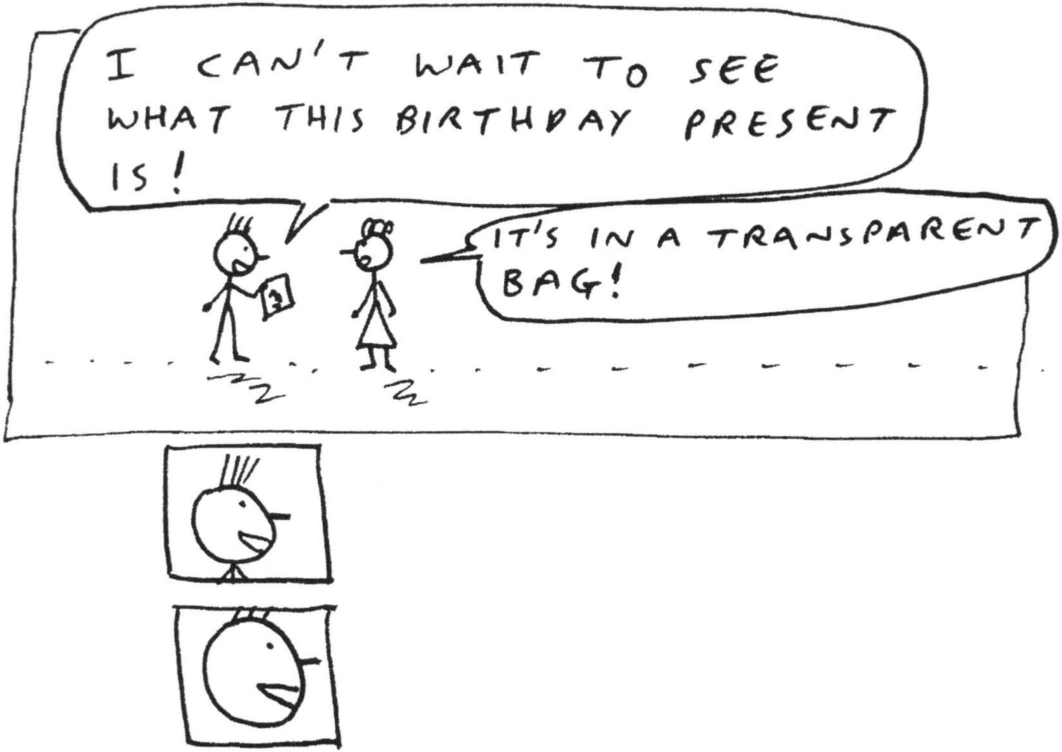
I CAN'T WAIT TO SEE WHAT THIS BIRTHDAY PRESENT IS!
IT'S IN A TRANSPARENT BAG!

WE CALL HIM "THE ANAESTHETIST," BECAUSE OF HIS ABILITY TO SEND PEOPLE TO SLEEP!

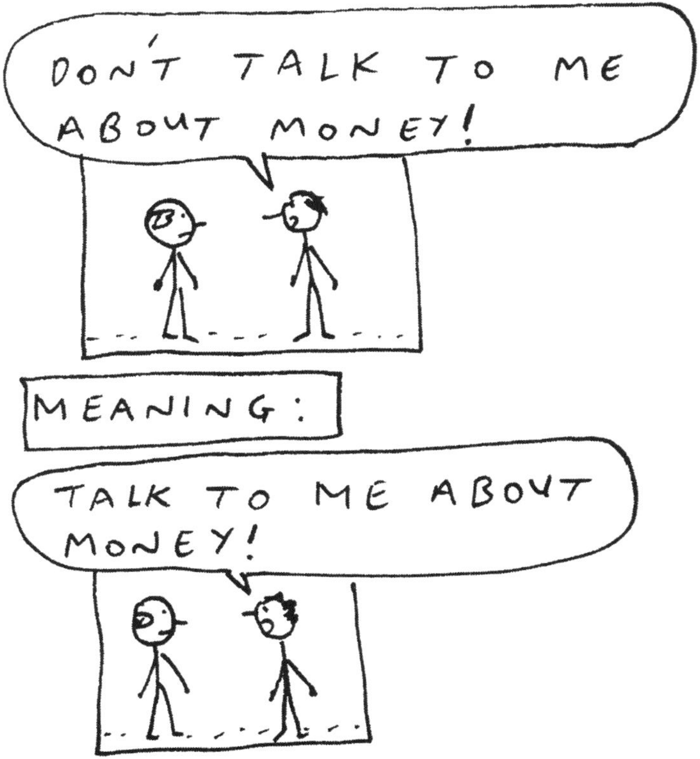
DON'T TALK TO ME ABOUT MONEY!
MEANING:
TALK TO ME ABOUT MONEY!

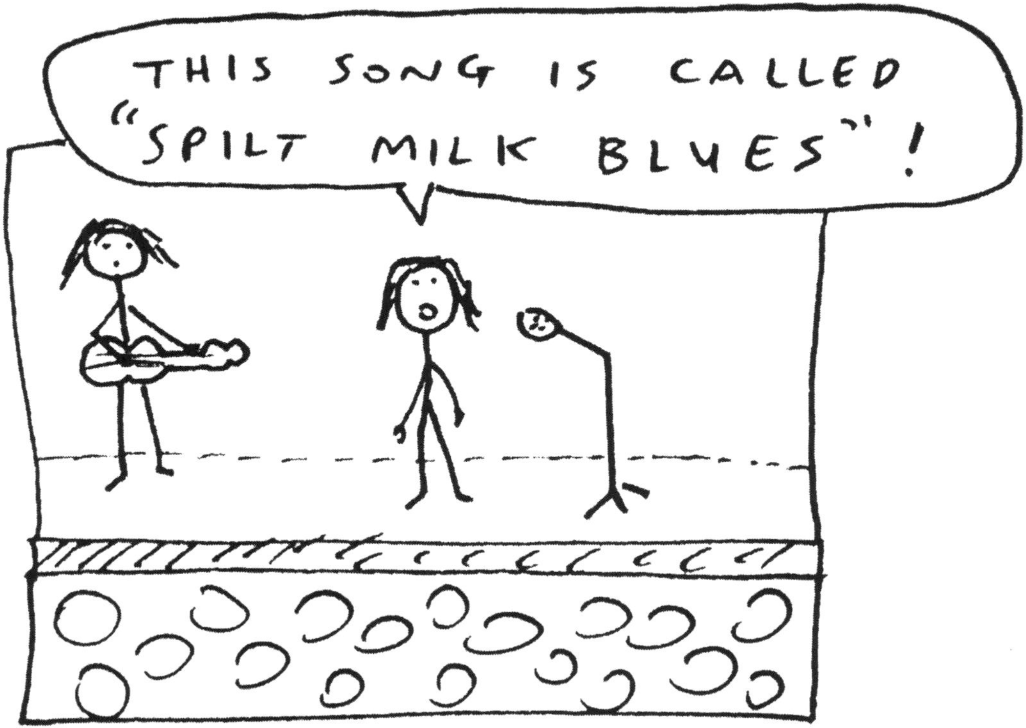
THIS SONG IS CALLED "SPILT MILK BLUES"!

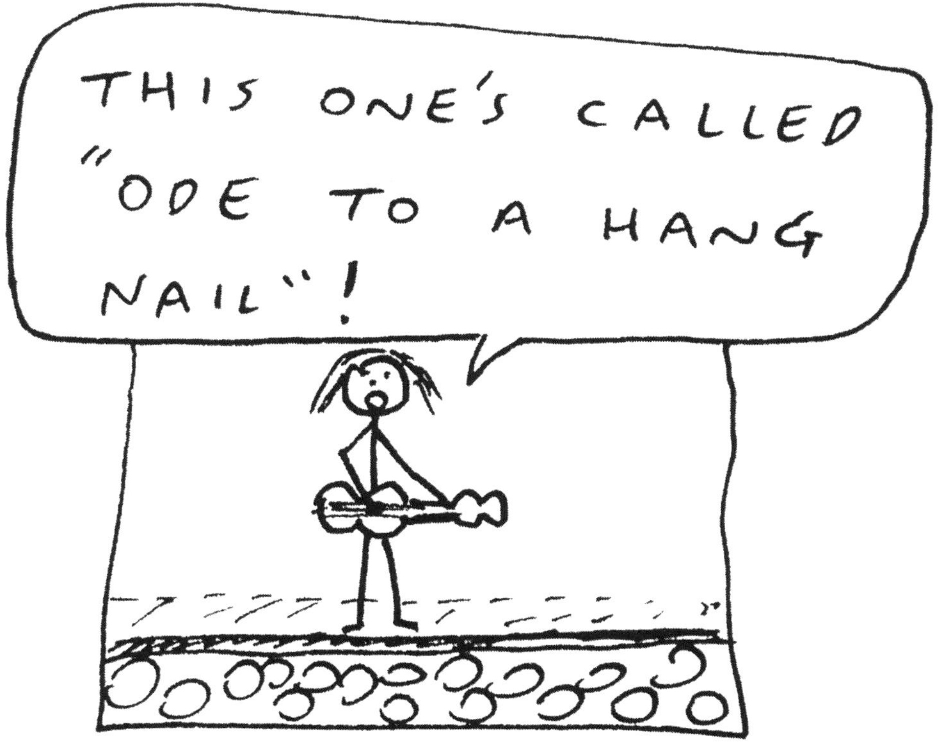
THIS ONE'S CALLED "ODE TO A HANG NAIL"!

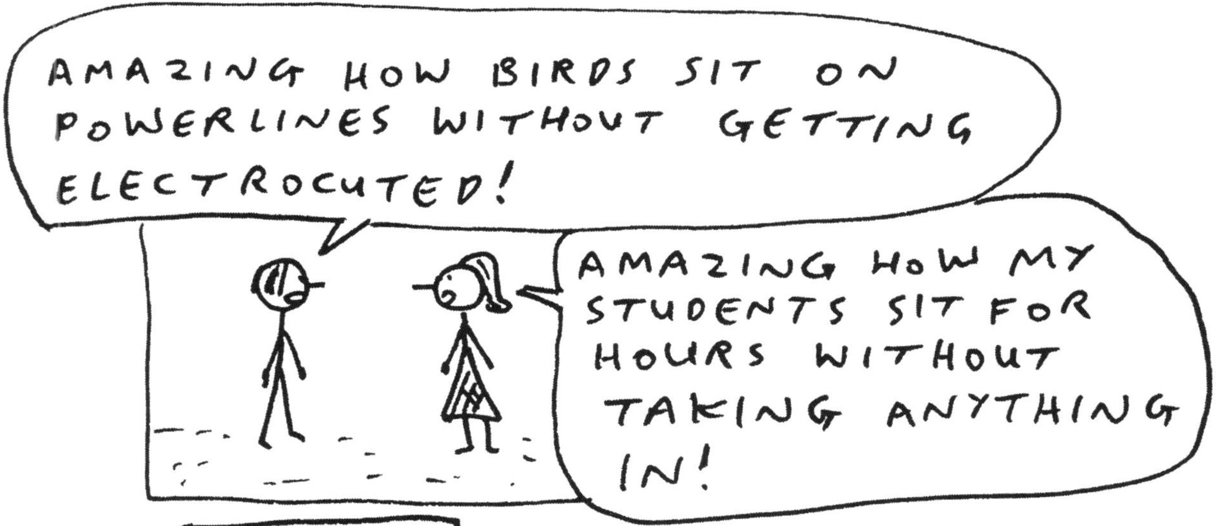

TEACHER TALK

I WILL SEE YOU BRIGHT AND EARLY TOMORROW MORNING!
ONE OF THOSE

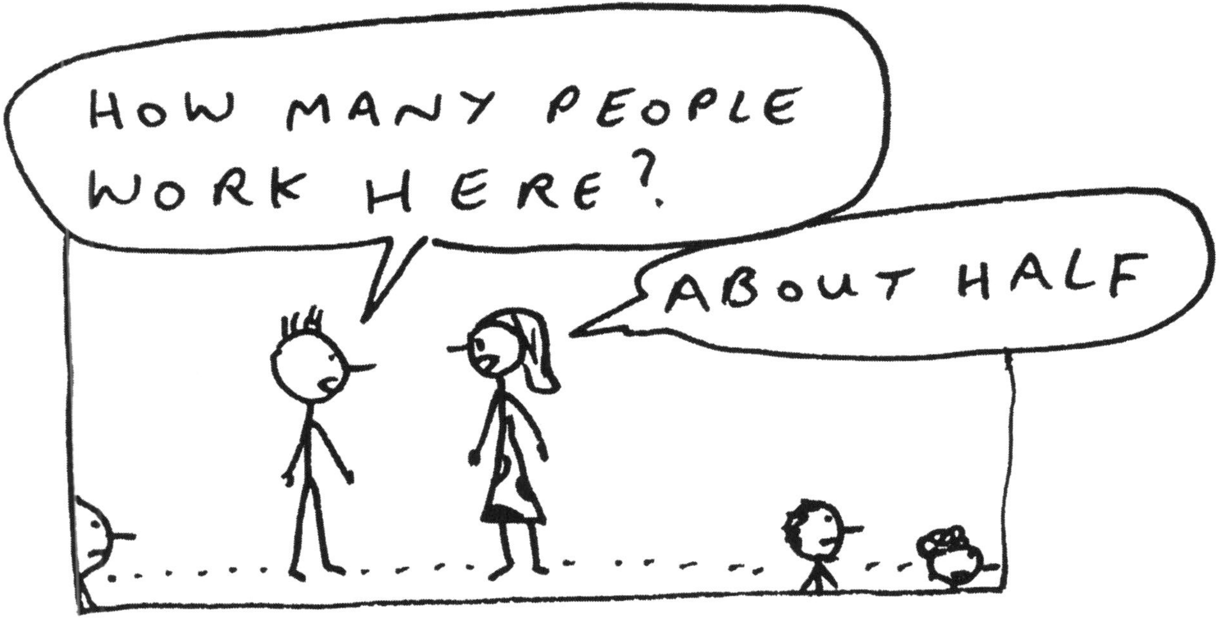
HOW MANY PEOPLE WORK HERE?
ABOUT HALF

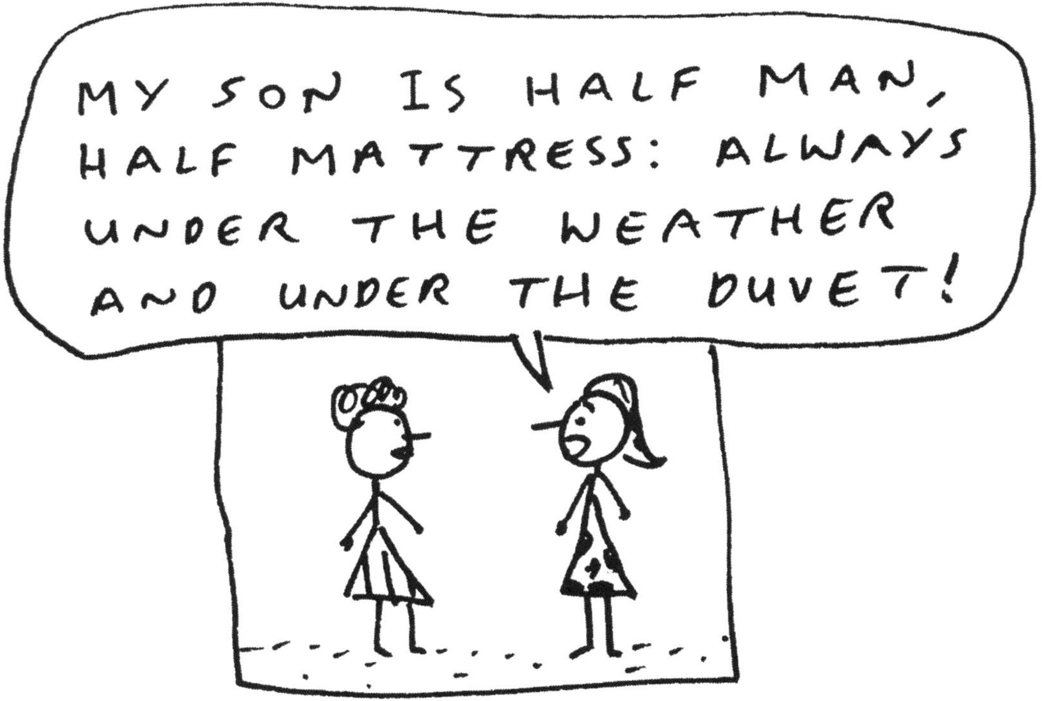
MY SON IS HALF MAN, HALF MATTRESS: ALWAYS UNDER THE WEATHER AND UNDER THE DUVET!

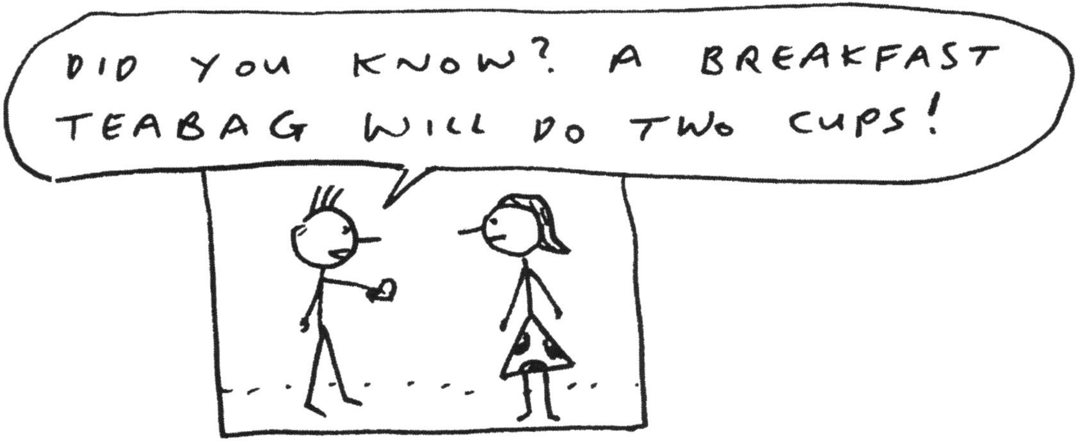

EDDIE SOLVES THE GLOBAL FINANCIAL CRISIS

AS MARY ENTERED THE PARK, A BALL UNFORTUNATELY HAD HER NAME ON IT...
MAR

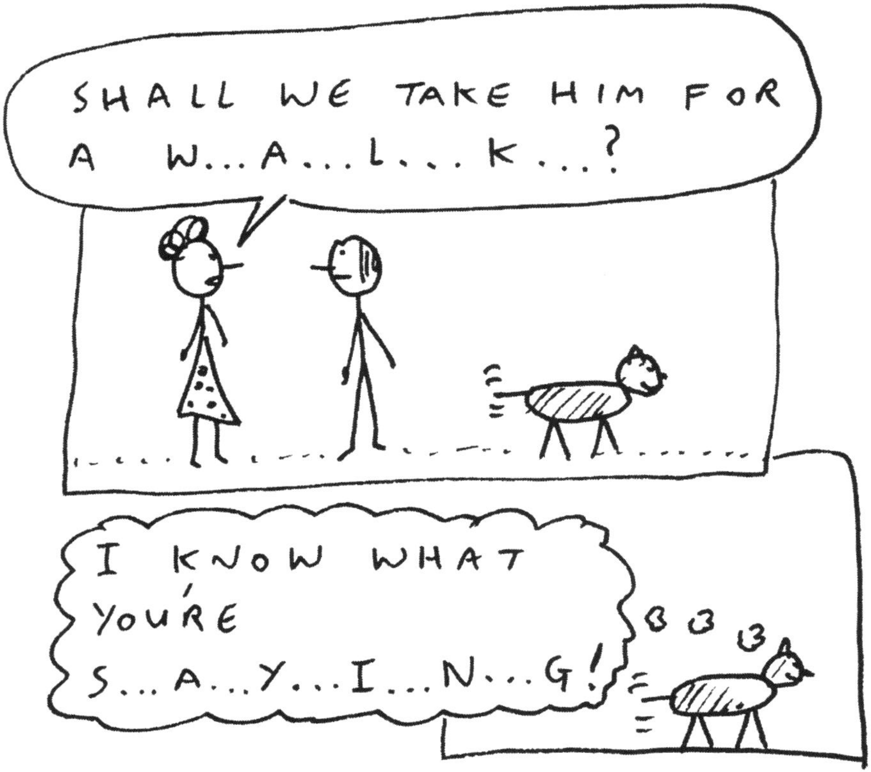
SHALL WE TAKE HIM FOR A W...A...L...K...?
I KNOW WHAT YOU'RE S...A...Y...I...N...G!

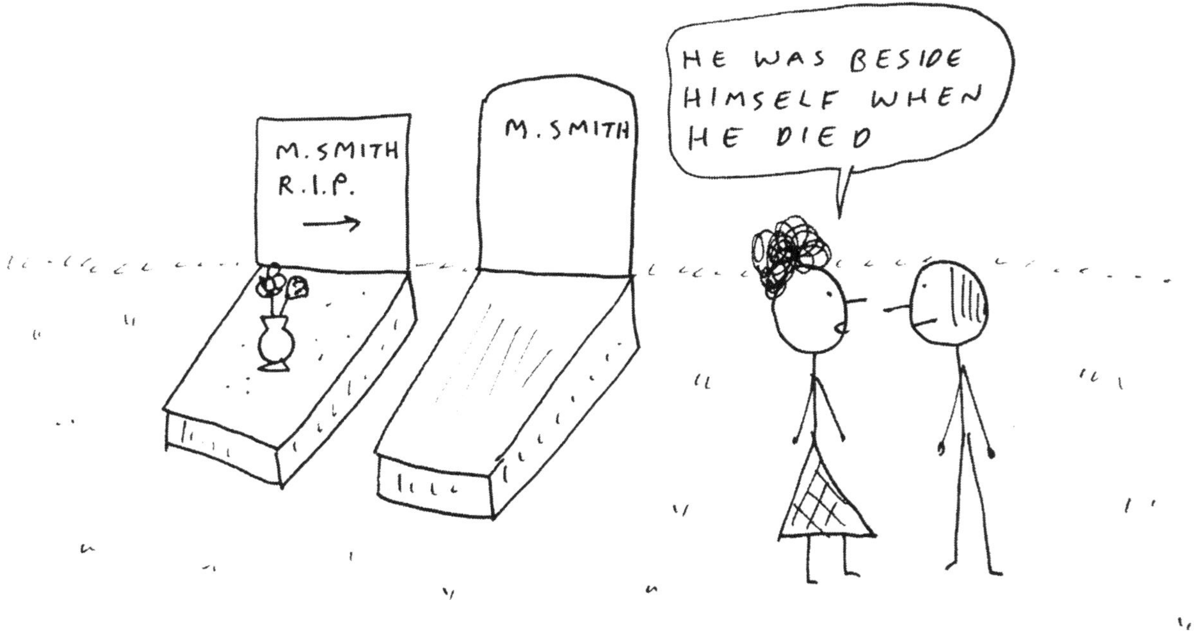
M.SMITH
R.I.P.
M.SMITH
HE WAS BESIDE HIMSELF WHEN HE DIED

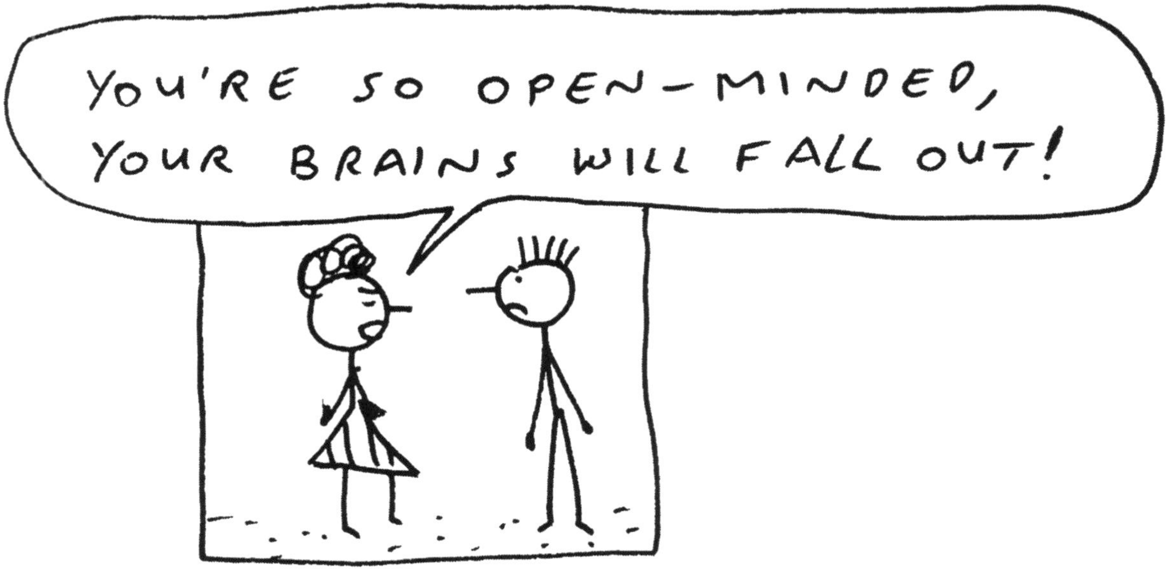
YOU'RE SO OPEN-MINDED, YOUR BRAINS WILL FALL OUT!

HOSPITAL
I WAS SUNBATHING WHEN MY WINDOW BOX COLLAPSED UNDER ME
?

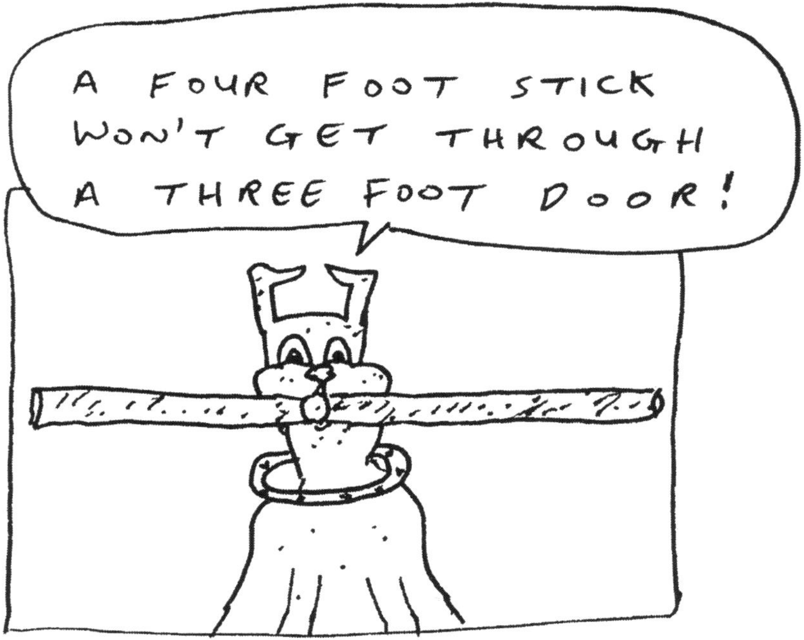

DOG SCHOOL

A CLOSER LOOK WON'T HELP YOU RESOLVE THE PROBLEM...
IT'LL JUST MAKE IT LOOK BIGGER!

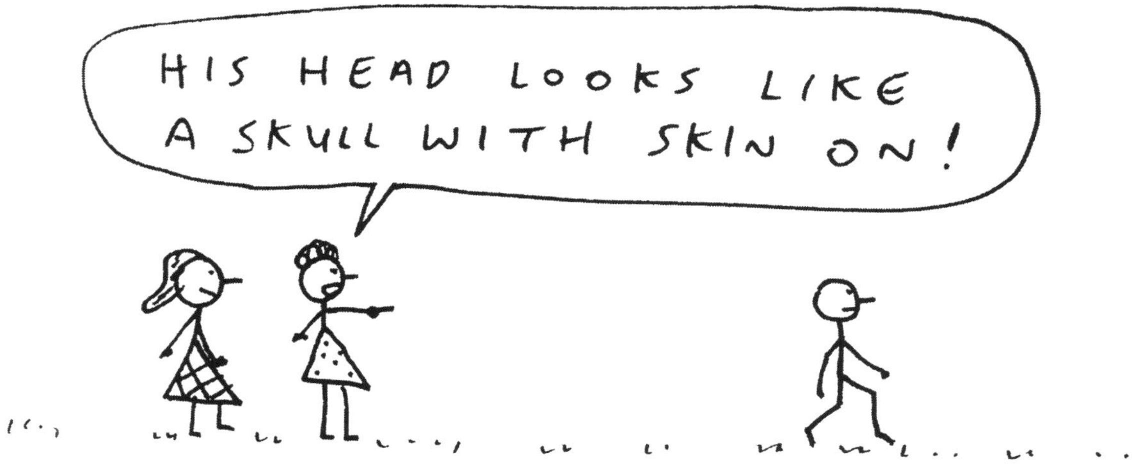
HIS HEAD LOOKS LIKE A SKULL WITH SKIN ON!

THREE HABITS OF HIGHLY EFFECTIVE PEOPLE:

① ALWAYS PUTS THE LID BACK ON THE TOOTHPASTE TUBE

② SPREADS TOWELS NEATLY ACROSS THE RADIATOR

③ PUTS DIRTY WASHING IN THE BASKET, NOT ON THE FLOOR

I MIGHT CROSS EVERY "I" AND DOT EVERY "T," BUT I AM AN EAR TO CRY ON, AND A SHOULDER TO TALK TO
KIND TEACHER

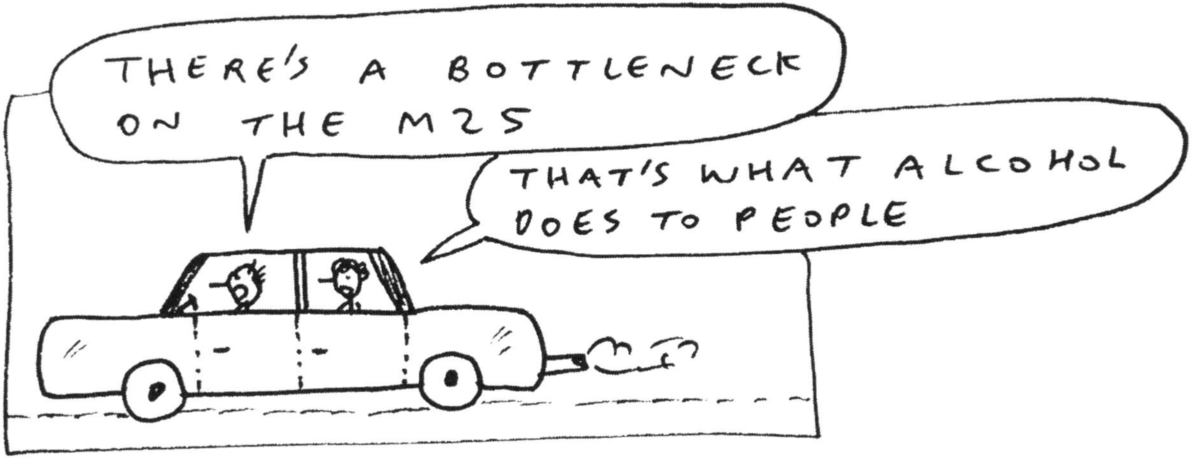
THERE'S A BOTTLENECK ON THE M25
THAT'S WHAT ALCOHOL DOES TO PEOPLE

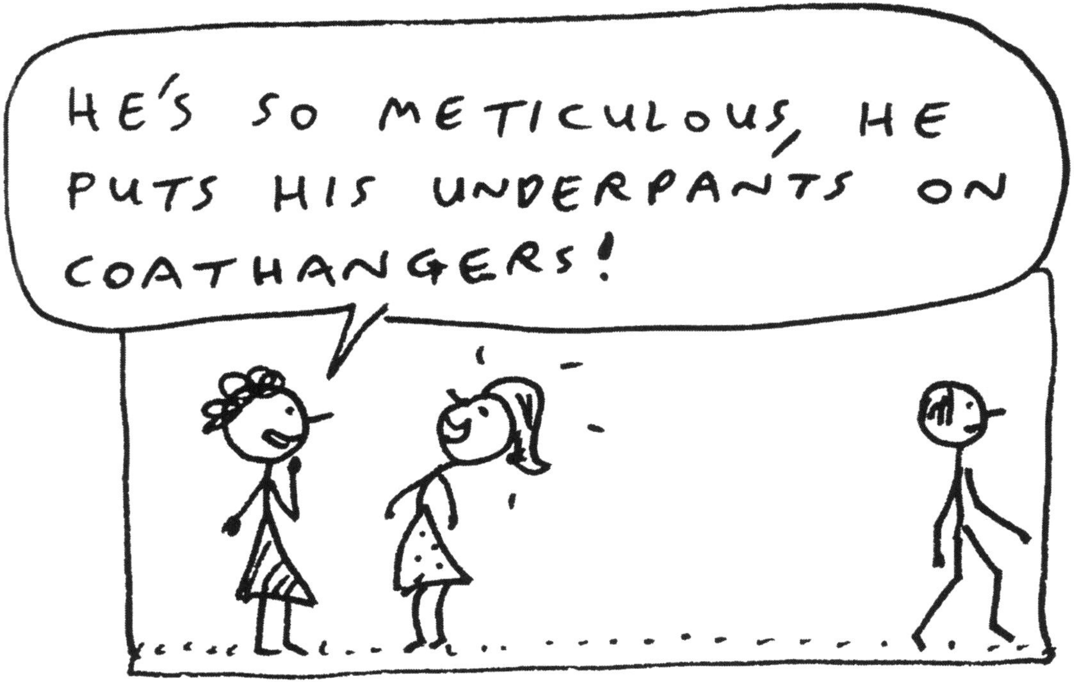
HE'S SO METICULOUS, HE PUTS HIS UNDERPANTS ON COATHANGERS!

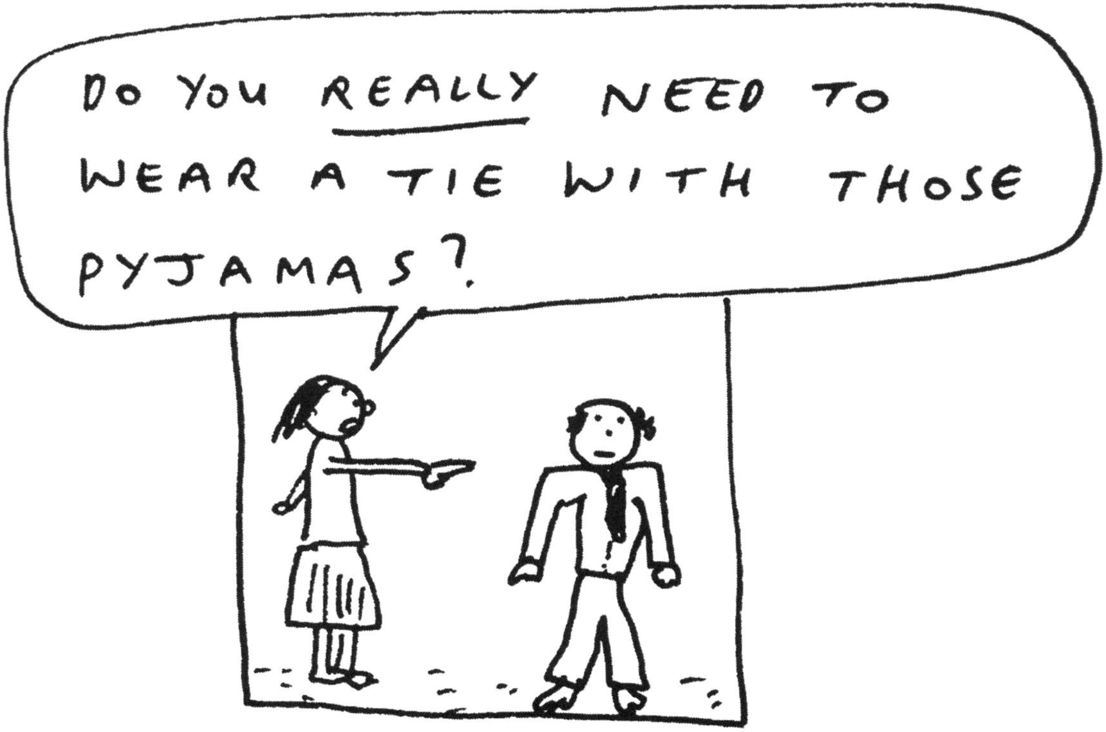
DO YOU REALLY NEED TO WEAR A TIE WITH THOSE PYJAMAS?

HE WEARS REFLECTIVE ARM BANDS WHEN HE'S ON HIS EXCERCISE BIKE!

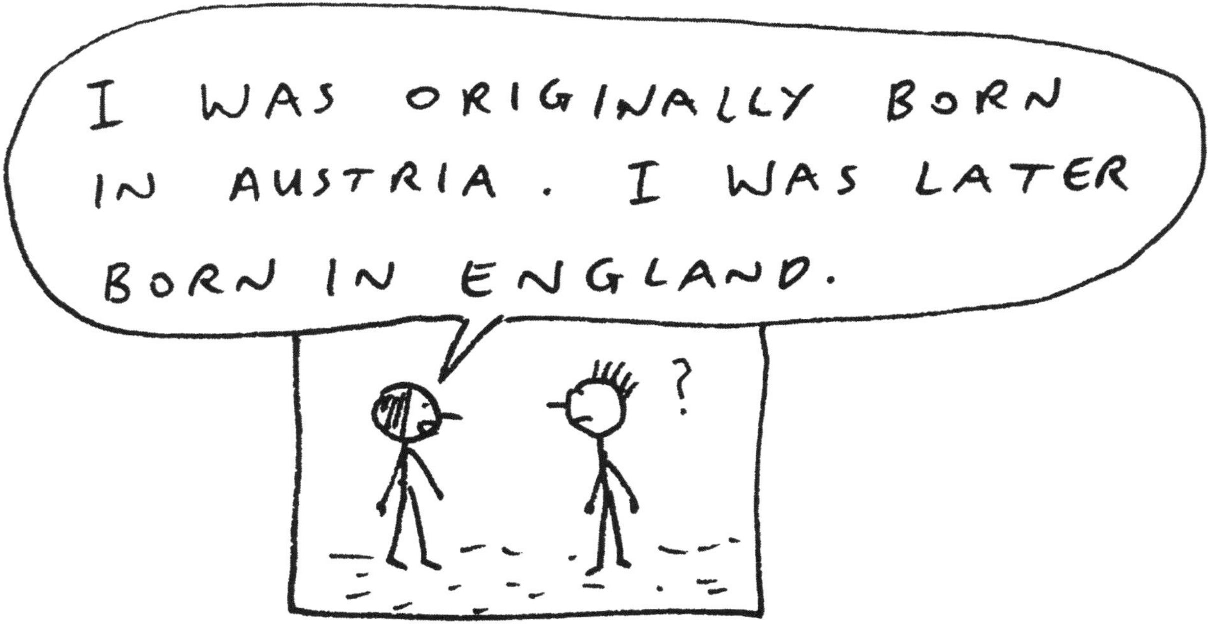
I WAS ORIGINALLY BORN IN AUSTRIA. I WAS LATER BORN IN ENGLAND.
?

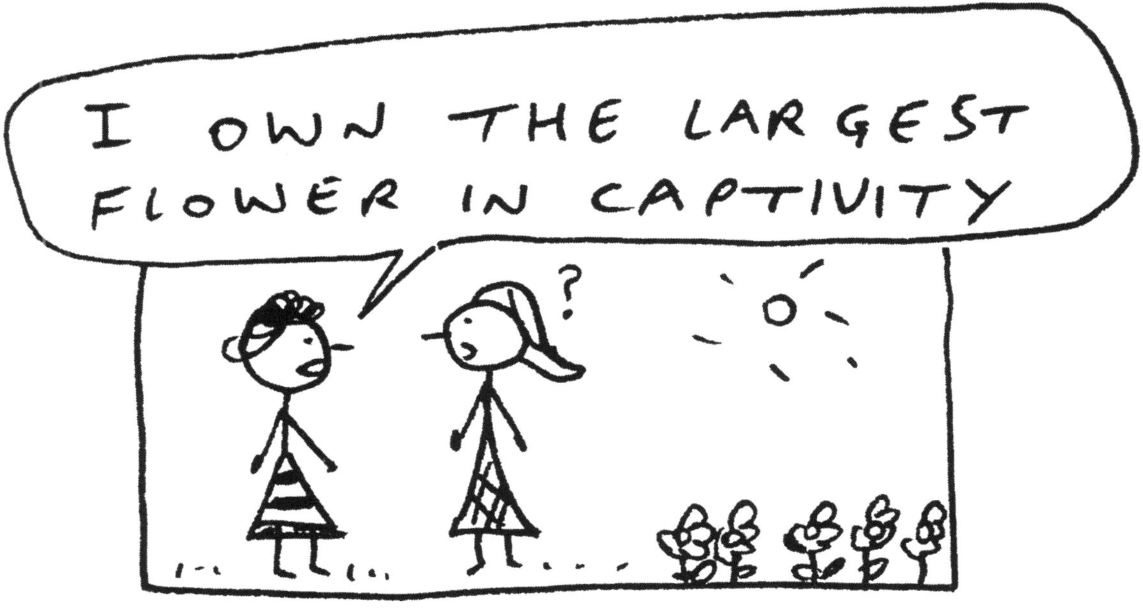
I OWN THE LARGEST FLOWER IN CAPTIVITY
?

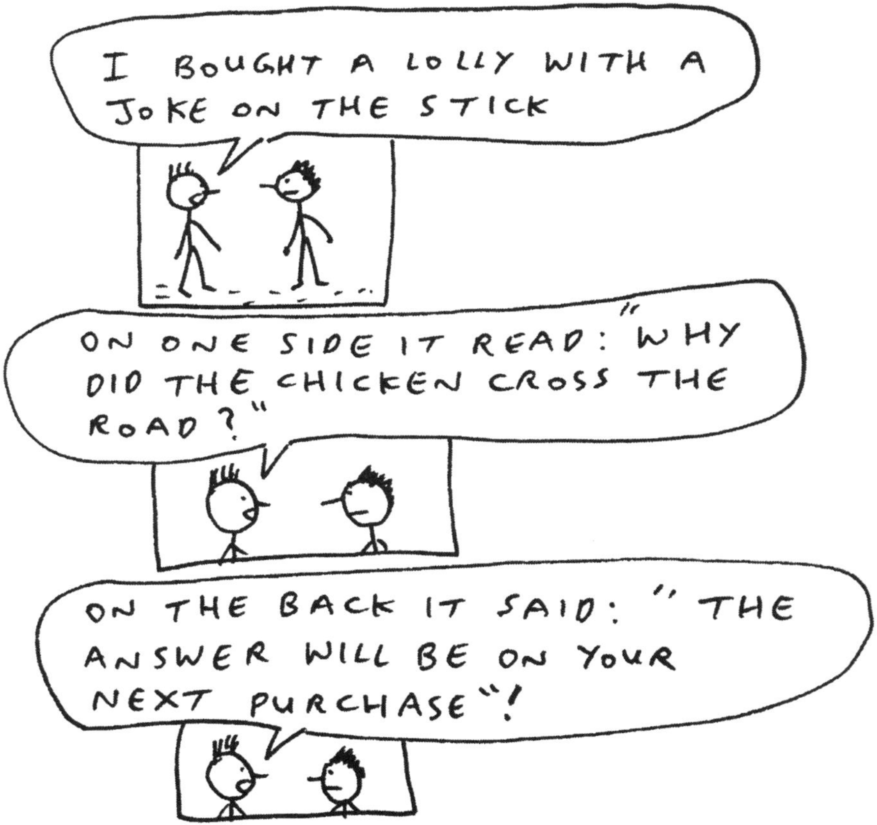
I BOUGHT A LOLLY WITH A JOKE ON THE STICK
ON ONE SIDE IT READ: "WHY DID THE CHICKEN CROSS THE ROAD?"
ON THE BACK IT SAID: "THE ANSWER WILL BE ON YOUR NEXT PURCHASE"!

BOOK SHOP
I'D LIKE A BOOK ON HOME IMPROVEMENT PLEASE
DO IT YOURSELF?
NO - I WANT YOU TO ORDER IT FOR ME

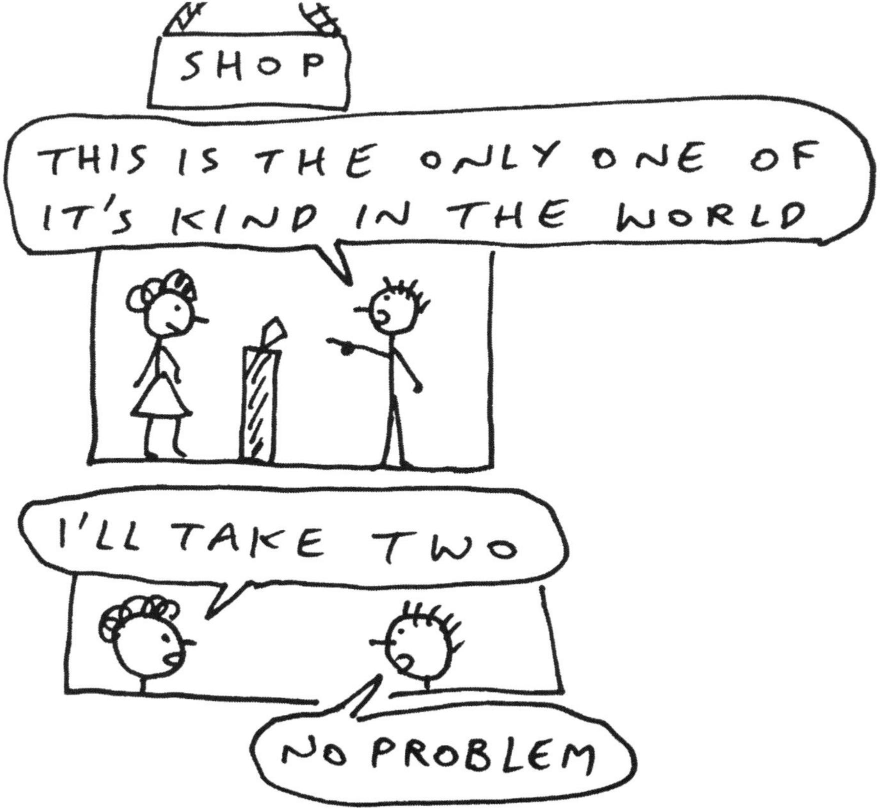
SHOP
THIS IS THE ONLY ONE OF IT'S KIND IN THE WORLD
I'LL TAKE TWO
NO PROBLEM

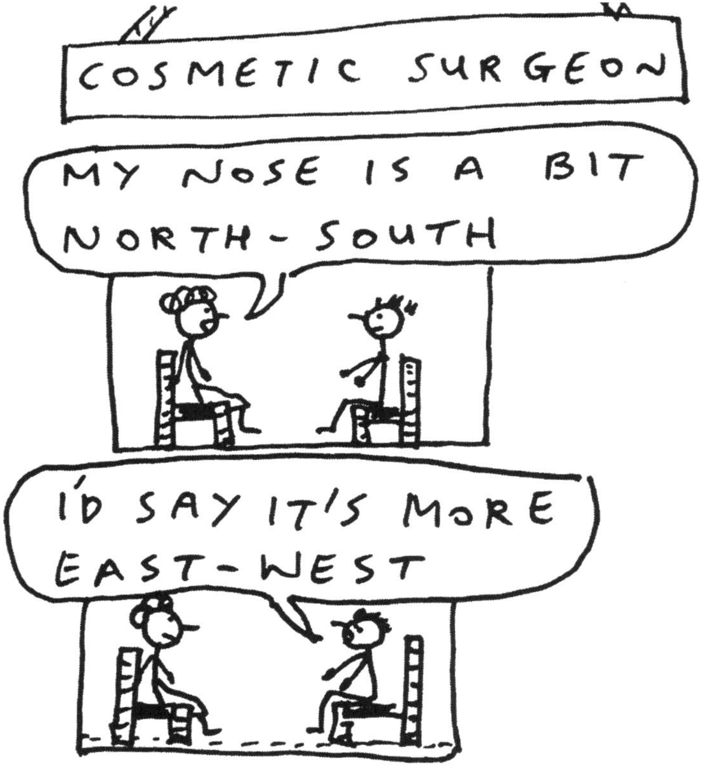
COSMETIC SURGEON
MY NOSE IS A BIT NORTH-SOUTH
I'D SAY IT'S MORE EAST-WEST

WHEN YOU CAN'T REMEMBER WHO THIS PERSON IS...
Hi! So... are you still... doing what you used to do?
yup
And you're... still with... those people?

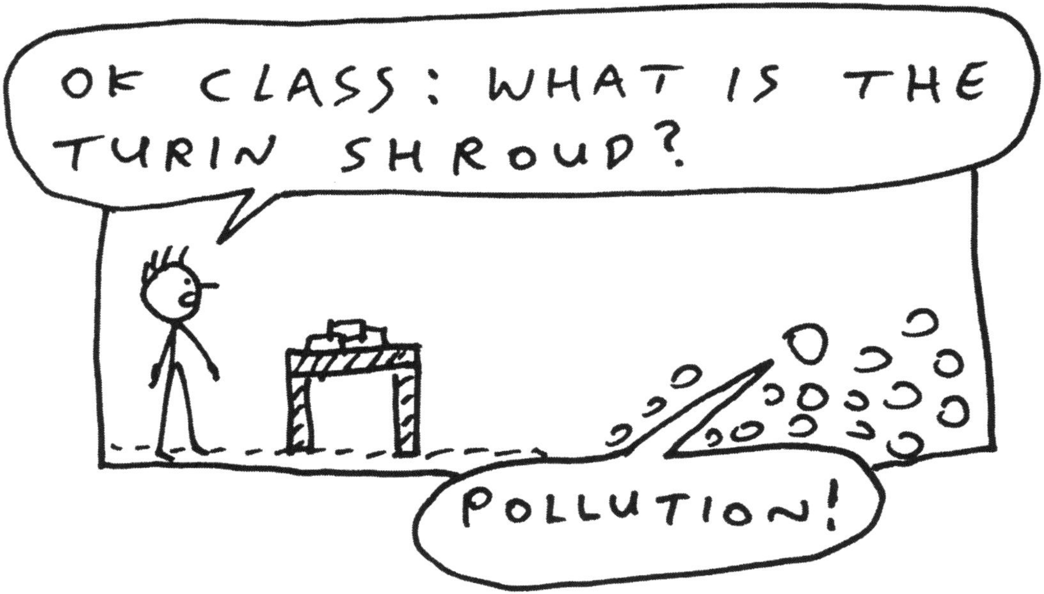
OK CLASS: WHAT IS THE TURIN SHROUD?
POLLUTION!

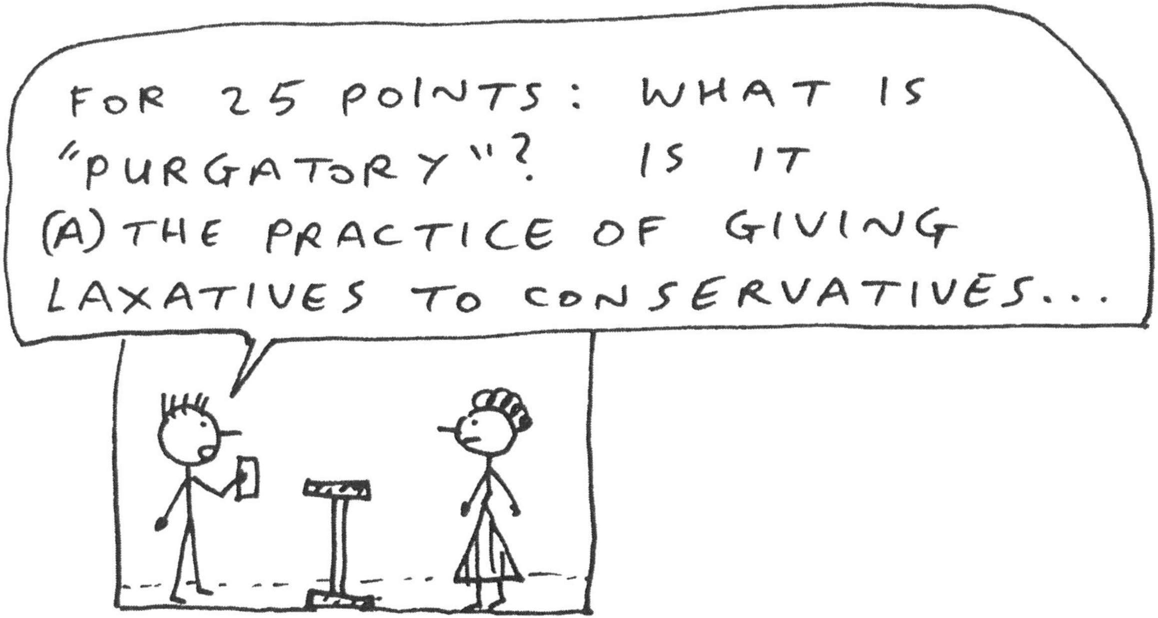
FOR 25 POINTS: WHAT IS "PURGATORY"? IS IT (A) THE PRACTICE OF GIVING LAXATIVES TO CONSERVATIVES...

AND STILL TO COME: ONE MAN'S CONVERSION FROM BURGERS 'N' BUNS TO VERGERS 'N' NUNS!
NEWS

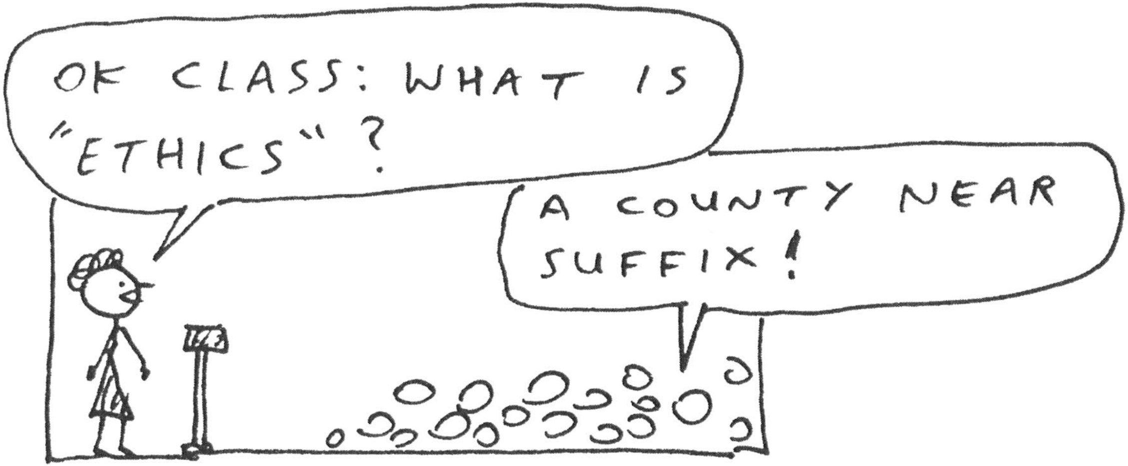
OK CLASS: WHAT IS "ETHICS"?
A COUNTY NEAR SUFFIX!

...AND ON OUR RETURN JOURNEY, THE SCENERY WILL BE THE SAME, BUT ON THE OTHER SIDE...
TOUR GUIDE

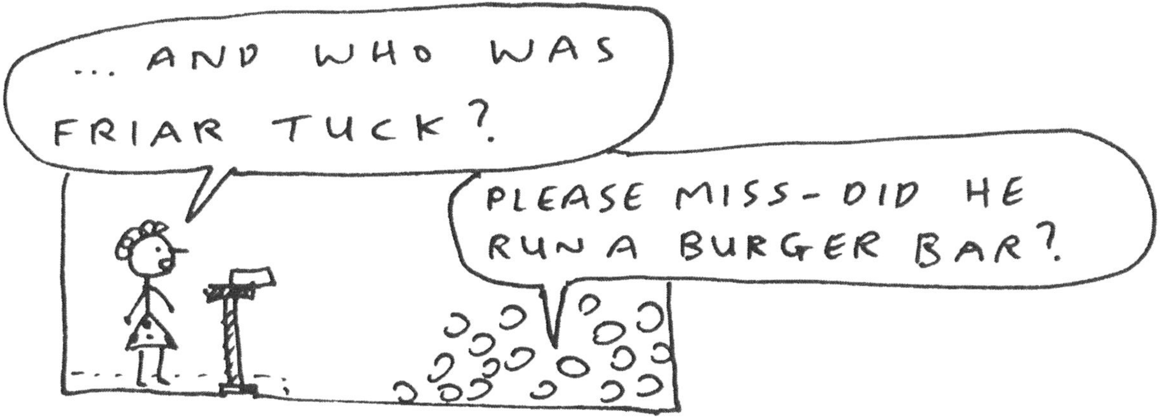
... AND WHO WAS FRIAR TUCK?
PLEASE MISS - DID HE RUN A BURGER BAR?

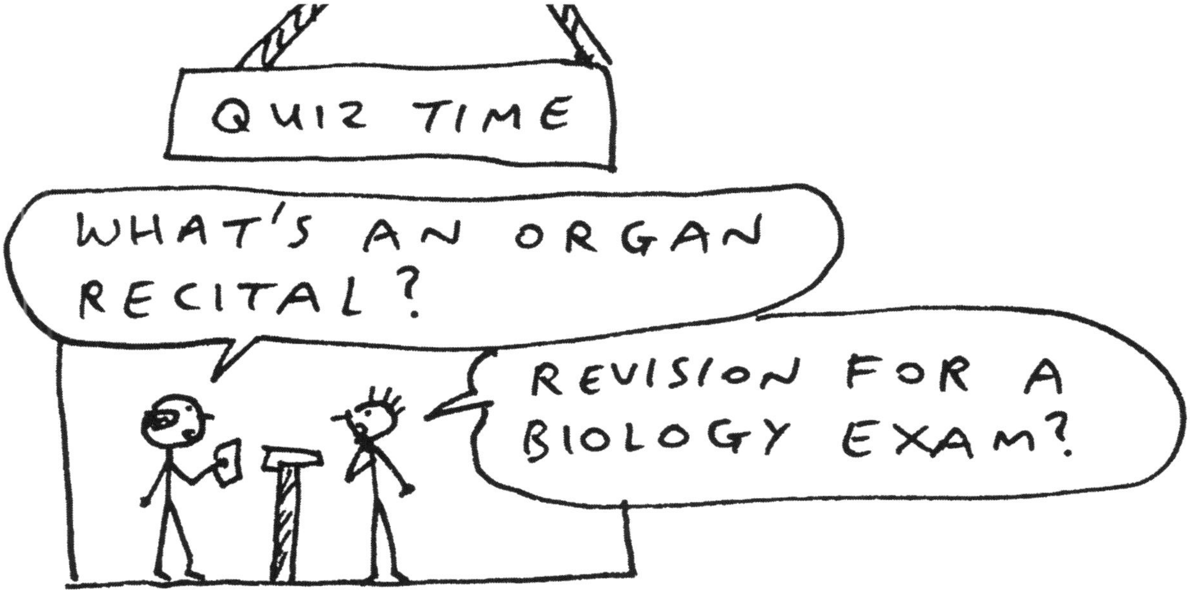
QUIZ TIME
WHAT'S AN ORGAN RECITAL?
REVISION FOR A BIOLOGY EXAM?

YOU KNOW ME: EARS TO THE GROUND, NOSE TO THE WIND AND FINGERS ON THE PULSE..!

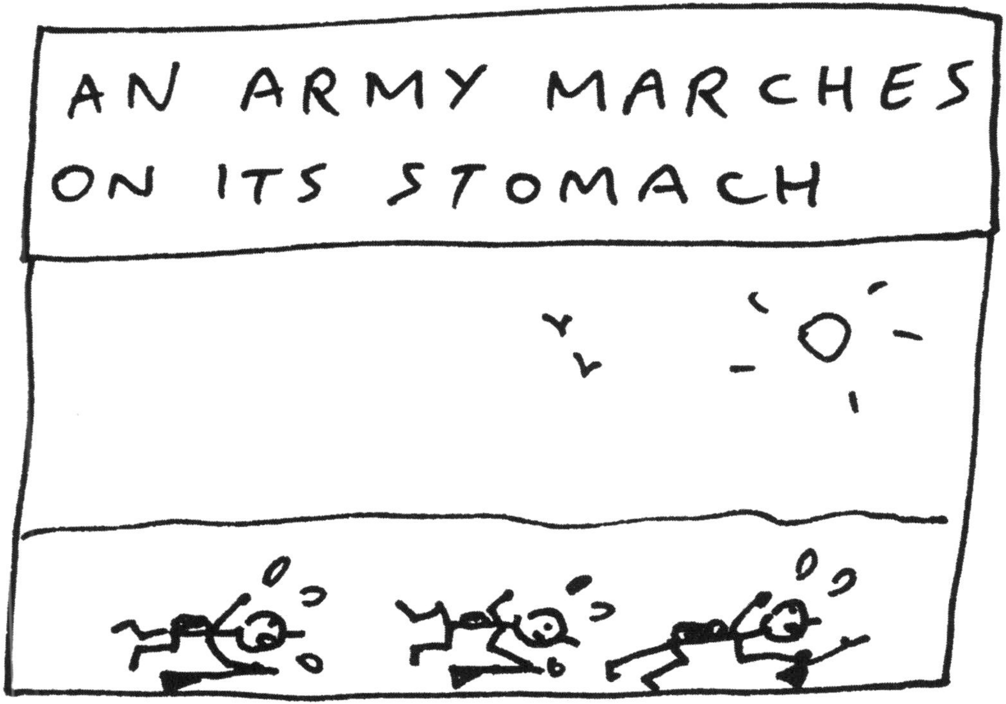
AN ARMY MARCHES
ON ITS STOMACH

WE PRAY FOR YOUNG MEN AS THEY ENTER THE CHURCH WITH GRACE. MAY THEY GO OUT WITH JOY AND FELICITY

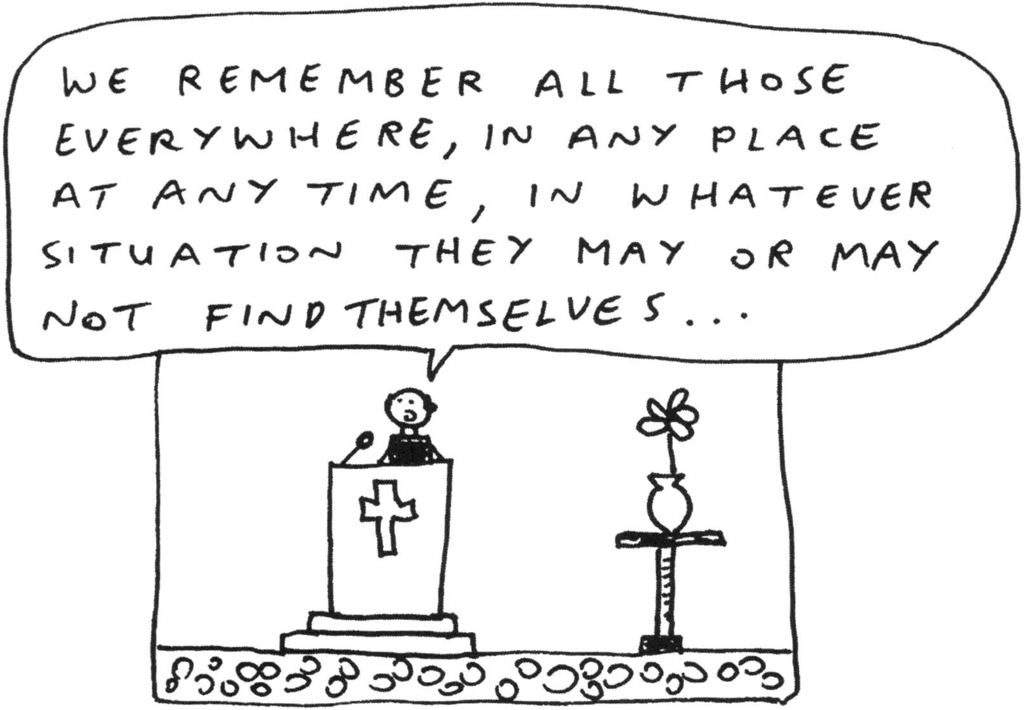
WE REMEMBER ALL THOSE EVERYWHERE, IN ANY PLACE AT ANY TIME, IN WHATEVER SITUATION THEY MAY OR MAY NOT FIND THEMSELVES...

THE MINUTES
MR. JEFFREYS CHAIRED THE MEETING UNTIL SEATS WERE PROVIDED...

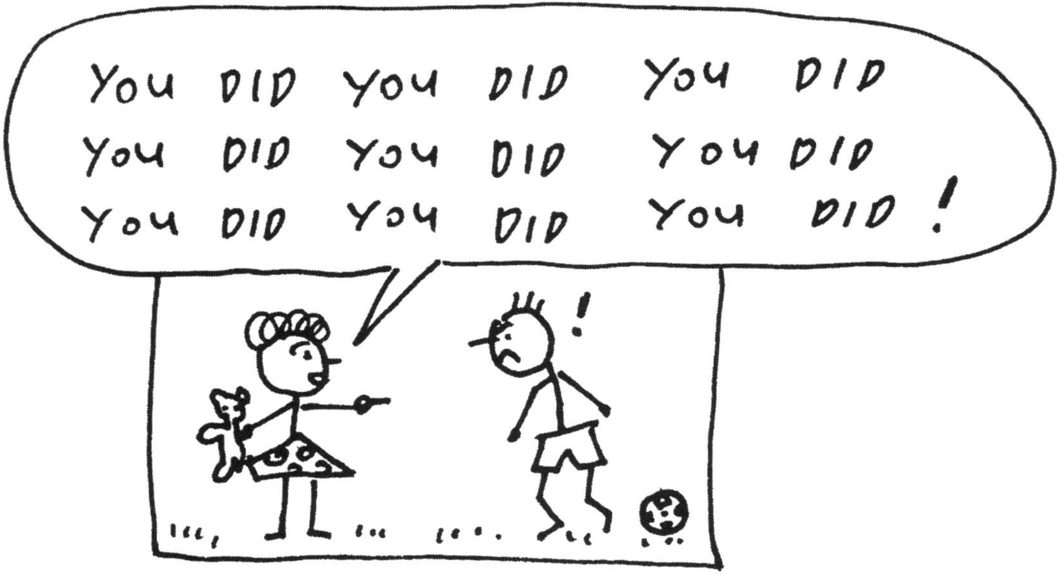
YOU DID YOU DID YOU DID YOU DID YOU DID YOU DID YOU DID YOU DID YOU DID!
!

KIDDY CONFLICT

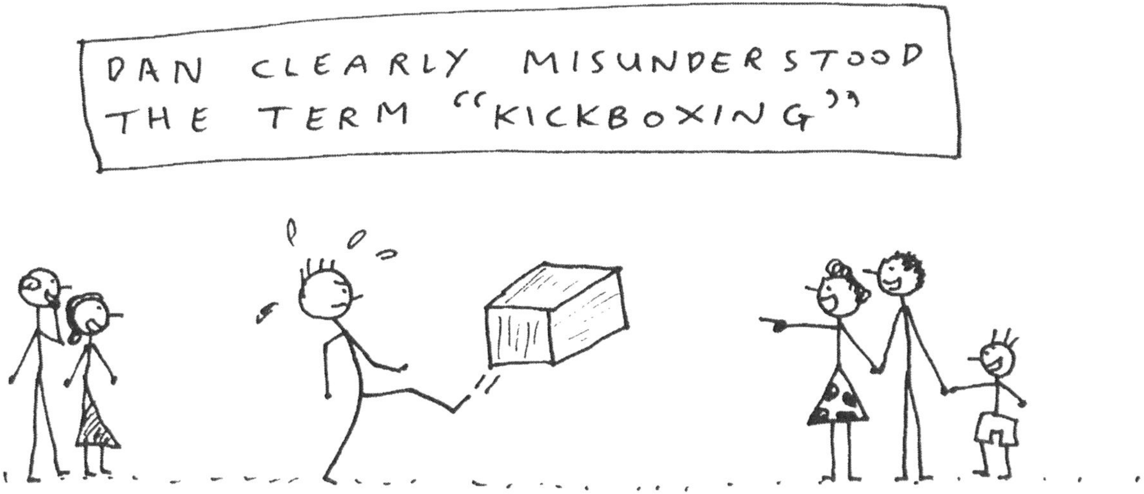
DAN CLEARLY MISUNDERSTOOD THE TERM "KICKBOXING"

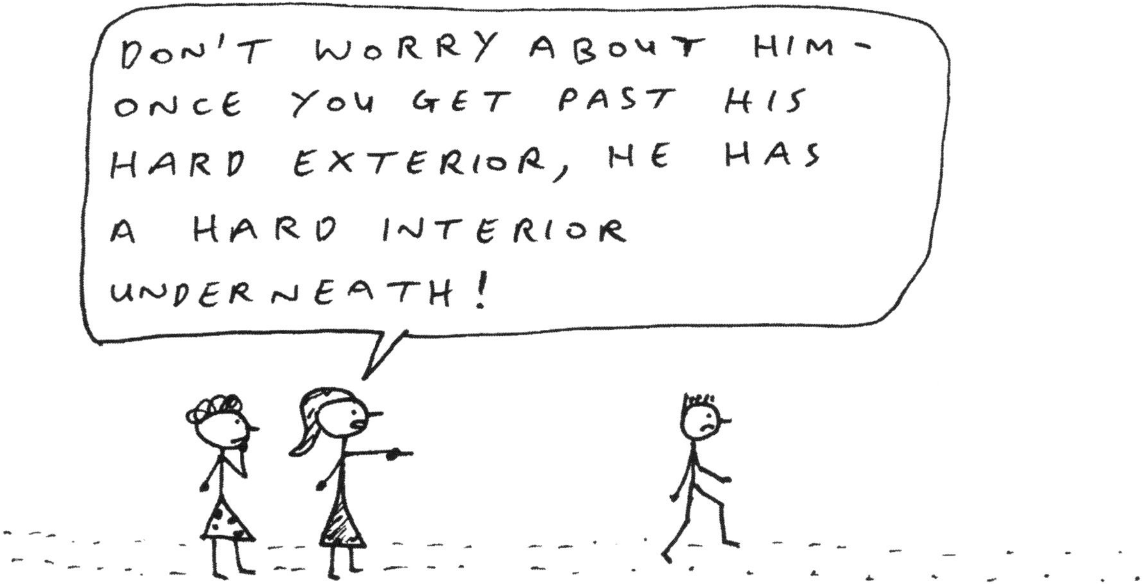
DON'T WORRY ABOUT HIM - ONCE YOU GET PAST HIS HARD EXTERIOR, HE HAS A HARD INTERIOR UNDERNEATH!

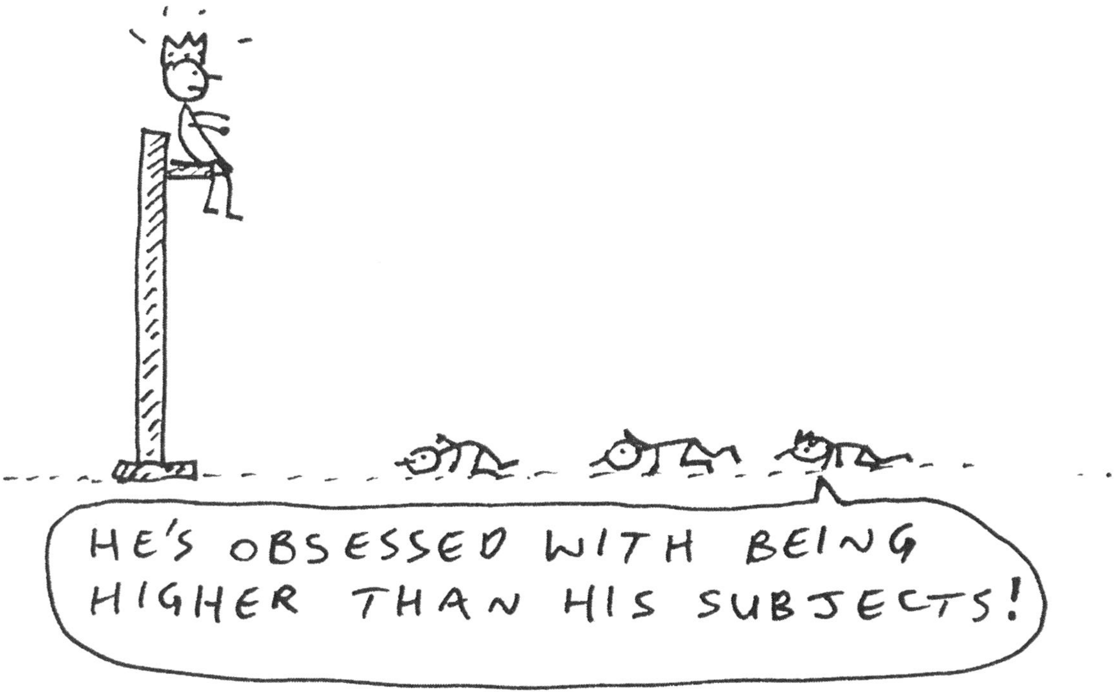
HE'S OBSESSED WITH BEING HIGHER THAN HIS SUBJECTS!

WHY DO YOU HAVE FLORAL WALLPAPER UP THERE?
'COS I'M TIRED OF STARING BLANKLY AT THE CEILING

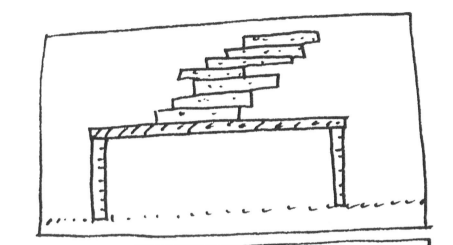

THE LEANING TOWER OF PIZZA

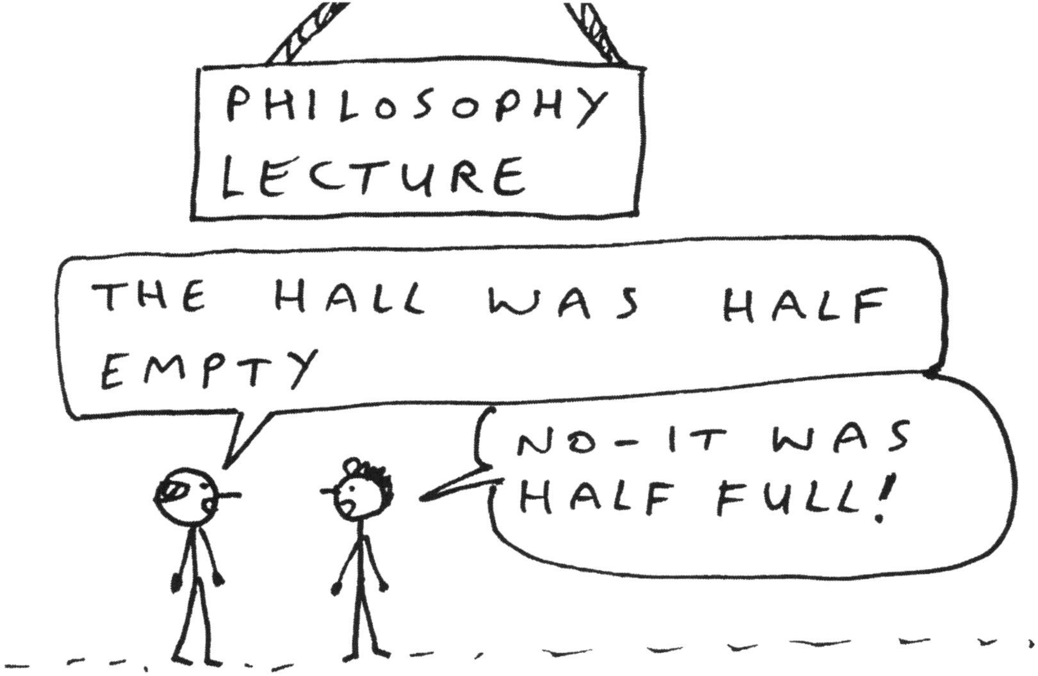
PHILOSOPHY LECTURE
THE HALL WAS HALF EMPTY
NO-IT WAS HALF FULL!

LOST PROPERTY
WE'VE FOUND A PAIR OF GLASSES. IF THEY'RE YOURS - PLEASE SEE ME (IF YOU CAN!)
...AND THE MISSING TISSUES HAVE BEEN FOUND. HANKS FOR LOOKING

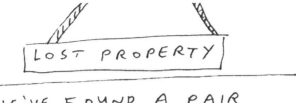

WE HAVE NOT SUPPLIED OUR ADDRESS FOR CONTACT – BUT IF YOU WRITE TO US, WE WILL GIVE IT TO YOU
ADVERT

MY GRANDAD'S JUST DIED AT THE AGE OF 127
WHY DID HE DIE?
IT'S A TOTAL MYSTERY

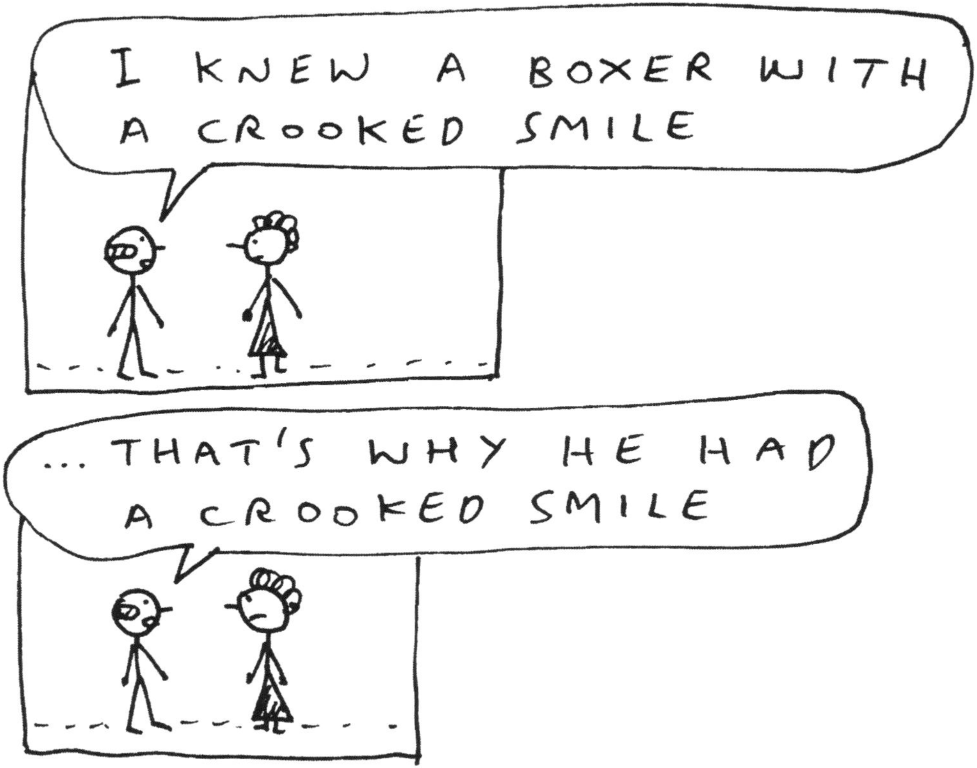
I KNEW A BOXER WITH A CROOKED SMILE
... THAT'S WHY HE HAD A CROOKED SMILE

THESE TOILETS ARE OUT OF USE. WE APOLOGISE FOR ANY INCONTINENCE CAUSED

SICKNESS POLICY
PLEASE NOTE: BROKEN LIMBS ARE AN ACCIDENT, NOT AN ILLNESS
...AND IF YOU CAN CRAWL ACROSS THE FLOOR, YOU ARE STILL ABLE TO "GET ABOUT"

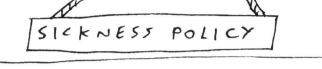

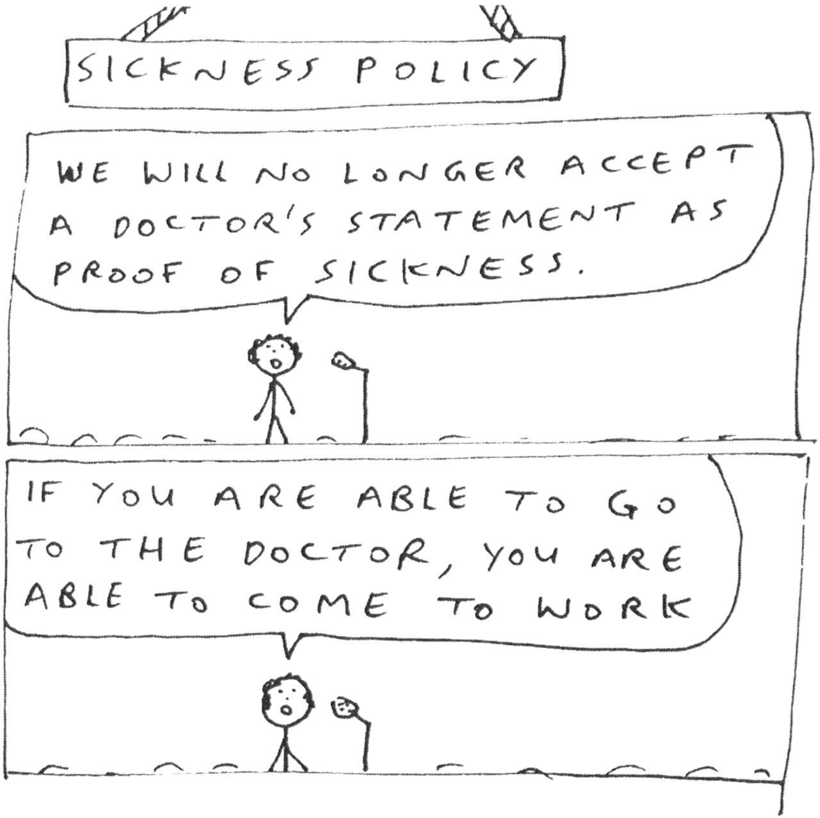
SICKNESS POLICY
WE WILL NO LONGER ACCEPT A DOCTOR'S STATEMENT AS PROOF OF SICKNESS.
IF YOU ARE ABLE TO GO TO THE DOCTOR, YOU ARE ABLE TO COME TO WORK

MY BOOK IS NOW A CONDENSED, ABRIDGED VERSION WHICH HAS BEEN ENLARGED AND EXPANDED FOR A WIDER AUDIENCE
?

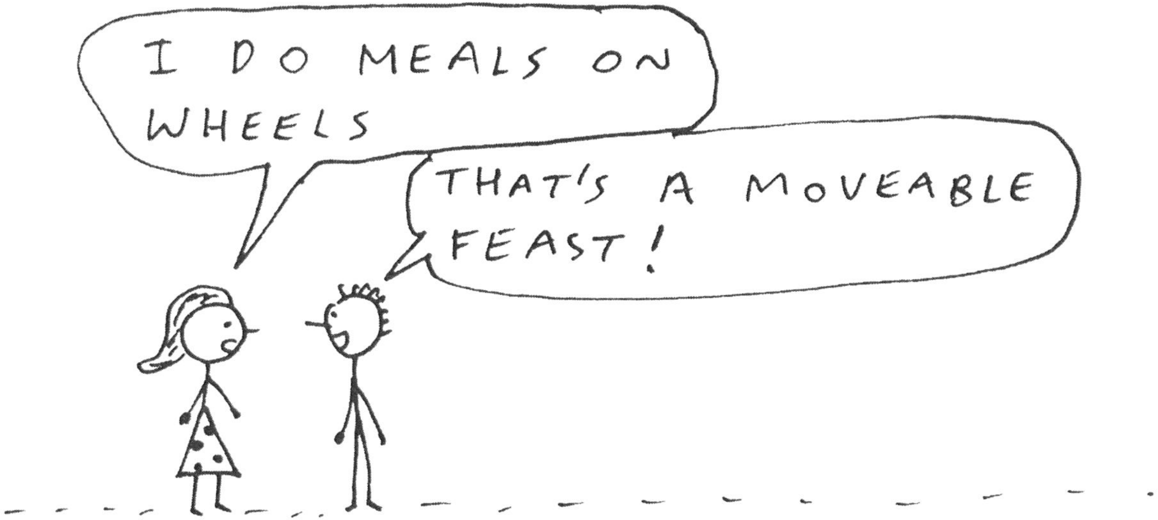
I DO MEALS ON WHEELS
THAT'S A MOVEABLE FEAST!

NO ONE ON HIS DEATHBED SAID HE WISHED HE'D SPENT MORE TIME AT THE OFFICE
PARTICULARLY IF HE WAS A MILKMAN!

OUR BUSINESS - PAST, PRESENT AND FUTURE
THAT COVERS ALL THE OPTIONS!

BUSINESS CONFERENCE
EXISTING USERS WILL NOTICE OUR WEBSITE HAS CHANGED. NEW USERS WILL NOT.

THIS IS JUST THE BEST THING EVER!

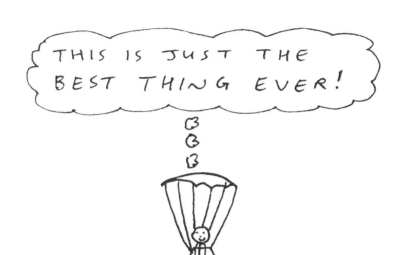

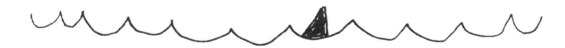

INSOLE COMPANY
WHEN YOU LEAVE, IT'S GONNA BE HARD FINDING SOMEONE TO FILL YOUR SHOES!

HE ONLY SMILES WHEN HE HAS WIND
THIRTY YEARS LATER

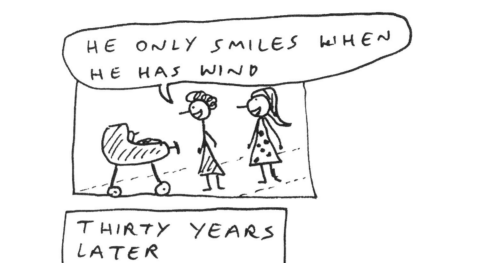

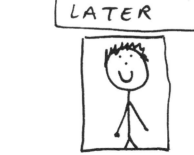

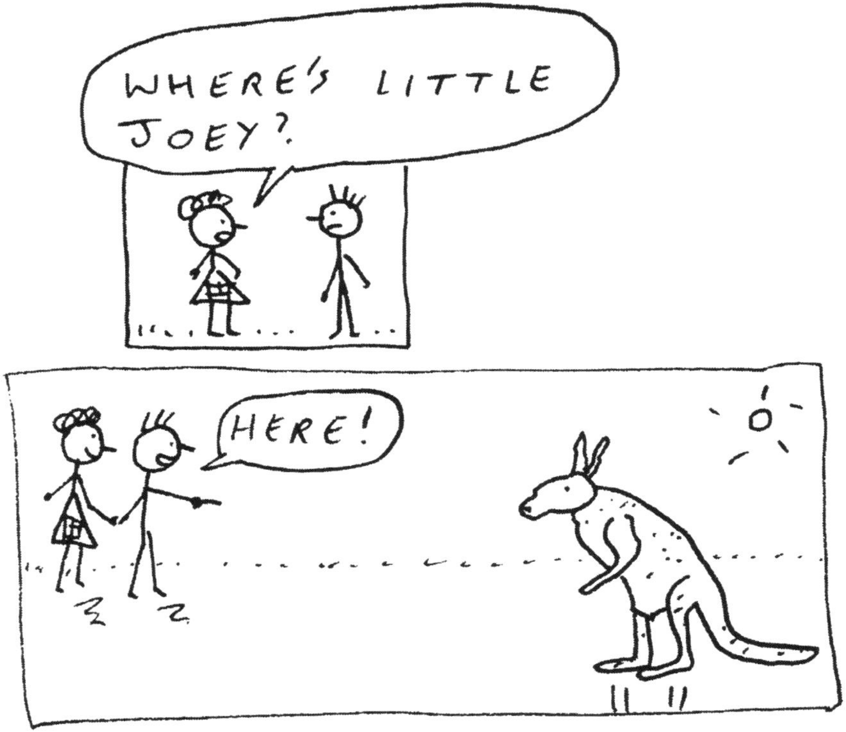
WHERE'S LITTLE JOEY?
HERE!

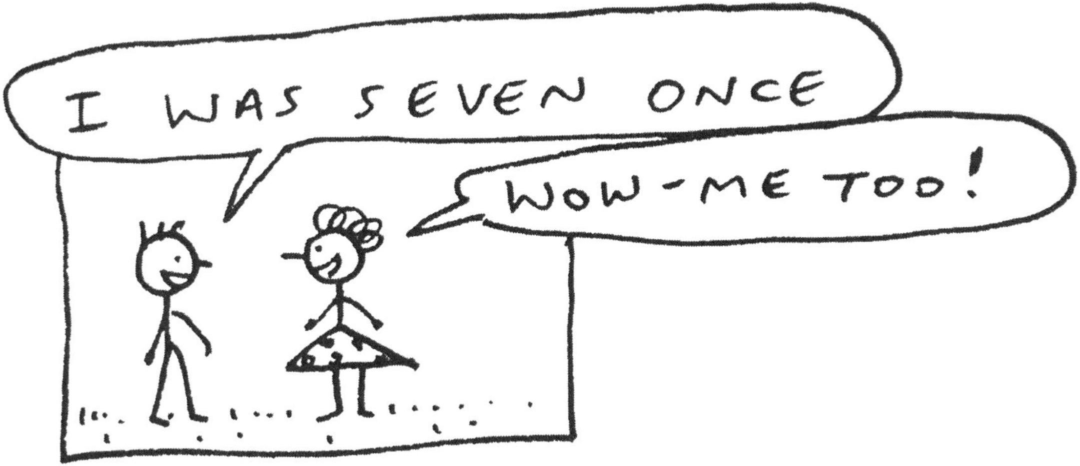
I WAS SEVEN ONCE
WOW - ME TOO!

YOUNG LOVE

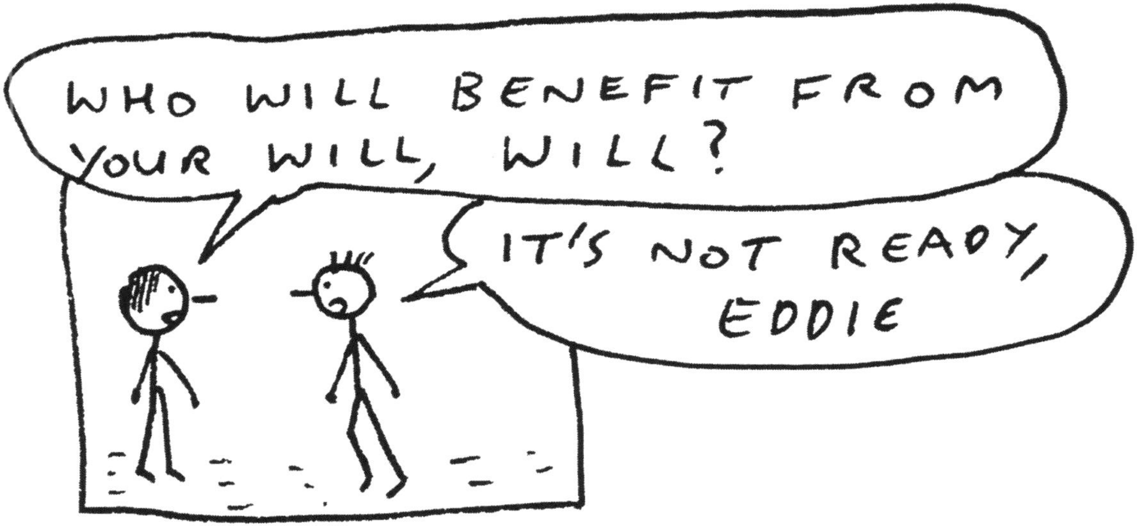
WHO WILL BENEFIT FROM YOUR WILL, WILL?
IT'S NOT READY, EDDIE

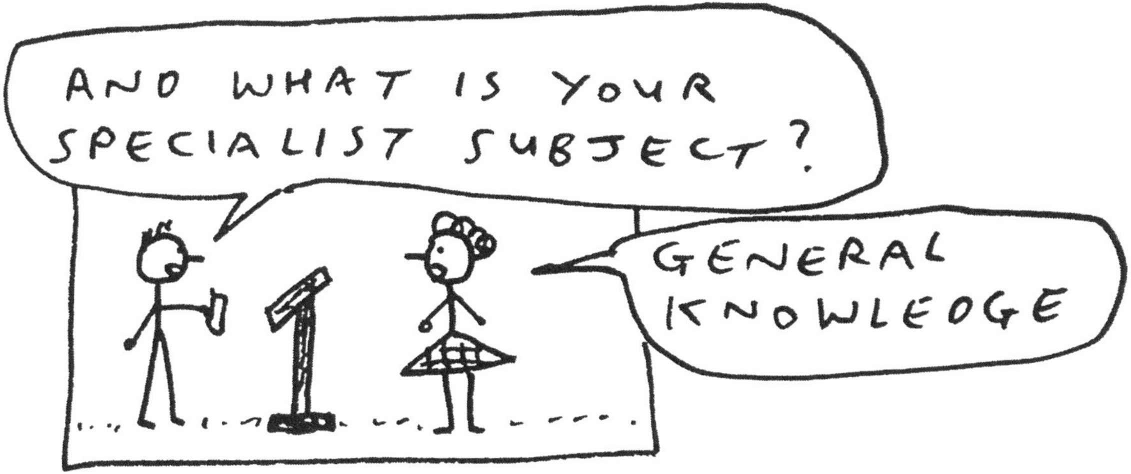

QUIZ NIGHT

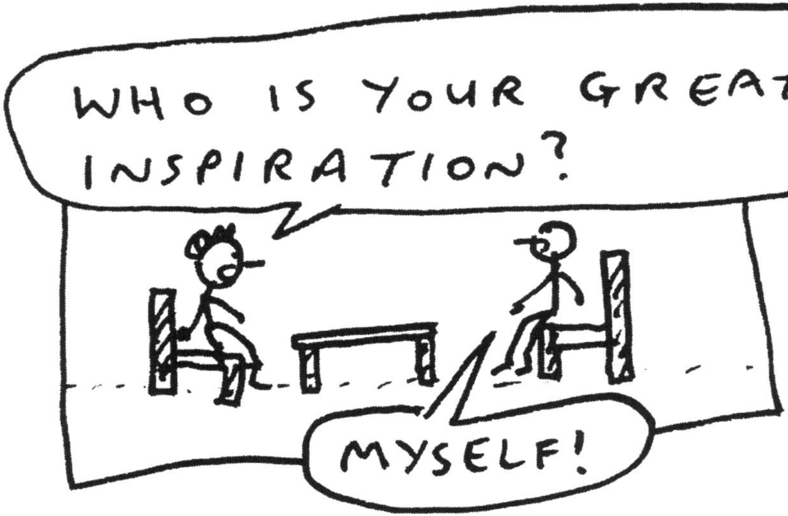

TYPICAL CELEB INTERVIEW

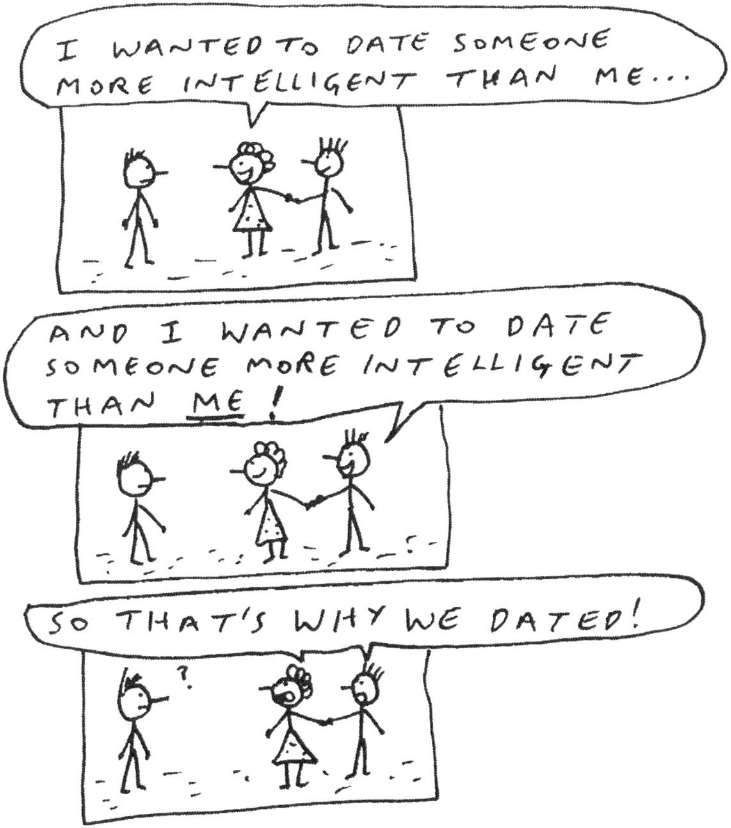
I WANTED TO DATE SOMEONE MORE INTELLIGENT THAN ME...
AND I WANTED TO DATE SOMEONE MORE INTELLIGENT THAN ME!
?
SO THAT'S WHY WE DATED!

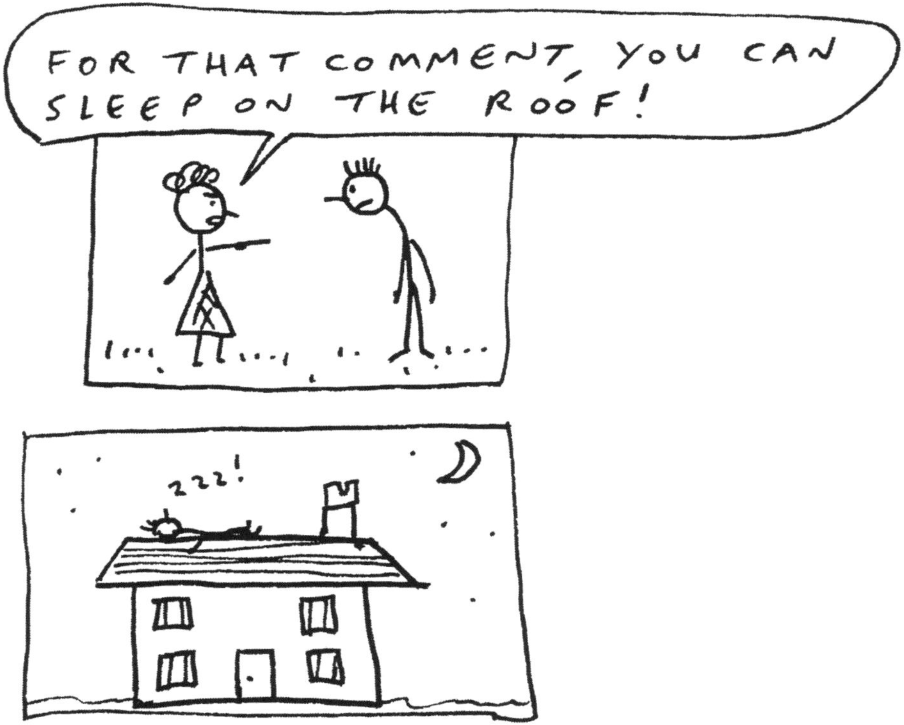
FOR THAT COMMENT, YOU CAN SLEEP ON THE ROOF!
ZZZ!

NIGHT ON THE TILES

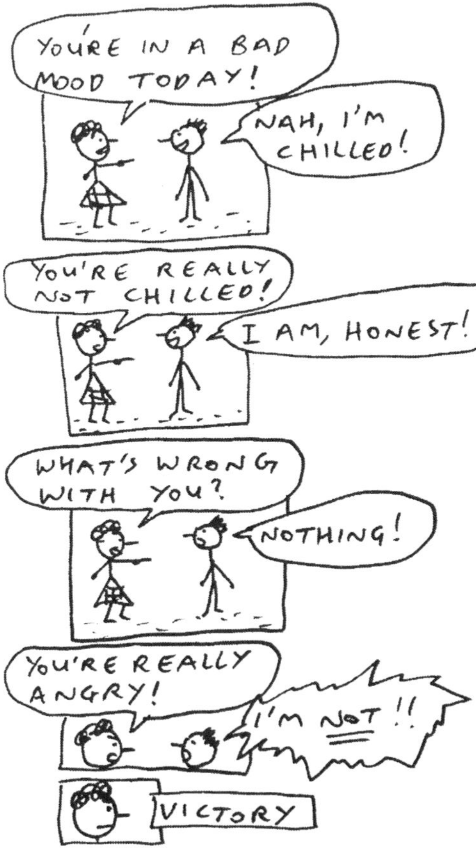
YOU'RE IN A BAD MOOD TODAY!
NAH, I'M CHILLED!
YOU'RE REALLY NOT CHILLED!
I AM, HONEST!
WHAT'S WRONG WITH YOU?
NOTHING!
YOU'RE REALLY ANGRY!
I'M NOT!!
VICTORY

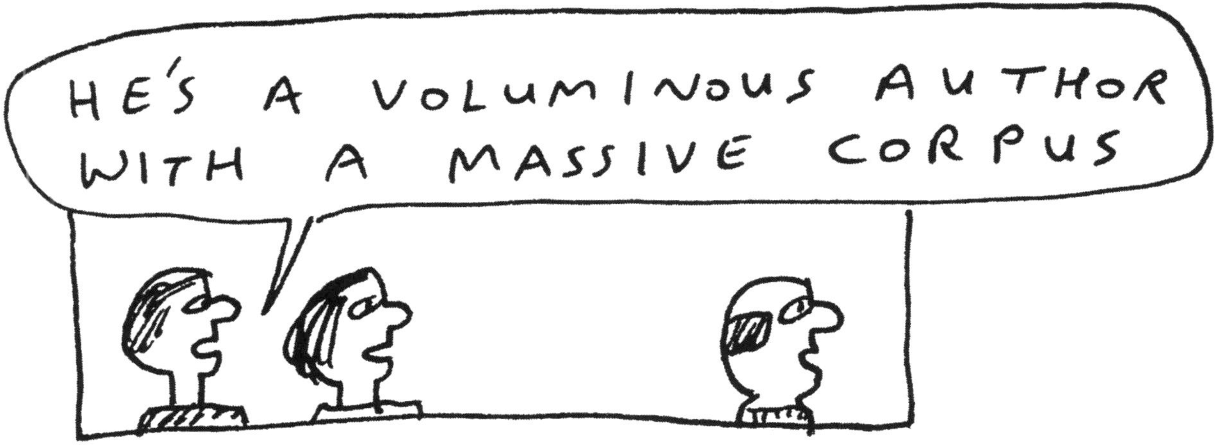
HE'S A VOLUMINOUS AUTHOR WITH A MASSIVE CORPUS

WE'RE ABOUT TO FILM THE PROFESSOR
MAKE SURE HE SITS IN FRONT OF A BOOKCASE, AND KEEP FOCUSSING ON HIS HANDS!

I CHANGED MY SURNAME TO GENTS. IT WAS THE ONLY WAY I COULD GET AN OFFICE WITH MY NAME ON!

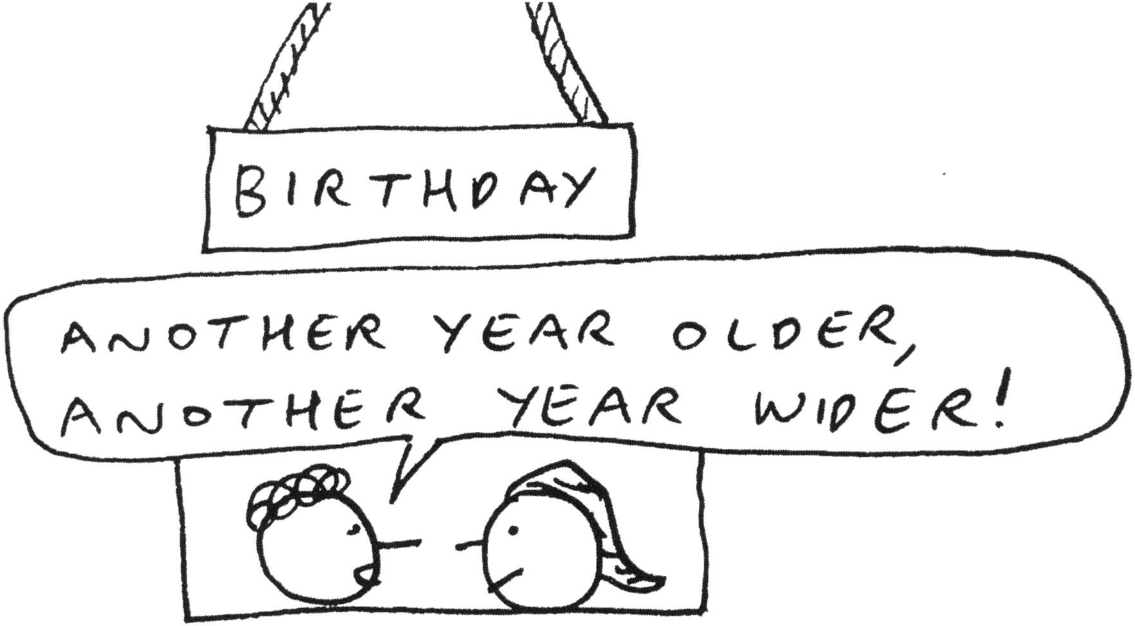
BIRTHDAY
ANOTHER YEAR OLDER, ANOTHER YEAR WIDER!

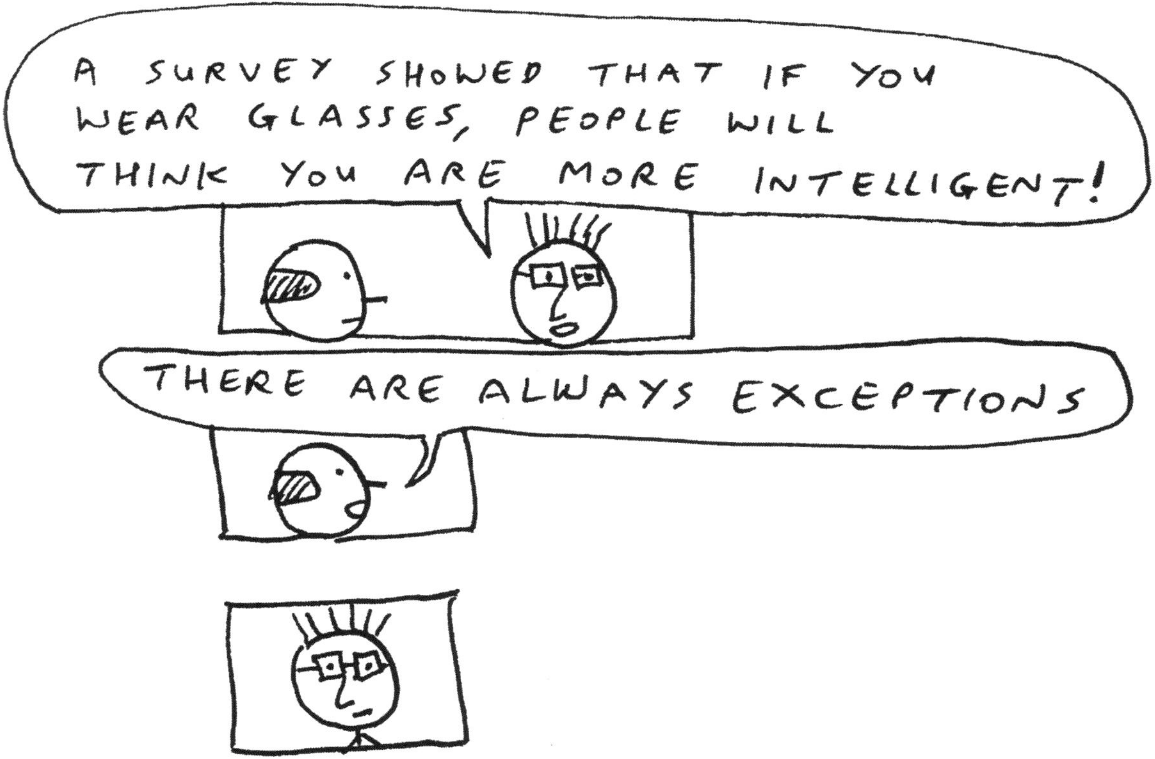
A SURVEY SHOWED THAT IF YOU WEAR GLASSES, PEOPLE WILL THINK YOU ARE MORE INTELLIGENT!
THERE ARE ALWAYS EXCEPTIONS

I THINK MY SPEECH TOTALLY ROCKED!
YOU HAVE A BIG BLOB OF MAYONNAISE ON THE CORNER OF YOUR MOUTH
!

THEY SAY A GOOD LAUGH IS EQUIVALENT TO 20 MINUTES ON THE TOILET!
SILENCE

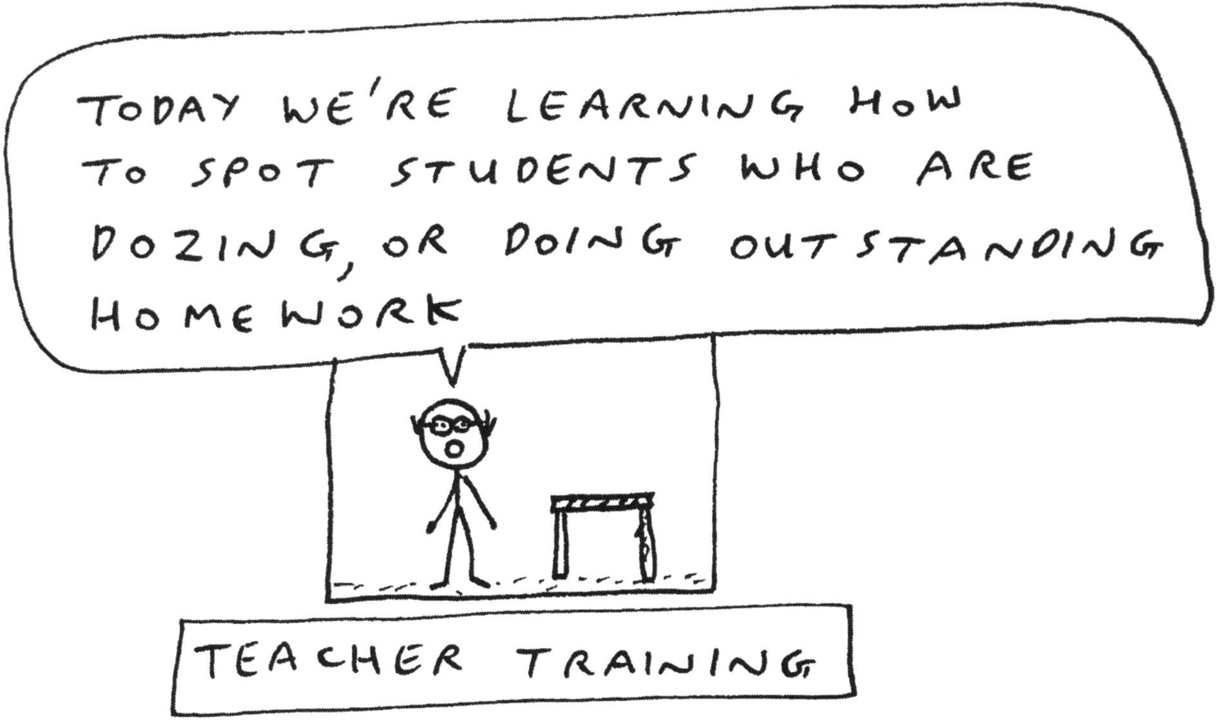
TODAY WE'RE LEARNING HOW TO SPOT STUDENTS WHO ARE DOZING, OR DOING OUTSTANDING HOMEWORK
TEACHER TRAINING

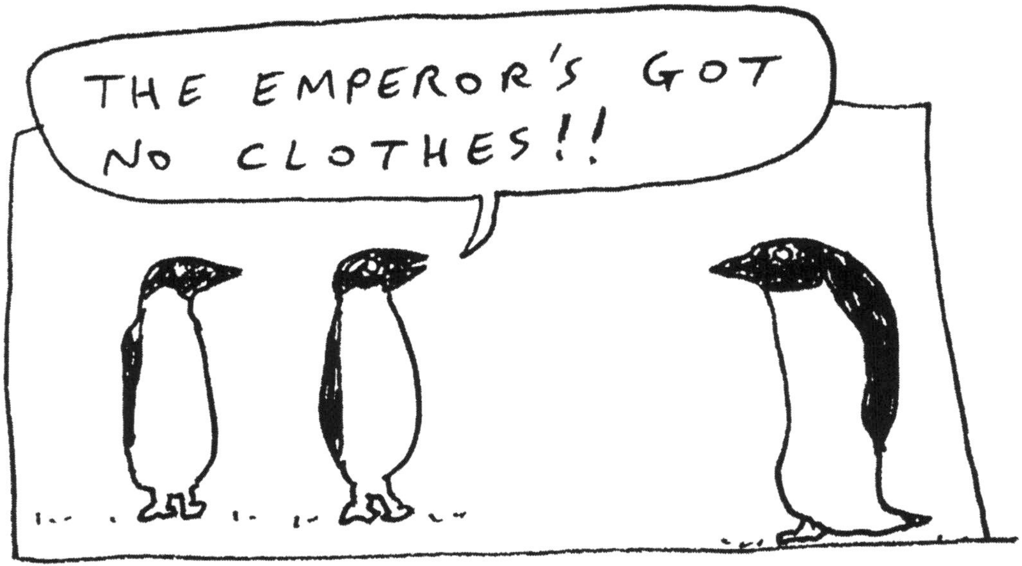
THE EMPEROR'S GOT NO CLOTHES!!

PENGUIN JOKE

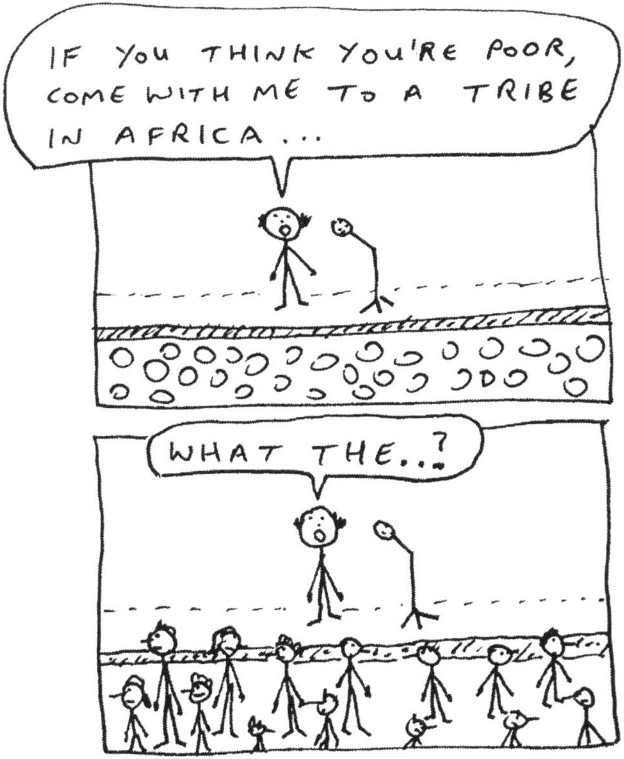

LITERALISTS

AMERICA
TWO MILES

COLUMBUS
DISCOVERS
AMERICA

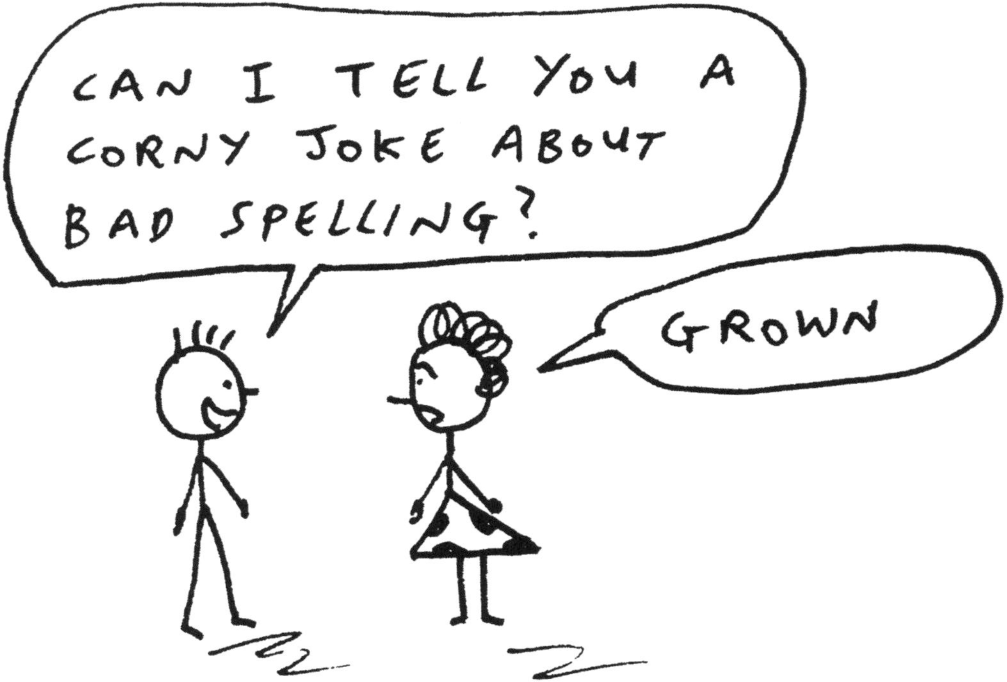
CAN I TELL YOU A CORNY JOKE ABOUT BAD SPELLING?
GROWN

NO LEVITATION ALLOWED
THEY'VE EVEN PUT SPIKES ON THE CEILING!

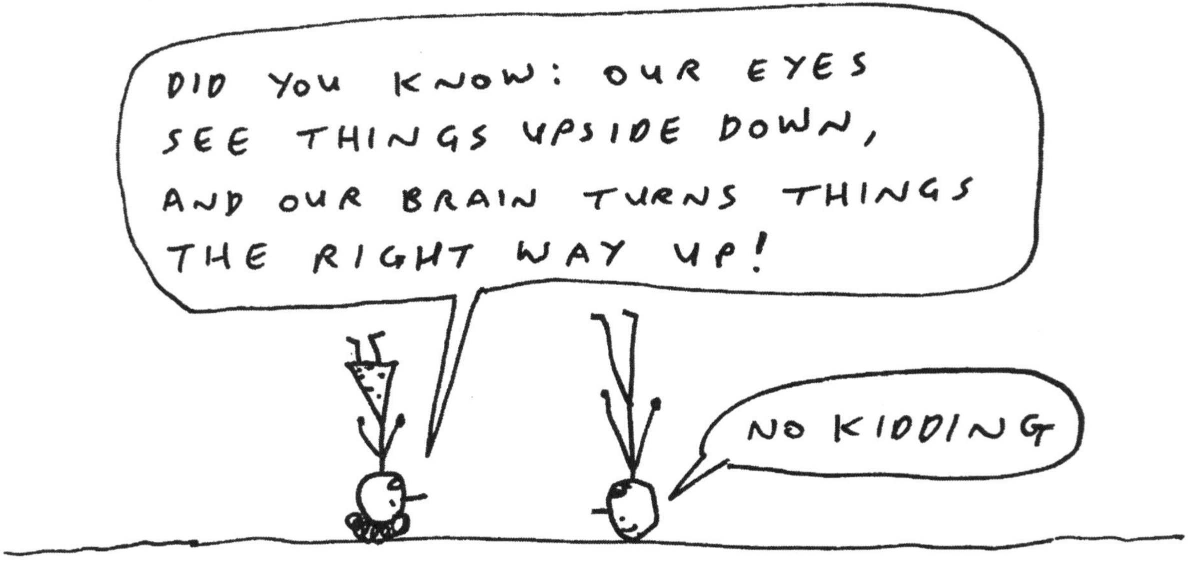
DID YOU KNOW: OUR EYES SEE THINGS UPSIDE DOWN, AND OUR BRAIN TURNS THINGS THE RIGHT WAY UP!
NO KIDDING

INTRODUCTION TIME
HELLO. MY NAME IS AGNES, AND I AM COMING FROM SWEDEN!
WHEN?
NOW!

CITIZEN'S ADVICE
YOU NEED TO TAKE A STEP BACK TO TAKE A STEP FORWARD!

I'D SWEAR THAT SHOP ASSISTANT'S SHOE LACES WERE TIED TOGETHER!
WELL, HE WAS FALLING OVER HIMSELF TO HELP YOU!

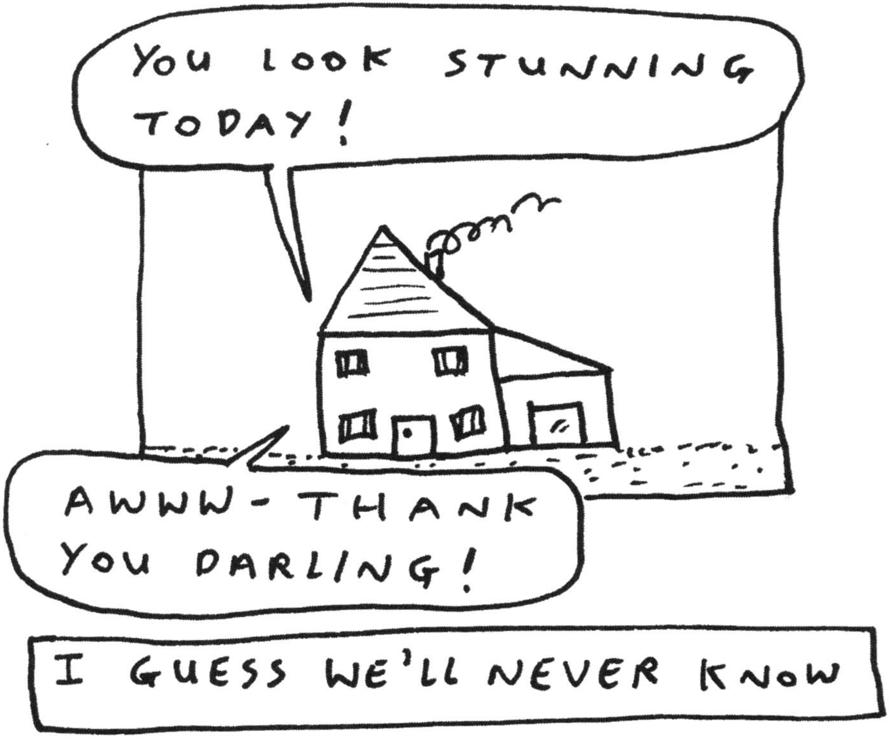
YOU LOOK STUNNING TODAY!
AWWW - THANK YOU DARLING!
I GUESS WE'LL NEVER KNOW

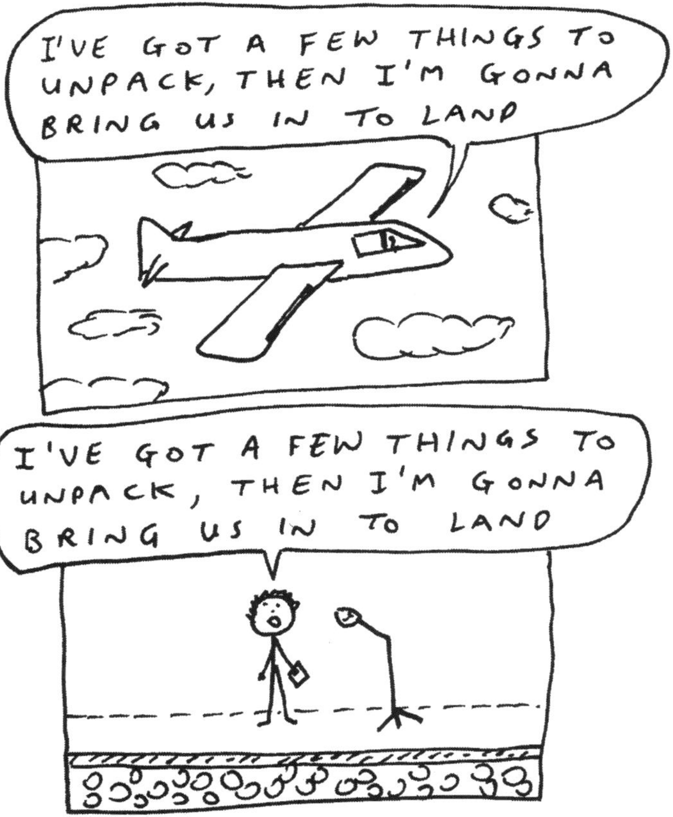
I'VE GOT A FEW THINGS TO UNPACK, THEN I'M GONNA BRING US IN TO LAND
I'VE GOT A FEW THINGS TO UNPACK, THEN I'M GONNA BRING US IN TO LAND

THAT BEAUTIFUL FRENCH WOMAN JUST SAID TO ME, "JE T'ADORE"!!
NAH-SHE SAID "SHUT THAT DOOR"!

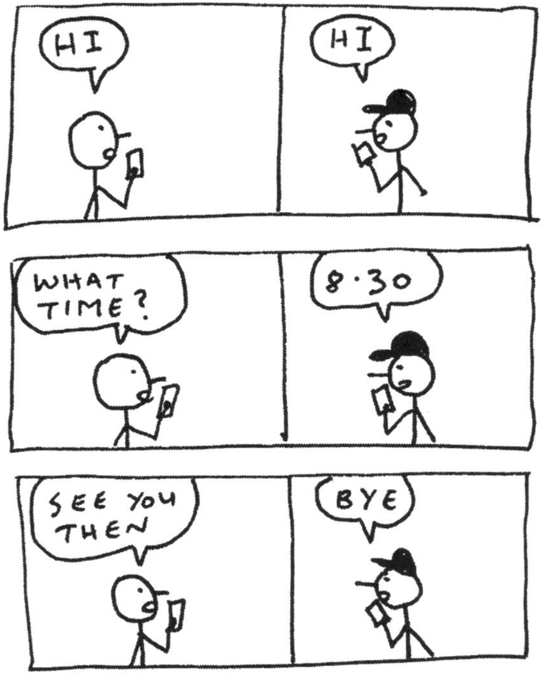
HI
HI
WHAT TIME?
8·30
SEE YOU THEN
BYE

MALE PHONE CONVERSATION

I LOVE IT WHEN THERE'S GALLONS OF SUNSHINE!
OH, YOU ARE A SILLY GOOSE!

IT LOOKS LIKE RAIN
WHAT DOES?
THE RAIN

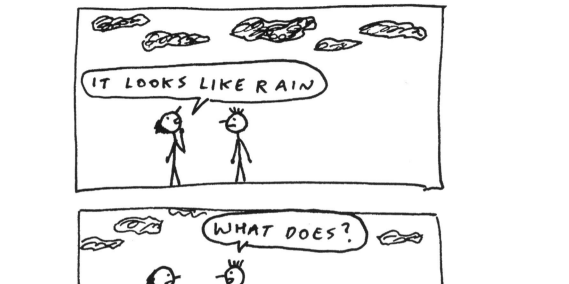

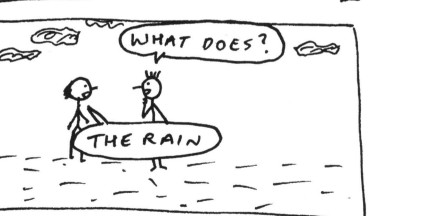

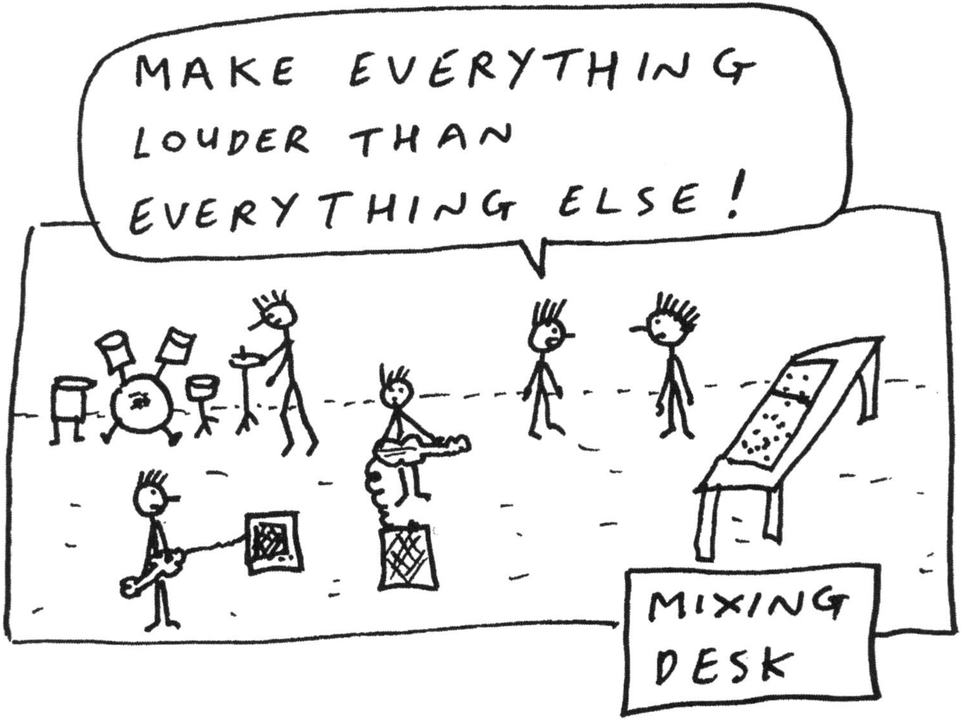
MAKE EVERYTHING LOUDER THAN EVERYTHING ELSE!
MIXING DESK

THERE ARE A HUNDRED BILLION GALAXIES IN THE UNIVERSE ...
... AND YET I STRUGGLE TO FIND A PLACE TO PARK!

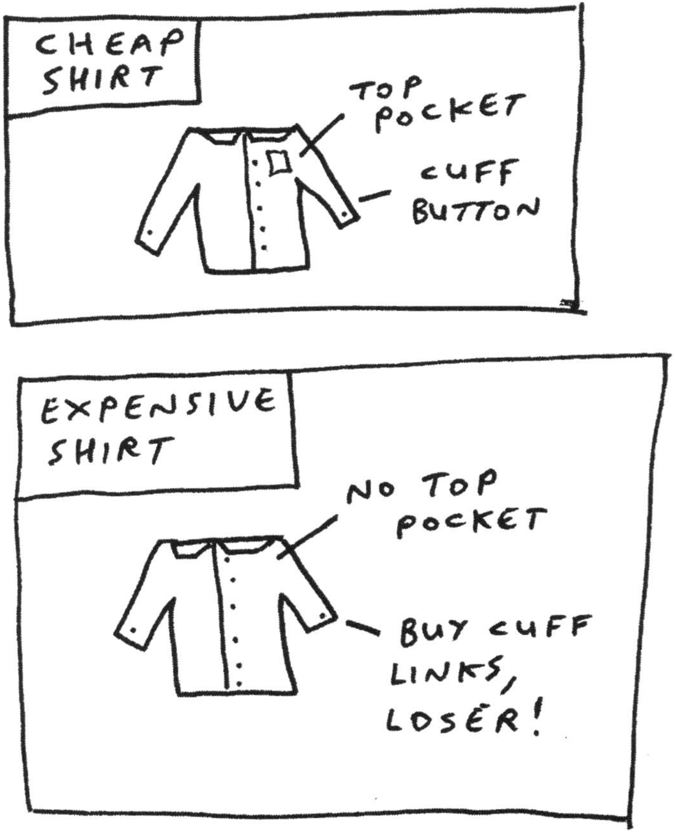
CHEAP SHIRT
TOP POCKET
CUFF BUTTON
EXPENSIVE SHIRT
NO TOP POCKET
BUY CUFF LINKS, LOSER!

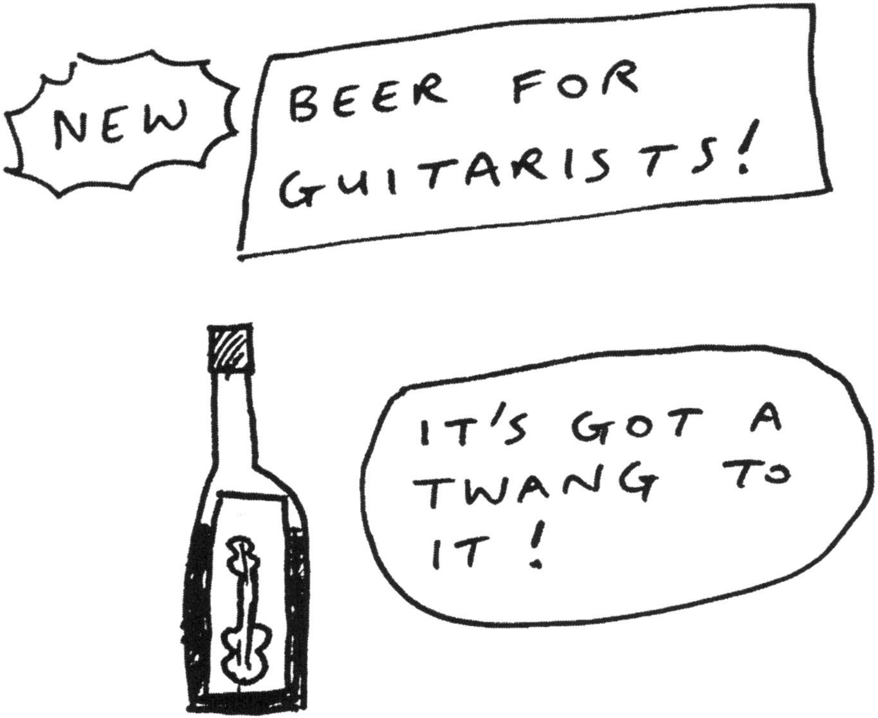
NEW
BEER FOR GUITARISTS!
IT'S GOT A TWANG TO IT!

LET'S SIT ON A ROCK UNDER A TREE BY A BRIDGE OVER A RIVER NEAR A LAKE ON A HILL!
YES, LET'S!
PLAY TIME

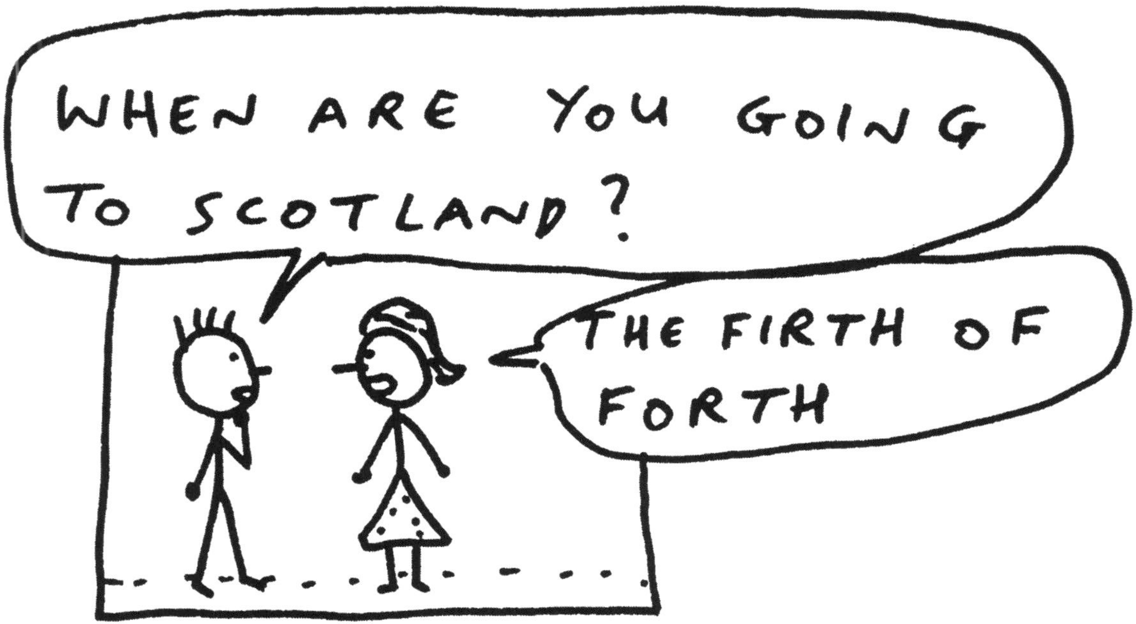
WHEN ARE YOU GOING TO SCOTLAND?
THE FIRTH OF FORTH

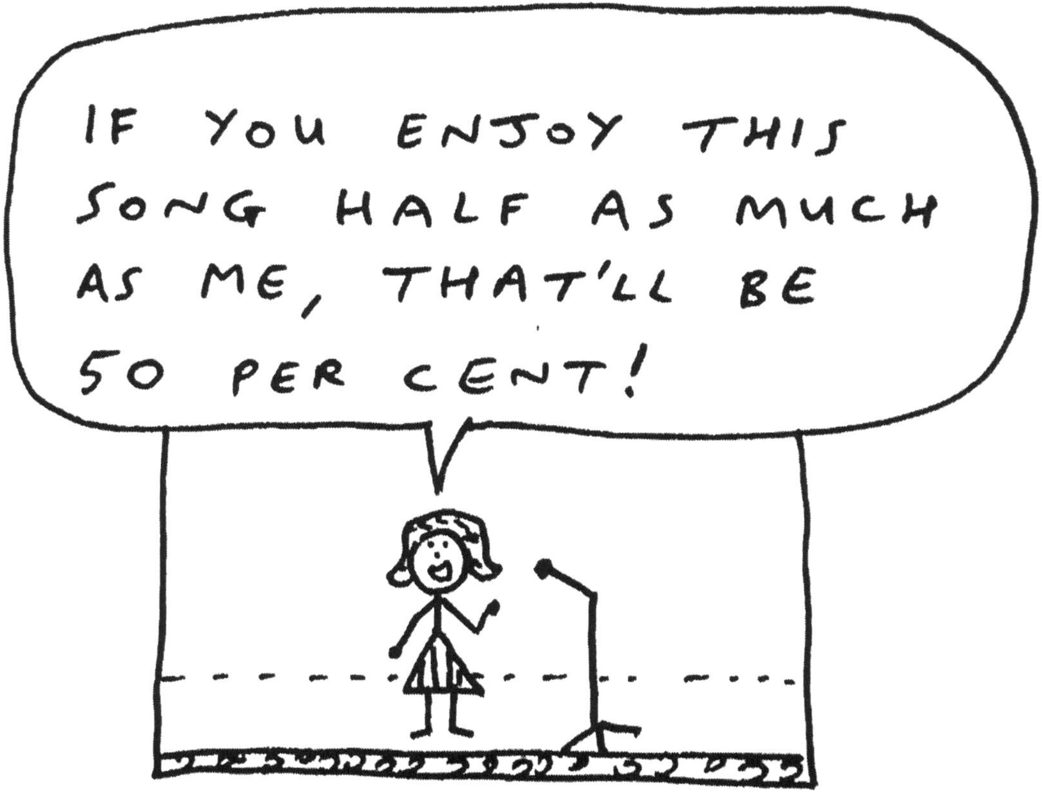
IF YOU ENJOY THIS SONG HALF AS MUCH AS ME, THAT'LL BE 50 PER CENT!

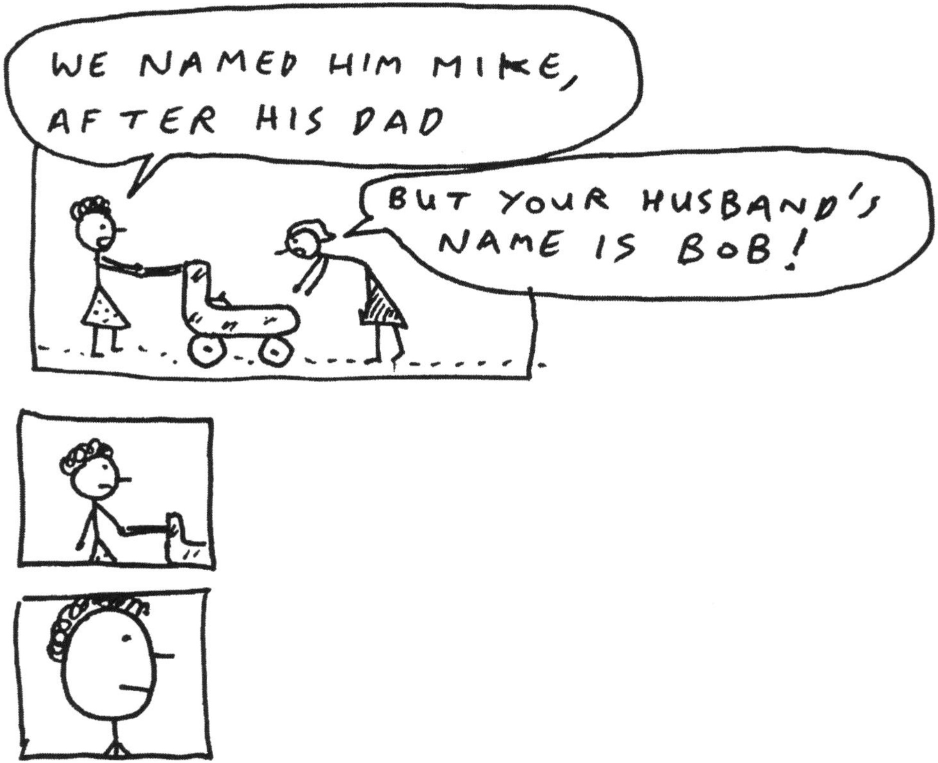
WE NAMED HIM MIKE, AFTER HIS DAD
BUT YOUR HUSBAND'S NAME IS BOB!

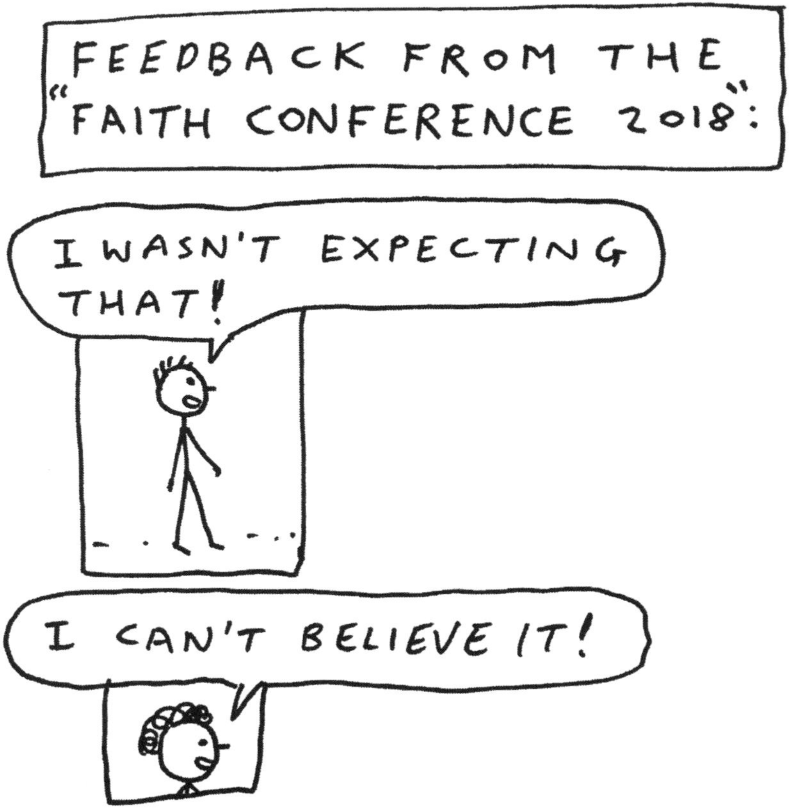
FEEDBACK FROM THE "FAITH CONFERENCE 2018":
I WASN'T EXPECTING THAT!
I CAN'T BELIEVE IT!

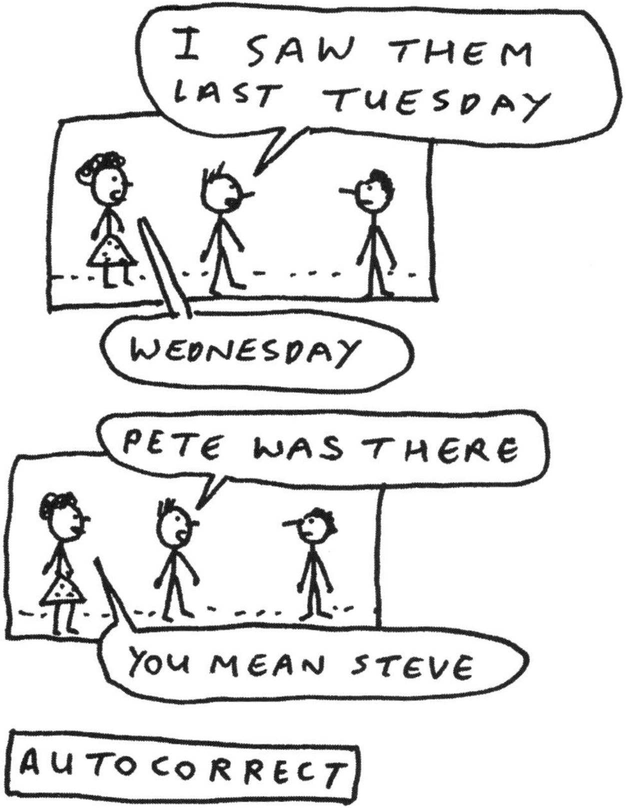
I SAW THEM LAST TUESDAY
WEDNESDAY
PETE WAS THERE
YOU MEAN STEVE
AUTOCORRECT

YOU RING THEM
NO, YOU
BUT YOU'LL KEEP INTERRUPTING ME AND TELLING ME WHAT TO SAY

DOCTORS
I GET OUT OF BREATH ON ESCALATORS

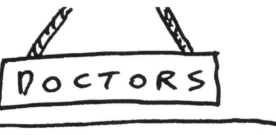

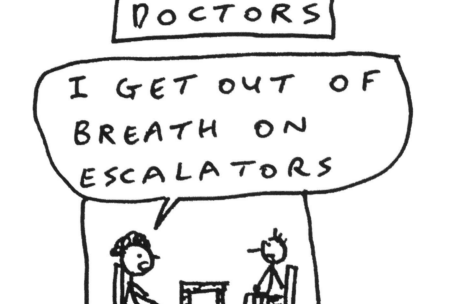

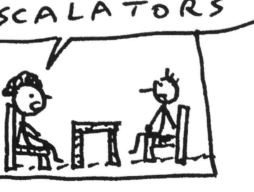

EVERY MOVEMENT IN HISTORY HAS HAD ITS LUNATIC FRINGE

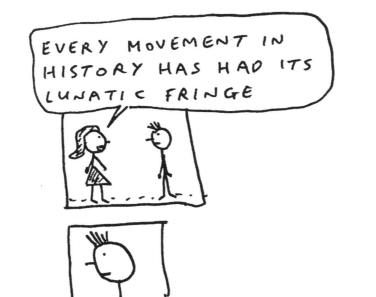

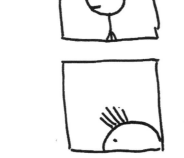

HEY BOB - THERE'S A GREY HAIRED, OVERWEIGHT MAN WHO'S TORMENTED WITH REGRET AND WONDERING WHERE THE YEARS WENT, TO SEE YOU
RECEPTIONIST

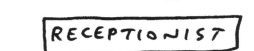

I REALLY DON'T WANNA SEE YOU, BUT I GOTTA EARN A LIVING
I'M PRE-OCCUPIED WITH WHAT I'M GONNA COOK FOR DINNER

TRUTH DRUG

I'LL BRING IT IN, THE NEXT TIME I COME TO WORK!
HEY, ROGER! WE'LL HAVE TO MEET UP SOME TIME!
NEVER HAPPENS

I REALLY THOUGHT I'D PASSED THE ACTING AUDITION!
I SPOKE TOO SOON

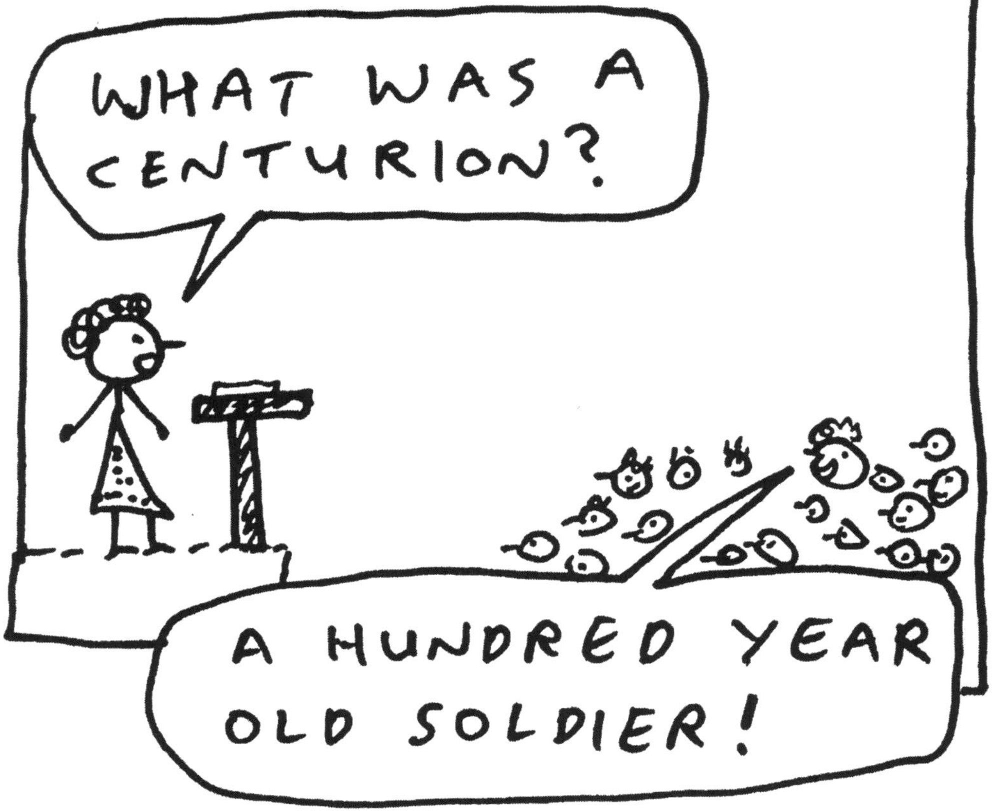
WHAT WAS A CENTURION?
A HUNDRED YEAR OLD SOLDIER!

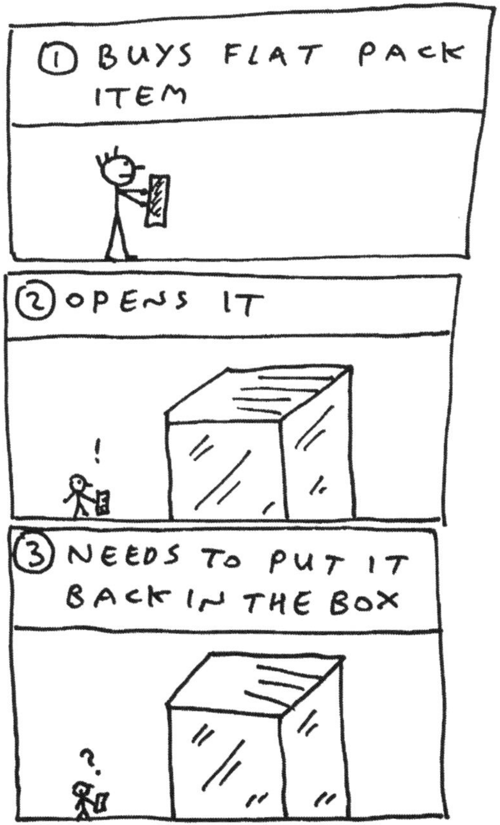
1 BUYS FLAT PACK ITEM
2 OPENS IT
!
3 NEEDS TO PUT IT BACK IN THE BOX
?

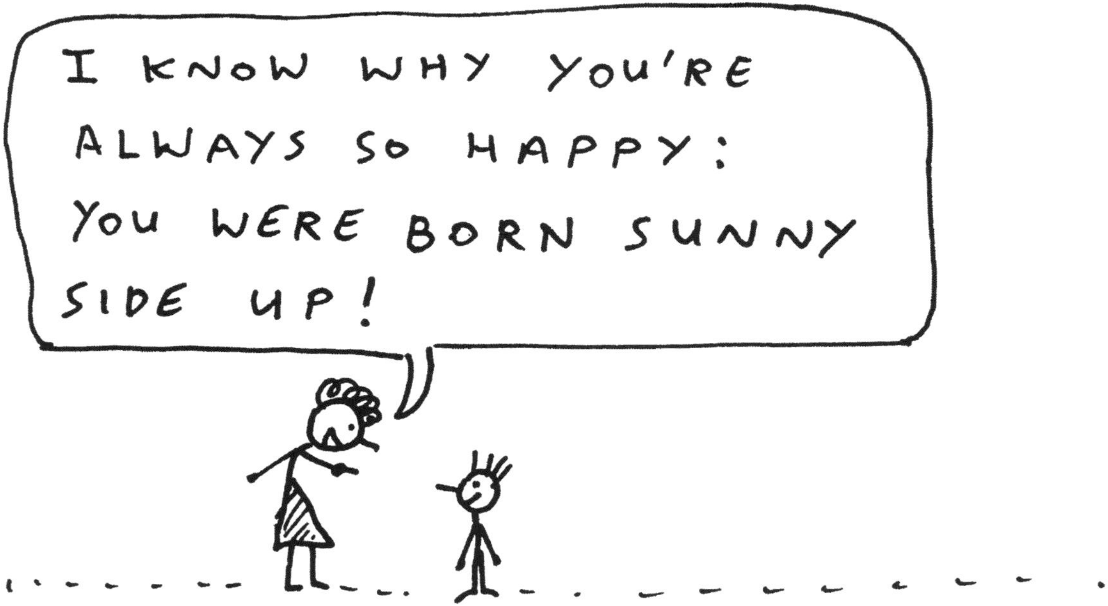
I KNOW WHY YOU'RE ALWAYS SO HAPPY: YOU WERE BORN SUNNY SIDE UP!

WHEN YOUR FRIEND HAS A FUNNY HAIRCUT:

RELAXATION CLASSES
I WANT YOU TO RELAX AT THE COUNT OF THREE...
ONE... TWO... THREE...
NOW!!!
!
!
!

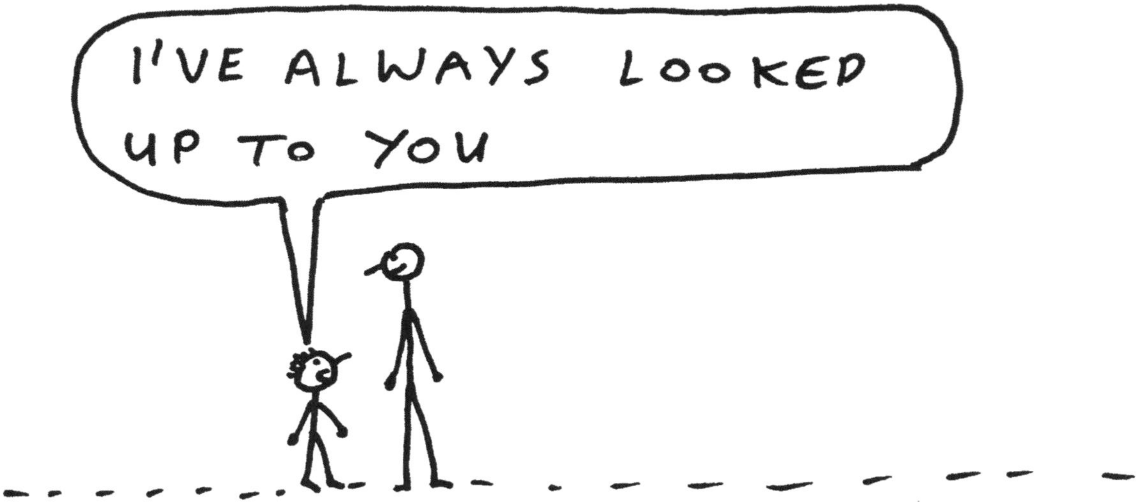
I'VE ALWAYS LOOKED UP TO YOU

IT GOES WITHOUT SAYING, NEEDLESS TO SAY... BUT IT'S WORTH SAYING, THAT...

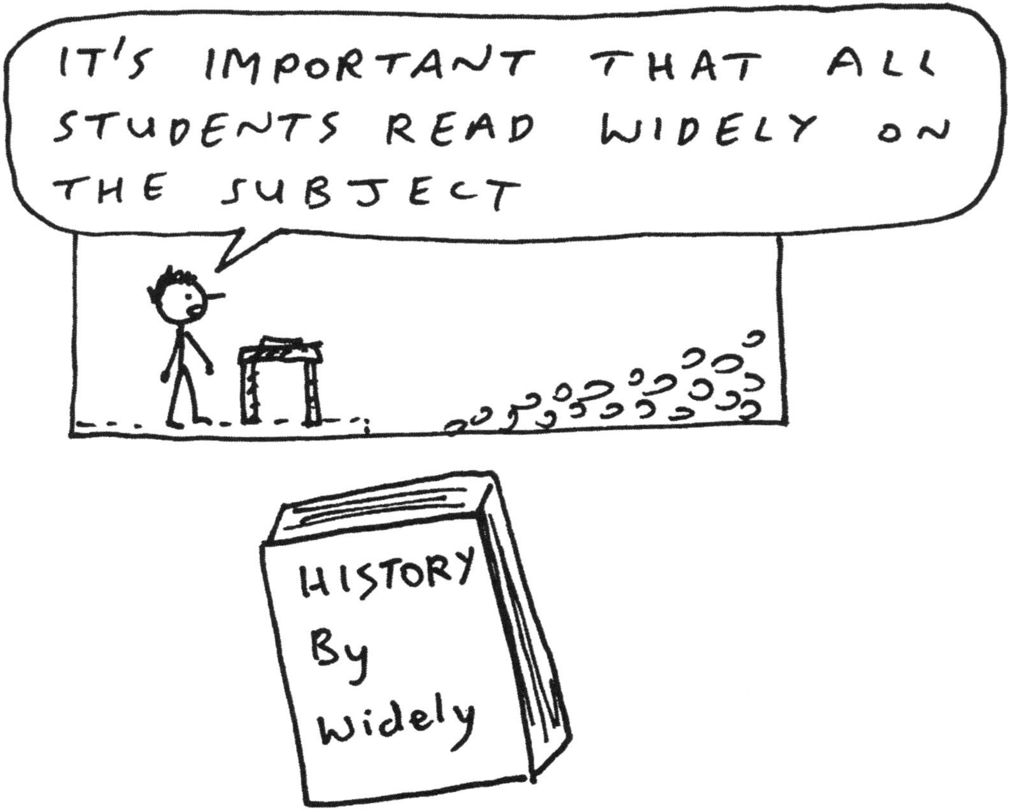
IT'S IMPORTANT THAT ALL STUDENTS READ WIDELY ON THE SUBJECT
HISTORY
By
Widely

A SMALL THOUGHT IS LIKE A BIG THOUGHT, ONLY SMALLER

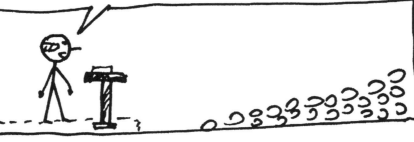

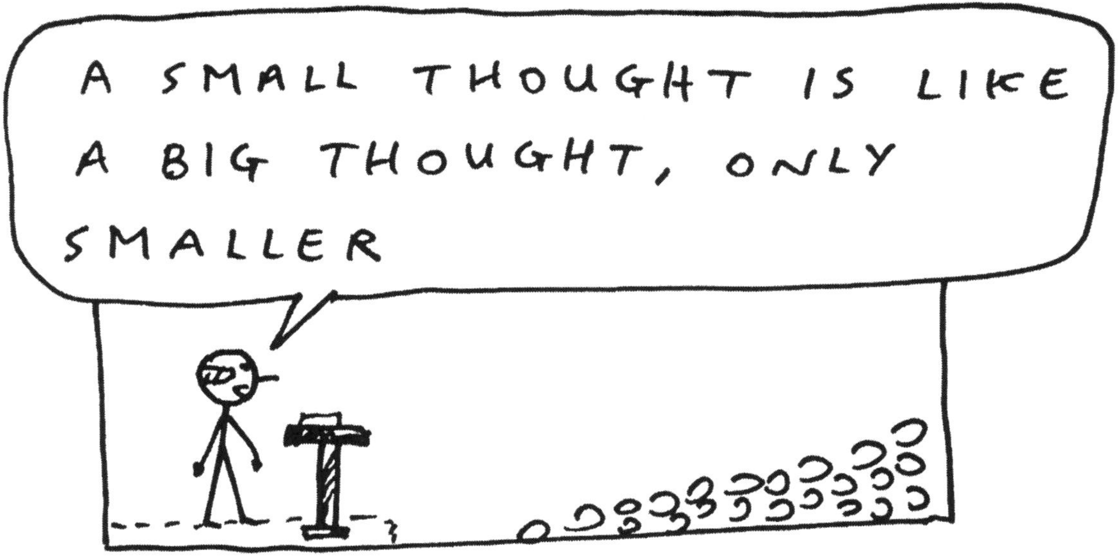

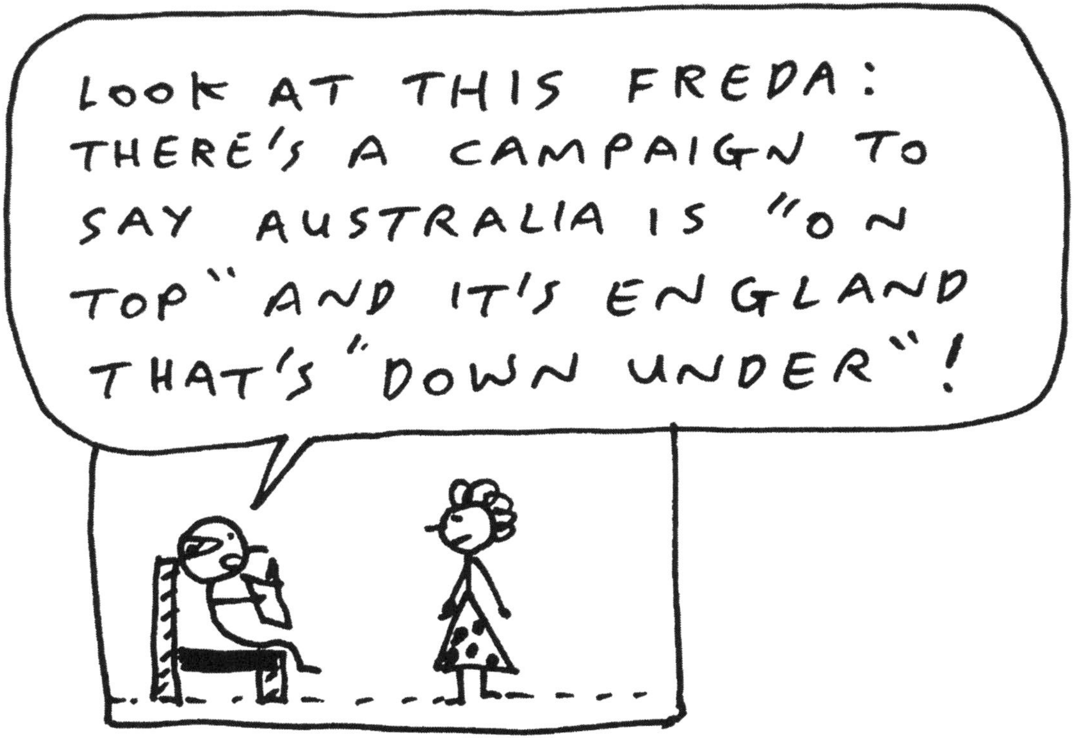
LOOK AT THIS FREDA: THERE'S A CAMPAIGN TO SAY AUSTRALIA IS "ON TOP" AND IT'S ENGLAND THAT'S "DOWN UNDER"!

YOU'LL BE OK IF YOU TOE THE LINE, KEEP YOUR NOSE CLEAN AND YOUR HEAD ABOVE WATER. THEN IF YOUR FACE FITS AND YOU'RE IN THE RIGHT PLACE AT THE RIGHT TIME, YOU'LL MAKE THE GRADE!

1. THINK OF A NUMBER BETWEEN 19 AND 46. NOW $\div 2 \times 6 + 32 \div 4 \times 30 - 16 + 19 - 42 \times 11 \div 9 + 27 - 56 \times 30 - 16 + 11$

2. WHAT WAS THE ORIGINAL NUMBER?

3. YOU'VE FORGOTTEN

4. I WIN

PICK A CARD—ANY CARD
AT THIS STAGE, YOU CAN TELL ME WHAT IT WAS
THREE OF HEARTS
CORRECT!

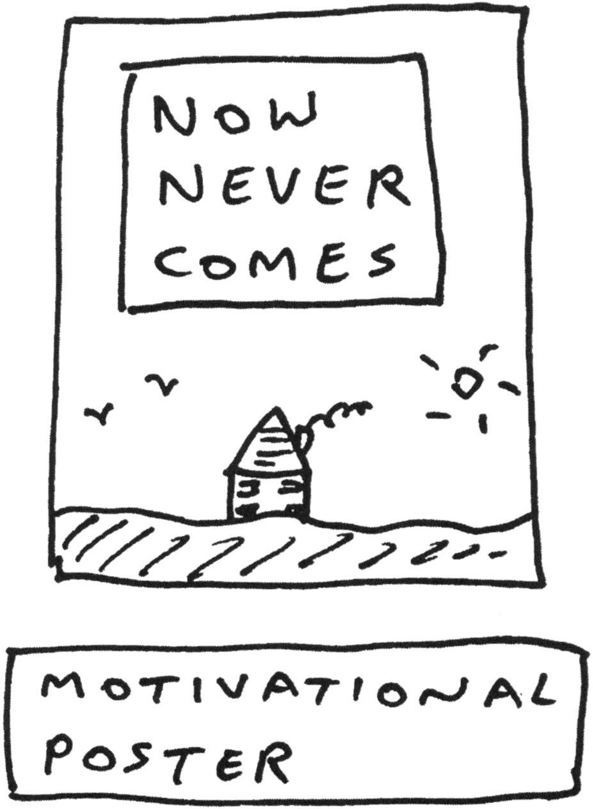
NOW NEVER COMES
MOTIVATIONAL POSTER

UNLESS IT HAD ENTERED MY MIND, I WOULD NEVER HAVE THOUGHT OF IT!

Ed's shoes were brand spanking new, squeeky clean, bright as a button and shiny as a new pin

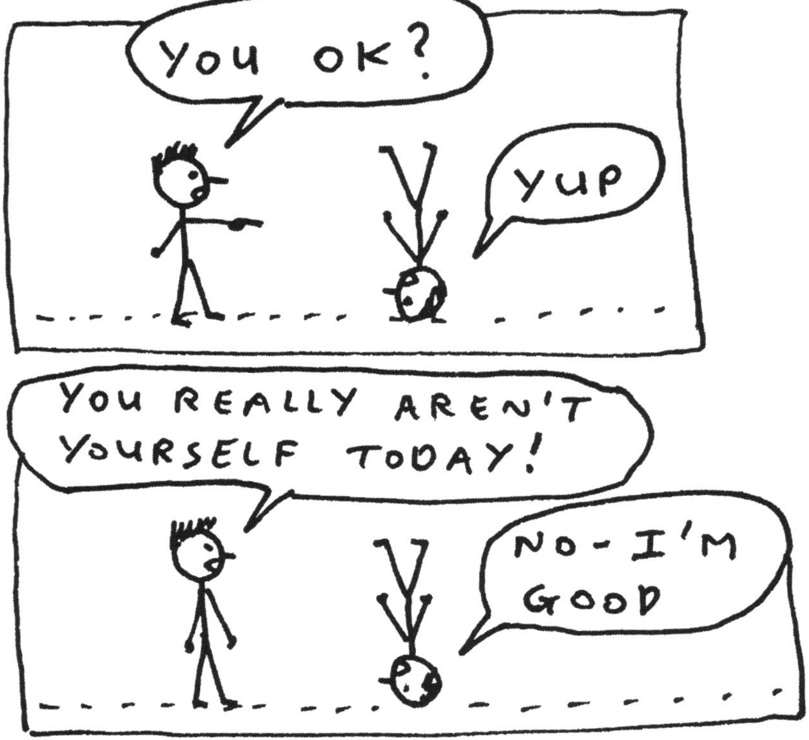
YOU OK?
YUP
YOU REALLY AREN'T YOURSELF TODAY!
NO - I'M GOOD

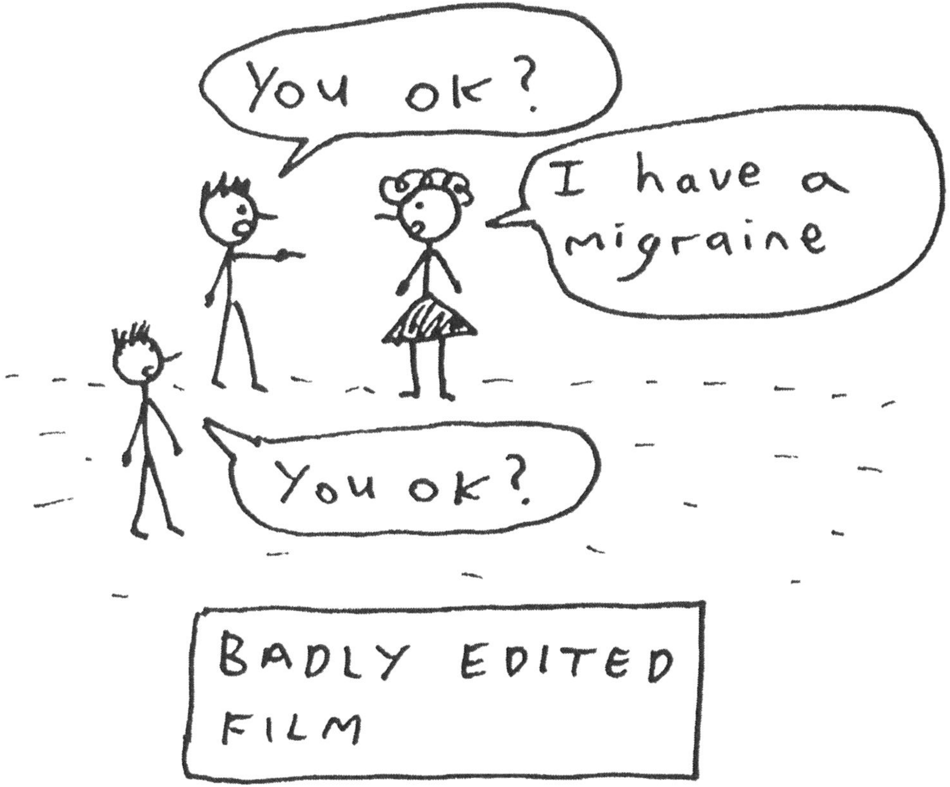
You ok?
I have a migraine
You ok?
BADLY EDITED FILM

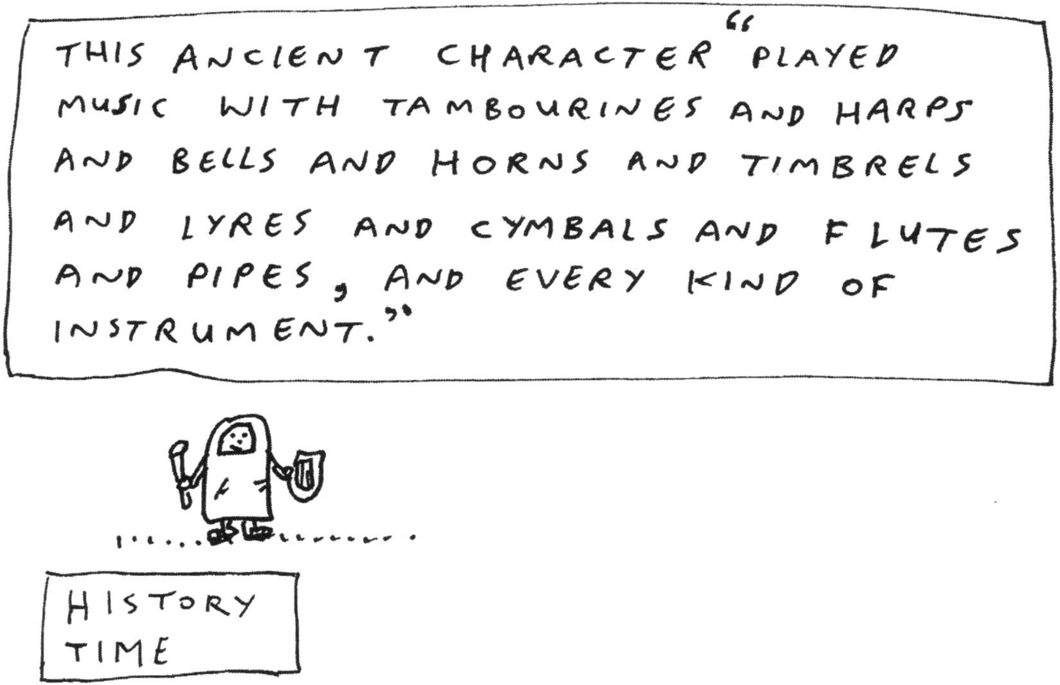
THIS ANCIENT CHARACTER "PLAYED MUSIC WITH TAMBOURINES AND HARPS AND BELLS AND HORNS AND TIMBRELS AND LYRES AND CYMBALS AND FLUTES AND PIPES, AND EVERY KIND OF INSTRUMENT."
HISTORY TIME

HERE COMES AN AMBASSADOR! WHERE'S A BRASS BAND WHEN YOU NEED ONE!

DOGMAS AND CATECHISMS

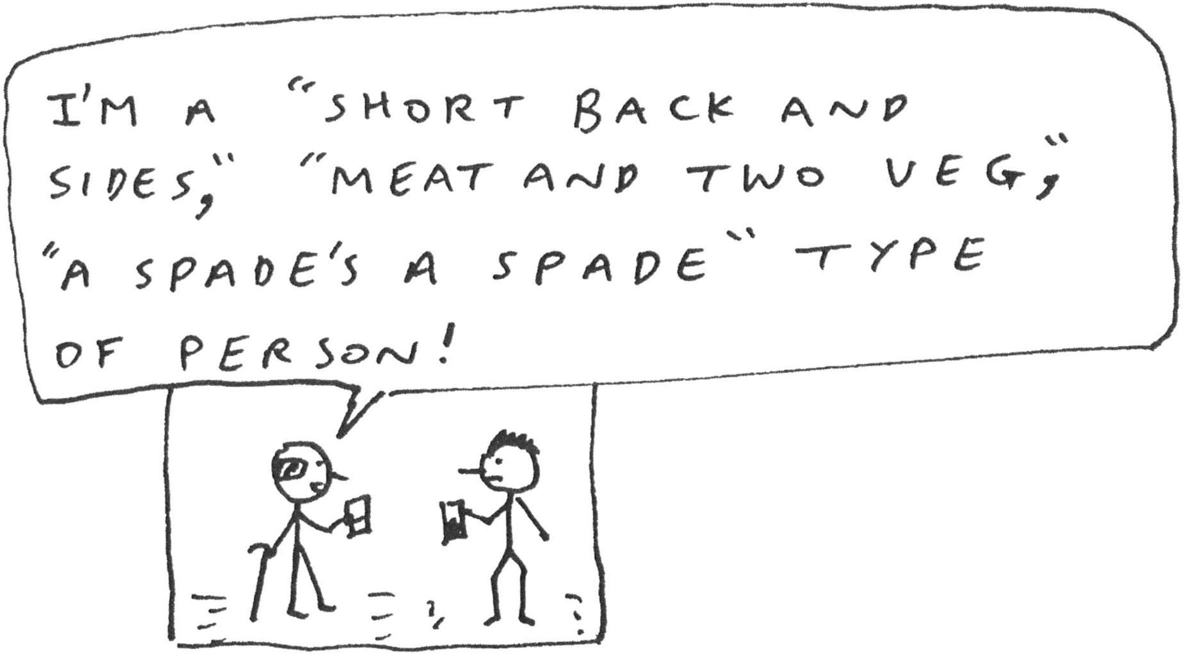
I'M A "SHORT BACK AND SIDES," "MEAT AND TWO VEG," "A SPADE'S A SPADE" TYPE OF PERSON!

ONE MINUTE TO NINE: I'M NOT AT WORK. ONE MINUTE PAST FIVE, I'M NOT AT WORK. IN MY LUNCHOUR, I'M NOT AT WORK. AND I DON'T TAKE MY WORK HOME WITH ME. BUT NINE TO FIVE, I AM AT WORK. AND I'LL DO ANYTHING FOR ANYBODY...

BY RUNNING AT 4 m.p.h. TOWARDS THE BACK OF THE TRAIN, YOU CAN BE TRAVELLING 196 m.p.h. IN THE OPPOSITE DIRECTION ...

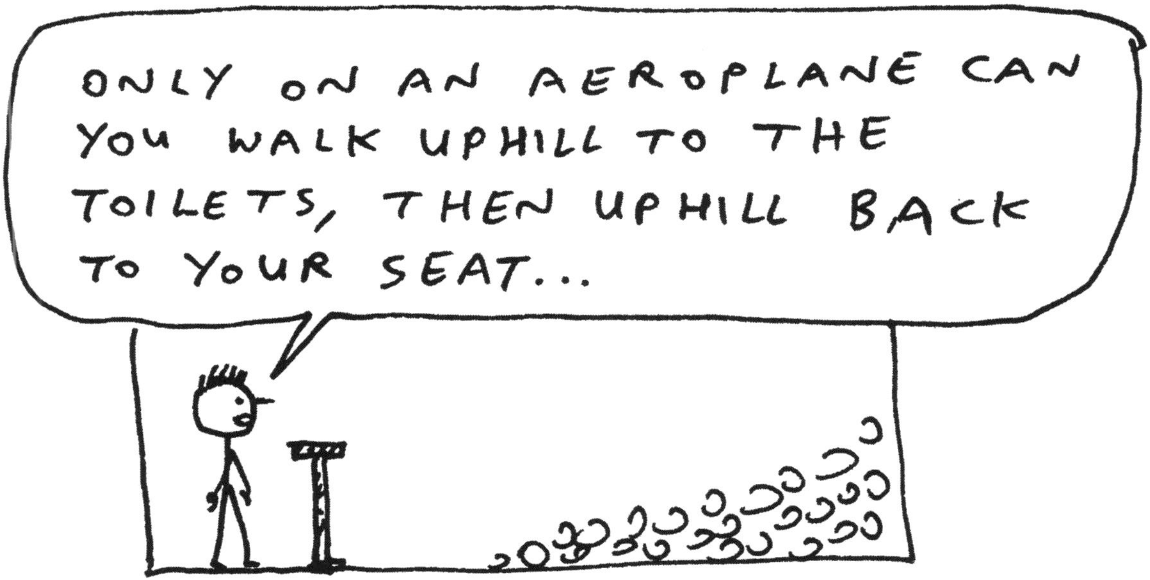
ONLY ON AN AEROPLANE CAN YOU WALK UPHILL TO THE TOILETS, THEN UPHILL BACK TO YOUR SEAT...

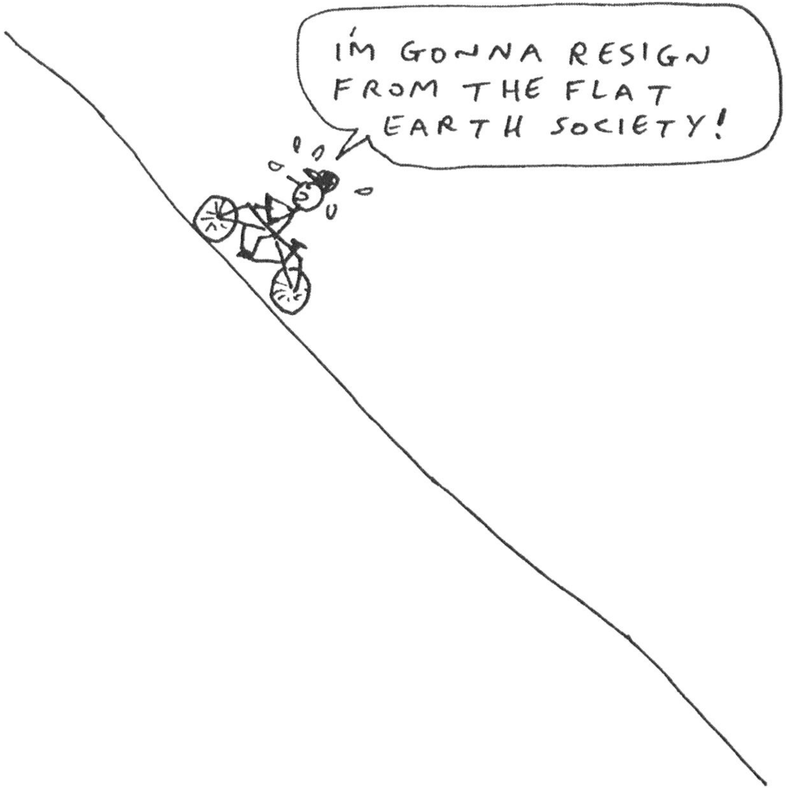
I'M GONNA RESIGN FROM THE FLAT EARTH SOCIETY!

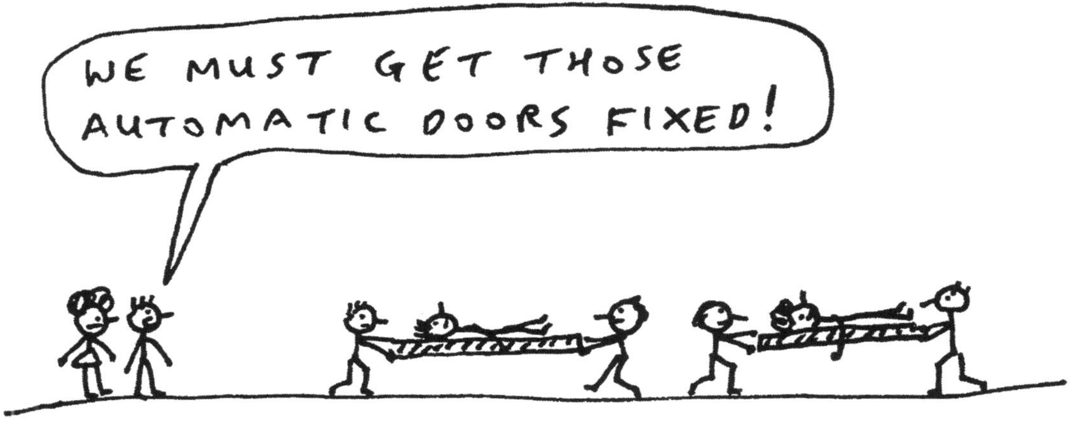
WE MUST GET THOSE AUTOMATIC DOORS FIXED!

THERE ARE TWO TYPES OF HUMOUR: AQUEOUS AND VITREOUS. (FUNNY 'HA HA' AND FUNNY 'PECULIAR')

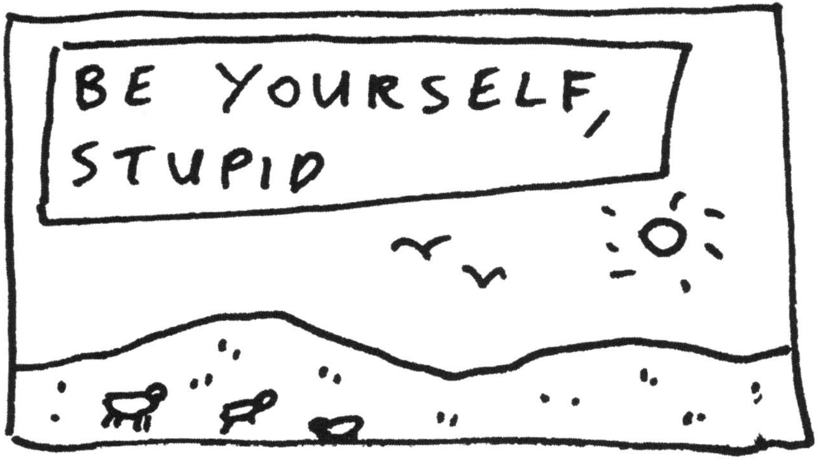

MOTIVATIONAL POSTER

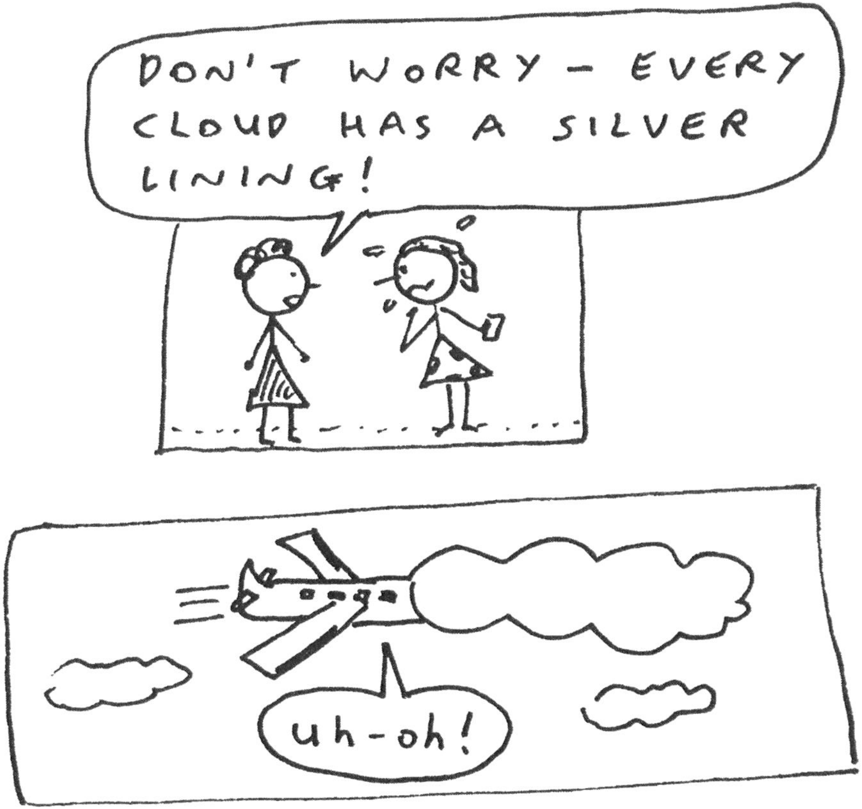
DON'T WORRY – EVERY CLOUD HAS A SILVER LINING!
uh-oh!

SAMUEL PEPYS: THE
PATRON SAINT OF
PERSONAL ORGANISERS

NEWTON SAID "TO EVERY ACTION THERE IS AN EQUAL AND OPPOSITE REACTION"
I VERY MUCH DOUBT THAT!

THIS CITY HAS A HISTORY THAT DATES BACK TO IT'S ORIGINAL COMMENCEMENT
WOW
TOUR GUIDE

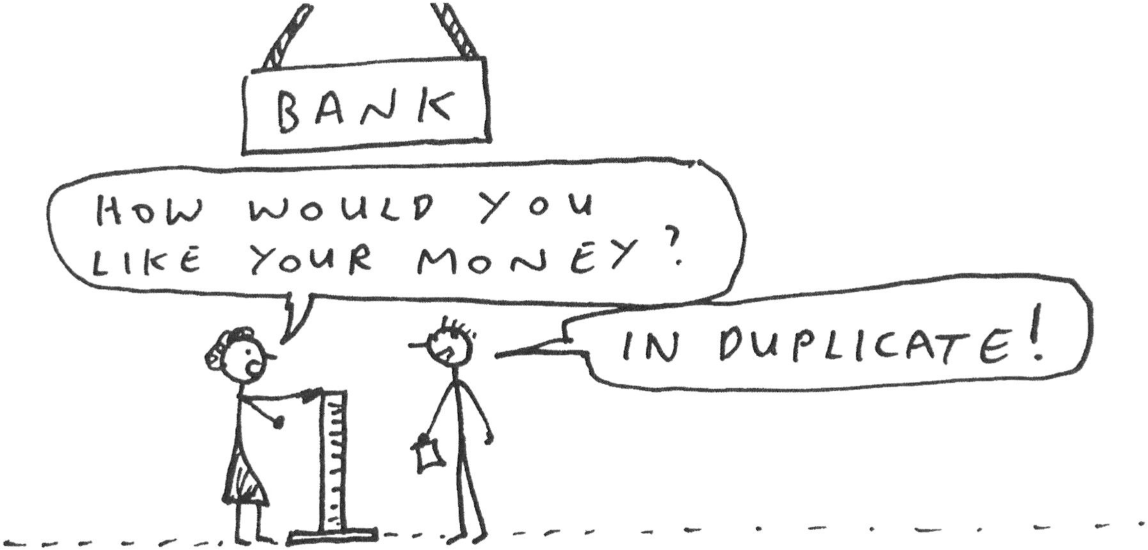
BANK
HOW WOULD YOU LIKE YOUR MONEY?
IN DUPLICATE!

THE SUN AND THE MOON ARE BOTH IN THE SKY. I WONDER HOW THEY'RE MANAGING IN AUSTRALIA...

I WONDER HOW THEY INVENTED MUSICAL SCORE
PREVIOUSLY:
HEY- LOOK AT THOSE BIRDS ON THE TELEPHONE WIRES!

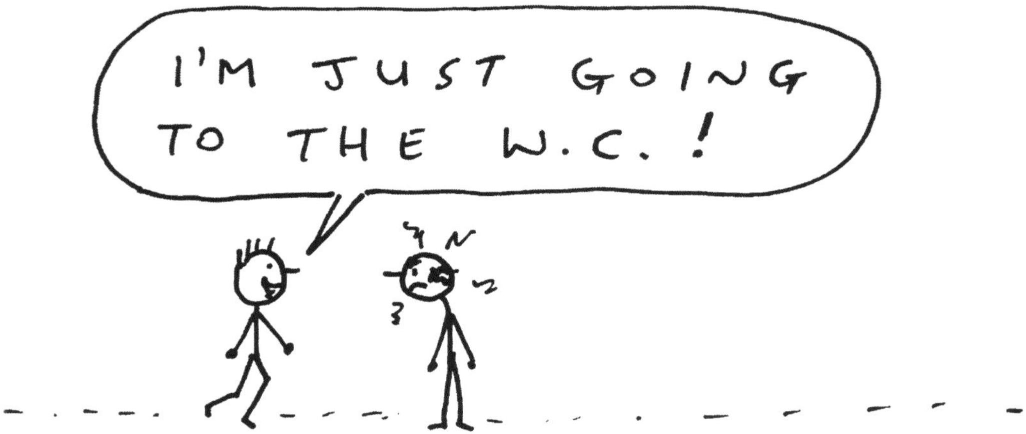
I'M JUST GOING TO THE W.C.!

HOW TO WIND UP CHURCHILL

ALSO IN THIS SERIES

VOL. 2 - CARTOON HEADCASE: MAKING THE WHOLE WORLD LAUGH

ABOUT THE AUTHOR

JOHN KING IS A SUCCESSFUL COMEDY GENIUS WITH TWO SUCCESSFUL BOYS AND A SUCCESSFUL CAT. WHILST HE DID NOT RECEIVE ANY FORMAL QUALIFICATIONS AT SCHOOL, HE DID RECEIVE AN ATTENDANCE CERTIFICATE. JOHN ENJOYS MUSIC, FILMS AND CURRIES - AND SPENDING TIME WITH JOY. HE IS AN ACTIVE MEMBER OF A LOCAL CHURCH. OH – AND HE DOES CARTOONS.